CIVIC CENTER

Also by James D. Scurlock

Maxed Out: Hard Times in the Age of Easy Credit

KING LARRY

The Life and Ruins of a
Billionaire Genius

James D. Scurlock

Scribner

New York   London   Toronto   Sydney   New Delhi

SCRIBNER
A Division of Simon & Schuster, Inc.
1230 Avenue of the Americas
New York, NY 10020

Copyright © 2012 by James Scurlock

First Scribner hardcover edition January 2012

SCRIBNER and design are registered trademarks of The Gale Group, Inc., used under license by Simon & Schuster, Inc., the publisher of this work.

For information about special discounts for bulk purchases, please contact Simon & Schuster Special Sales at 1-866-506-1949 or business@simonandschuster.com.

The Simon & Schuster Speakers Bureau can bring authors to your live event. For more information or to book an event, contact the Simon & Schuster Speakers Bureau at 1-866-248-3049 or visit our website at www.simonspeakers.com.

Designed by Carla Jayne Jones

Manufactured in the United States of America

1   3   5   7   9   10   8   6   4   2

Library of Congress Control Number: 2011019548

ISBN 978-1-4165-8922-8
ISBN 978-1-4165-9394-2 (ebook)

For my mother, Marianne Scurlock

Contents

Contents

Contents

*I*had not heard the name Larry Lee Hillblom until his eulogy appeared on the front page of the *Wall Street Journal,* above the fold and under the headline "Heir Freight: How the Strange Life of a DHL Founder Left His Estate a Mess." In my two decades as a *Journal* devotee, I'd never read any article more than once, but the moment I'd finished the last word of that piece, I started again from the top. Here was the tale of an eccentric multimillionaire who had disappeared in a small-plane crash one year earlier and of the already epic battle for his fortune—money that he had not seemed to care very much about in his lifetime. The reporter had woven the various aspects of Hillblom's convoluted life into a narrative but had failed to resolve its glaring contradiction: Why would a hugely successful entrepreneur exile himself to an obscure island in the middle of nowhere at the dawn of his career? Imagine, for example, Bill Gates moving to Bhutan after the release of Microsoft Windows, or Henry Ford heading into the Alaskan tundra after the first Model T rolled off the assembly line at River Rouge.

The *Wall Street Journal* article teetered on a small shelf in the back of my mind for nearly a decade, slipping further and further from present concerns but refusing to leave my consciousness. Hillblom's mysteries multiplied with time. Why had no one written about the man who had made globalization possible? Only after months of research would I learn that a biography had been in the works years earlier but was smothered by piles of lawsuits and confidentiality agreements that arose from what has been called the World Cup of probate. An unintended consequence of his notoriety was that it allowed him to remain anonymous. After a burst of publicity in the late 1990s that included two more *Wall Street Journal* articles, a *Dateline NBC* special, and a 10,000-word exposé of his sex life in *GQ*, Hillblom disappeared a second time. The story of his death is now far more familiar than the story of his life. That thousands of less important businessmen have become household names by hiring publicists to embed them on CNBC, ghostwriters to distill their success into ten catchphrases (*humility* is a popular one), and agents to book them on the speaking circuit would bother Hillblom not at all. Those who worked for Larry, as a friend of his once admonished, appeared on the covers of magazines; Larry did not. Another friend bristled when I mentioned the *Wall Street Journal* article that had inspired me; Larry, she said, would have hated it. DHL's first general counsel told me that Hillblom was just not capable of examining his life.

"You're looking at the luckiest guy in the world!" (Courtesy of Michael W. Dotts)

But that does not preclude us from doing so. How a peach farmer's stepson from a flyover town in California's Central Valley linked continents, abolished centuries-old institutions, and became fabulously wealthy is fascinating stuff. That his accomplishments interested him so little makes him all the more compelling.

Not that he was, as most assume, reclusive or even antisocial. Hillblom was as relentless socially as he was in business. He loved meeting new people—particularly young women and fellow adrenaline junkies—as long as they struck him as authentic. He could cut it up at a disco, though he was a disaster at karaoke. (Here, unfortunately, we are soul mates.) He abhorred luxury hotels, opting to crash on friends' couches or floors. If those were unavailable, he found the cheapest motels or the YMCA, which he claimed was far safer than the Ritz; after all, no criminal would go looking for a rich target at the Y. Picturing his long, pencil-thin body cocooned in one of those self-enclosed first-class "suites" that have become fashionable among the jet set is difficult. On the ground, he eschewed limousines for taxis and sidewalks. He may have prized his anonymity, but he lived far more openly than most men whose net worths flirt with ten figures. He wandered Asia's concrete jungles on foot, among the masses, without bodyguards or an entourage of minions. He was often alone. Even the behavior that would become so controversial after his death was, during his lifetime, hidden in plain sight. On more than one occasion, I was speechless when a former friend or business associate denied behavior that Hillblom had flaunted before others. Not that it matters. Hillblom's hopelessly outdated will confirmed what one of his lawyers would confide to me after our final interview: "Larry didn't give a shit what happened after he died. He'd be dead."

Others do give a shit. Hillblom—at least, his initial—is emblazoned on tens of thousands of delivery vans, airplanes, and trucks worldwide. The foundation bearing his name gives away millions of dollars every year for medical research, and at least two women named their children after him. But more than a decade past the meltdown of his empire, Larry Hillblom remains radioactive. Family members refused to meet with me. When, by chance, I was seated next to DHL's director of media relations at a charity party, the man groaned, "I guess my job is to convince you not to write your book." DHL's new owners, the German postal monopoly Deutsche Post, fear the retelling of Hillblom's life as a potential PR disaster—a concern that is not a little ironic, considering the billions that the company has lost trying to make DHL a household name in the United States. The terse official corporate telegram announcing Hillblom's disappearance is evidence of how difficult it would be to assess the legacy. "Larry was a true visionary who helped create the air express industry," it read. "While Larry will be greatly missed, DHL's day-to-day operations will not be affected. Our business continues as usual."

By then, as one of the company's vice presidents told me, Hillblom had become a legend, something not quite real. In America, Fred Smith, the founder of FedEx, is considered the pioneer of the express industry, yet DHL's certificate of incorporation precedes FedEx's inaugural flight by half a decade. Smith, in fact, would not transport documents anywhere until Ronald Reagan occupied the White House—and only after Hillblom had engineered a landmark victory against the United States Postal Service affirming the right of private companies to transport time-sensitive documents. By the time DHL's better-known competitor flew over an ocean, Hillblom's network already connected more countries than the United Nations. Not only did DHL make it possible for banks to go global, American engineers to develop the oil fields of the Middle East, and multinationals to exist, DHL sometimes served as the only means of communication between enemy states. During the Iranian hostage crisis, for example, DHL's couriers flew in and out of Tehran without interruption. DHL couriers were also flying into Saudi Arabia, Vietnam, and North Korea long before it was acceptable—or legal—for American companies to do so. Probably the fastest-growing company in history when measured by pure geographical reach, DHL pioneered the notion of the truly global enterprise that flies under no country's flag. When it came to stating a nationality, Hillblom himself seemed either agnostic or polygamous. He carried at least three passports. Officially, he died a citizen of the Commonwealth of the Northern Mariana Islands, whose legal status is currently being challenged in the federal courts—a process that Hillblom himself started a quarter century ago.

DHL was not his only adventure and certainly not his favorite. Hillblom also created one of the first word processors, bought two major airlines, led the fight for deregulation, stymied American imperialism in the Western Pacific (no less a character than Jack Abramoff was hired to replace him), and brought American investment to Vietnam years before the embargo was lifted in 1994. Less significantly, but more fun, were his side jobs: bartender, Supreme Court justice, island ambassador, backhoe operator, and pawnshop owner, among them. That he is remembered for his sexual exploits rather than any of these things is testament to our fascination with the hedonistic.

More than a few of those I interviewed believe that his "death" was simply a ruse to avoid responsibility for his actions. Fifteen years later, the name still provokes. "I have nothing good to say about Larry Hillblom," one of DHL's original shareholders barked at me before hanging up the phone. A previously friendly shopkeeper on Saipan groaned that her island was home to "the only law library named after a known pedophile" when I told her the subject of my research. And then there is the CNMI bishop's bemused take on Hillblom: "Larry was my favorite heathen."

Can one book do justice to a man so complex? Hillblom was honored with no fewer than three memorial services, each representing a different facet of his life. He has been described as the head of an octopus whose tentacles flailed uncontrollably after he vanished. A few of those tentacles, like DHL, were hugely valuable. Others, like his interest in an island pawnshop, were little more than hobbies. Assets amounting to hundreds of millions of dollars were never recorded on paper; shares he owned were sometimes assigned to others without their knowledge. That there was more to Larry Hillblom than can be reconstructed from the printed record is certain, though his probate alone amounts to more than a million pages.

But here is my attempt at exhumation, regardless. *Not* to attempt it would be to expunge one of the most important men of the twentieth century from the historical record. For efficiency's sake, I must assume that Hillblom is actually dead, and not basking beneath a Southeast Asian sun somewhere surrounded by nubile young women, pineapples, and Vietnamese coffee, as many still believe, including agents of the Internal Revenue Service and the U.S. Department of State. I must disregard a former governor of Guam, who claimed to have seen Hillblom recently on a trip to Thailand, as well as an MIA organization that may or may not possess physical proof of Hillblom living in that country. Hillblom's estate chose not to verify the latter, despite paying out nearly two hundred million dollars to law firms, of which millions have been spent chasing less credible rumors.

But questioning his death certificate now does nothing more than make Hillblom a little more like his idols Howard Hughes and Elvis Pres-ley. There is mystery enough in his life without debating his death, so I will let him rest in peace somewhere at the bottom of the Western Pacific Ocean. What I will not do is allow him to disappear—at least not quite yet. . . .

A Final Round

Saipan, Commonwealth of the Northern Mariana Islands
May 20, 1995

By 9:00 a.m., the first waves of Japanese tourists had emerged from the bay below, shimmering aluminum tanks strapped to their backs reflecting patches of morning sun as blinding as halogen. On the sprawling golf course above, clusters of tanned men grazed a mass of former jungle carved into manicured greens. A handful paused to acknowledge a Tokyo-bound Boeing 747-400 loaded with newlyweds and a belly full of just-purchased Louis Vuitton luggage. The plane banked to the north, then disappeared into an azure sky as smooth as latex.

Bob O'Connor, a pristine Californian on the early side of middle age and possessed of the bronzed, chiseled features of a young Burt Lancaster, pushed a tee into the moist earth at the start of the eighteenth hole. As he stepped back to reach for a polished wood driver, he heard Larry snap, "Don't use that one."

O'Connor did as he was told—not because Larry Hillblom was his most important client, or because they were business partners in a half dozen ventures, but because he could trace nearly every accomplishment in his life thus far—with the notable exceptions of his wife and newborn daughter—back to the advice of the man standing beside him. O'Connor turned to his friend, tried his best not to stare at the right eye that had gone dark or the skin that the doctors in San Francisco had pulled so taut and smooth around his skull that his face seemed doll-like. *Surreal.* He was grateful to have his eyes diverted to the glimmering 2-iron that Larry extended with his gloved right hand.

O'Connor pulled back, uncurled his long frame, and hit a near-perfect drive. Then he slipped the gleaming shaft into his own bag.

"That's mine," he heard Larry say. And immediately, a sheepish O'Connor handed the 2-iron back to Larry's caddie.

Hillblom as best man at Bob O'Connor's wedding (Courtesy of Michael W. Dotts)

They boarded the little white cart a moment later and moved forward up the green. O'Connor hesitated to make conversation. Hillblom had been unusually curt that morning, snippy even, and the usual subjects had become minefields. O'Connor knew better than anyone how Larry compartmentalized his relationships. "Larry is my best friend but I know that I'm not Larry's best friend" is how he explained the asymmetry of their friendship to himself and others. True, Larry had agreed to be O'Connor's best man two years earlier and had even showed up at his wedding in a suit and tie—a concession that, as far as anyone knew, Micronesia's wealthiest man had made for only two other people: Senator Edward M. Kennedy and the secretary-general of the United Nations. And O'Connor was one of a handful of men who knew the true extent of Hillblom's wealth, something that even the Ivy League–trained researchers at *Forbes* magazine had missed. (They had estimated his fortune most recently at a mere $300 million.) On the other hand, O'Connor also knew that Larry's empire rested a little precariously. There was the $11 million in back taxes owed; the IRS investigation; the boy in Palau; the $9,000 checks that O'Connor's junior partner, Mike Dotts, cashed on Larry's behalf to pay for his extracurricular activities in Manila. Dotts was constantly calling DHL's legal office in San Francisco for more money. As rich as he was, Larry was probably insolvent.

O'Connor briefly considered a conversation about his new daughter. When he'd mentioned her in the past, Larry had seemed to soften unexpectedly, had seemed engaged even, which was a departure from the hostility that any talk of children—or marriage—typically inspired. Maybe, O'Connor hoped, Larry would finally settle down with his Filipina girlfriend, Josephine, and start a family. It had taken O'Connor nearly ten years to warm up to Josephine, but the idea of himself and Larry being fathers appealed to him. Maybe their kids would even play together one day.

"You know," Larry blurted suddenly. "You really ought to go flying with me tomorrow."

O'Connor laughed. *Never. Not in a million years would I go flying with you,* he said to himself. Few of those who knew Larry would fly with him. Less than two years before, Hillblom had nearly died when he crash-landed his little Cessna 182 on the neighboring island of Tinian, in part because he'd been in such a hurry to take off. And the first time Hillblom had landed his World War II–vintage seaplane on Saipan, the landing gear had collapsed—probably due to lack of maintenance, *id est,* Larry's cheapness. Hillblom treated his planes like most people treated their cars: jump in, start the ignition, and off you go. Checklists were a waste of precious time; maintenance logs were not worth keeping, much less reading. In one infamous case, Larry had forgotten to reattach the gas cap, only to think of it as he was hurtling down the runway at a hundred miles an hour.

O'Connor finally engaged. "Where are you going?"

"Pagan," Larry replied. Pagan was one of the small, uninhabited islands of the Northern Mariana Archipelago that linked Guam to Japan. The island's old military airstrip had been truncated by lava years ago, making it a notoriously tricky place to take off and land, but explorers were rewarded by black sand beaches and wild game. "I've got this new pilot," Larry continued. "A Vietnam vet. Flew fighter missions."

O'Connor nodded ambiguously. They took a few more strokes on the green. Larry's mind was never in the present, especially when he was putting. Occasionally, he skipped that part of the game altogether. He derived no pleasure from sinking the ball in the little cup. He preferred hitting it as hard and as far as possible.

A cluster of local politicians had already gathered in the clubhouse by the time they arrived; of course they intercepted Larry, wealth and power both being magnets. Larry had known every member of every legislature for at least a decade. He'd traveled to D.C. or New York with most of them. O'Connor was known too. He was the island's first registered lobbyist and the stocky, betel nut–chewing legislators were accustomed to his visits, usually on behalf of Hillblom. ("Larry's the brains and I'm the mouthpiece," O'Connor liked to say.) Today the brief conversation veered from how to prevent an imminent federal government takeover of the islands' minimum wage and immigration policies to how great Larry's new face looked. Avoided was the incident, a few months before, when Hillblom had been arrested for drinking at a legislative hearing. On the way to the police cruiser, he'd hurled expletives at a news camera and claimed he had a bomb. O'Connor's junior partner had bailed him out of what, in Saipan, passed for a jail.

Hillblom's clubs arrived first and he abruptly extricated himself.

By the time O'Connor's caddie showed up, the lawyer had reconsidered Hillblom's offer to go flying, mainly on account of his friend's promise that he would not pilot the airplane himself. A few hundred feet distant, O'Connor could see Larry's caddie walking back toward the clubhouse, empty-handed, and Larry's red Corolla crawling out from under the shadow of a coconut tree behind him. O'Connor shouted out his nickname, the one reserved for private conversations. Then he raised his hand and waved, but Larry wasn't looking back. He waited impatiently for the caddie to stuff his clubs into the back of his SUV, proffered the tip, jumped into the driver's seat, and fired up the engine.

When ignorance is bliss, 'tis folly to be wise. O'Connor repeated it silently, the mantra that had guided his life from the moment he'd become friends with Larry, the smartest man O'Connor had ever met or probably would meet—but also the most fun, the most blissful. Because Larry had taught him that the important thing in life was not to be happy but to be adventuresome.

O'Connor shifted into reverse, maneuvered out of the parking lot, drove the straightaway to Kagman Road a little too fast, passed the guard gate without a wave, hung a left, and sped by the farms, looking straight ahead. He weaved up into the hills of San Vicente, threading a narrow road bordered on both sides by thick jungles of knotted, pea-green tangan-tangan trees, past the abandoned castle, then down toward the flats of Dan-dan, where he spotted the Toyota paused at a stoplight in front of one of the island's ubiquitous video poker dens.

O'Connor brought his car alongside just as the light was turning green, but Larry barely glanced at him. O'Connor realized his friend, the perpetual teenager, had misread his intentions. Hillblom wanted to race. Of course he did. But as soon as Larry made a quick left turn ahead of the green light, O'Connor found himself blocked by oncoming traffic. He pressed on the accelerator and straightened the steering wheel, aiming for the townhome he shared with his new family.

The next morning arrived bright and hot. On the southern end of the island, the sun bounced off the airport's twin Polynesian-style terminals and heat rose from the tarmac in phantom waves. Guy Gabaldon, Saipan's second most famous resident, awaited its first in the area reserved for private aircraft. Gabaldon, a Mexican-American marine, had been stationed on the island during the tail end of World War II and never left. He'd become famous when he emerged from behind enemy lines followed by more than eight hundred demoralized Japanese troops who had surrendered to him after an unsuccessful banzai charge. His exploits had been memorialized in the 1960 film *Hell to Eternity* and, after a long wait, he'd received the Navy Cross Medal.

Gabaldon was standing next to his plane, watching another early riser crouched next to Larry Hillblom's latest toy, tinkering with one of the cowlings. SeaBees were impossible to miss, their propellers pointing back-ward from a small, round cabin, causing the fuselage to dip before looping back up to join the tail. In profile they resembled cartoon whales, and they were old but very reliable. Republic Aircraft Corporation had over-engineered them to such an extent that the company had gone bankrupt when it proved impossible to sell such a well-built airplane at a profit. The only flaw was that they were notoriously underpowered. Most owners had solved that problem by replacing the single engine with two wing-mounted propellers, but that made them trickier to fly.

Hillblom's SeaBee was a two-engine conversion, trimmed with light brown and orange racing stripes. It kept his pilot, a big American named Robert Long, plenty busy. Things were constantly falling off the plane; most recently the tail rudder had to be replaced. Hillblom had bought a twin just for spare parts, but many of the instruments were still unreliable and the gas line connecting the auxiliary tank didn't work. But maintenance was only one of the SeaBee's problems.

Gabaldon turned his attention back to his own plane. He was making his way through his checklist several minutes later when he heard the SeaBee's engines start up. He turned to notice Larry Hillblom and another man, a heavyset islander, standing next to the Pacific Aviation hangar. Gabaldon had agreed to follow Hillblom to Pagan that morning and he would give the relatively slow SeaBee a decent head start. They had been doing test runs between Saipan, Anatahan, and Pagan for nearly a month; Long had to be sure of the plane's range because Hillblom had ordered him to fly the SeaBee all the way to Vietnam and he'd have to do quite a bit of island-skipping to get there. All told, this morning's journey would be a little more than 450 nautical miles, which was pushing the SeaBee's fuel limits.

It took only a few minutes for Long to taxi the plane over, scoop up his passengers, and hustle to the end of the runway. When Gabaldon heard the throttle open up, he noticed that the engines did not sound quite right. Turning his gaze to the runway, Gabaldon watched as the SeaBee's wheels finally left the pavement and cleared the thin border of jungle before banking over the Philippine Sea. It seemed to him that the plane was not climbing as fast as it should. Like it was struggling to stay in the air.

Part I

The American Dream

The trouble with my life is that I do not think I am cut out to sit behind a desk.

—*Howard Hughes*

The Switch

By the time he reached his thirties, Larry Hillblom had invented a childhood in which he had been captain of his high school football team, a member of a radical liberal student group, and the son of a notorious bank robber executed in the electric chair at San Quentin. Like many things born of Hillblom's imaginative mind, this version of himself was not true but not totally false either. He had lettered in football as a cornerback—number 29—of the Kingsburg Vikings. He had been something of a radical in law school, though hardly a liberal one. And his father had died, when Larry was just three years old, but not at the hands of prison guards. Instead, the young man had suffered heatstroke while repairing a roof in Bakersfield on one of the hottest days in the summer of 1946. Whether he'd died before or after he'd hit the ground was something that no one, including his son, would ever know.

As for Larry himself, neighbors remember an infant so prone to wanderlust that he chewed through his wooden crib. And who could blame him? Kingsburg, the tiny Swedish enclave equidistant from San Francisco and Los Angeles along the 99 freeway, where his parents had bought a modest house, was hardly a suitable place for the man who would one day shrink the globe. Downtown was a double-wide strip of pavement framed by banks, a hardware store, and the occasional restaurant. The neighborhood a few miles distant where he would spent his childhood was dark and deathly quiet by 8:00 p.m. Hillblom saved the money that his stepfather, a farmer named Andy Anderson, paid him for driving a tractor, then he switched to more lucrative work at the peach cannery near the freeway, driving a forklift and ultimately becoming a supervisor. He had to go to the local community college's library to read the *Wall Street Journal,* which is how he learned to invest. "Someday," he told Dave Crass, his best friend from sixth grade on, "I'm going to move far away, and I won't write any letters." He thought a moment more before adding, "I'll call you once in a while, but I will not write any letters."

Crass did not take the remark personally. Hillblom was small, maybe five-nine the day they graduated from Kingsburg High, but he was clearly destined for big things. He worked harder than kids his age and he was more ambitious. Larry'd joke about how he was going to make a lot of money, and Crass never doubted that for a moment, particularly when, barely out of high school, his friend bought a Corvette with part of his stock market winnings. Larry was luckier, too, uncannily so. He always won the all-night poker games they played at Reedley, the local college they both attended as a stepping-stone to Fresno State. And he always won the dice games, which made no sense unless he was cheating. How he pulled that off was, like many things, a secret. Larry cherished secrets more than anything.

Back in Kingsburg, with half brother, Grant Anderson (*left*), and younger brother, Terry (*right*) (Courtesy of Michael W. Dotts)

In high school, they'd nicknamed Larry "Mountain Blossom" as a play on his last name. Freshman year, he was a skinny, stubborn, brainy mama's boy fond of plaid shirts, his teeth hidden by gleaming braces and blue eyes framed by thick glasses. A square who taught Sunday school, played the piano, and earned perfect grades . . . then, *poof!* One day he showed up without the glasses, a shiny ducktail peeking from behind his neck. He stopped trying so hard in class and went out for football, basketball, and golf. In a school as small as Kingsburg High, even a small kid like Larry could play varsity football. But Larry had refused to use his smallness to his advantage by avoiding his opponents. Instead he met the gorillas head-on, resulting in several concussions; more than once, his contact lenses popped out, and both teams were forced to crawl the field on their knees until they were located—an event memorialized by a half-page photograph in his senior yearbook.

But being a jock was not the goal. Larry wanted to be *popular,* and guys who played sports just happened to be more popular than guys who played the piano and studied in the library. The switch worked. Mountain Blossom won a plum role in the senior play, and he was voted class president. He dated girls too, though none seriously; relationships with the female species entailed an unacceptable level of risk. When he and Crass discussed marriage, Larry's most memorable observation was that he intended to marry a Catholic woman, because Catholics don't get divorced, meaning that his fortune would be safe.

Larry had been by his mother's side as she struggled to raise him and his younger brother, Terry, without a husband. They'd moved into a small apartment and she'd made money cleaning her friends' homes for two years before Andy Anderson married her. By then she'd developed a toughness that was unusual in a woman, particularly one from a bedroom community like Kingsburg. She could be sarcastic enough to make less confident women cry. Rather than sacrifice her son to the culture, as did so many mothers, she held on tighter and raised her standards. The center of his youth was the Concordia Lutheran Church, a stately brick edifice across the street from the high school where Helen and Andy were called founding members. There she reigned with a sharp tongue that her son would learn to emulate. "Oh, that Helen!" was a knowing refrain back then. She was ambitious for the church and for the community, also becoming a founding member of the Kingsburg Business and Professional Women's Club. And she was ambitious for Larry, who became skilled enough at the piano to substitute for the organist, and familiar enough with Scripture to deliver sermons on Sundays when the preacher was unavailable.

Helen resented prideful women but she was a terribly proud mother. On Halloweens, she rewarded Larry and his friends with hayrides. Vacations were spent in the foothills of the Sierra Nevada, where her three sons—Larry, Terry, and Grant Anderson—fished and swam in crystal-clear lakes as she sunbathed in a stylish black one-piece, beaming with pride, oblivious of Larry's latent hatred. "He talked about all of the nice things she'd done for him in a negative way," remembers one of his closer friends. "'So she's done all of these great things for me, *the bitch.*'"

When he moved out of the farmhouse and into an apartment at Fresno State, he declined to go home on the weekends like most of his friends. They would come back on Sunday night to find him shivering in a room without electricity, under a blanket, studying by candlelight. He purged his need for sleep and maternal love while fixating on careers that would take him far from the Central Valley—golf pro, at first, then actor, finally attorney. From that day forward, he aced every test, impressing his professors and ultimately earning himself an acceptance letter from UC Berkeley Boalt Hall School of Law, then the most prestigious public university in the country, and a universe away from home. Another switch.

Kingsburg, heralded by a water tower welded into a giant Swedish teakettle, is now a town of some ten thousand. Despite the inevitable additions of Taco Bell, McDonald's, and Starbucks, the modest Swedish enclave has retained much of its 1950s charm. Polka music serenades mostly empty sidewalks downtown. Cookie-cutter horses and maps of Sweden, from which most of the original settlers hailed, decorate the sides of two-story buildings. Churches are ubiquitous. The locals chat with strangers about that "something in the water" that brought them back, or how, if the Sun-Maid factory had just been built a little farther south, "the Burg" would be the raisin capital of the world rather than its football rival Selma, just to the north. By the time he left for law school, Hillblom had internalized its core values of modesty, frugality, and, above all, hard work, more than most, but if he carried any nostalgia for his childhood home at all, that would remain hidden. He maintained his job at the cannery, loading peaches at night, into his first few weeks at Boalt Hall, but only because he was unwilling to lose his seniority. Helen picked him up in the morning, drove him to school, then drove him back after his last class as he slept in the car. But when the canning season ended, his mother and Kingsburg faded from memory. He would return only a few times over the next couple of years before abandoning both for nearly a quarter century.

At Boalt Hall, he flipped yet another switch. He let his hair grow out, traded the contact lenses for a pair of frames that dominated his small features, and swapped polo shirts and khakis for bell-bottoms and tight T-shirts. Like most young men his age, by the time he reached the marijuana- and tear gas–infused East Bay air, he was ready to be seduced by sex, drugs, and rock 'n' roll, but there were more pressing items on his agenda than the diversions of youth.

"He was odd-looking and odd-sounding," recalls Steven Kroll, rolling a joint from a jar of homegrown weed. Kroll became Hillblom's first friend outside of the Central Valley and would fill a number of important roles in Hillblom's life, the first of which as his study partner in law school. "Larry had a twang." He smiles. "Country hick is what you might think, which is what I was but I didn't look it. . . ." A long inhale. "Larry and I were birds of a feather," Kroll continues. "He was a wonderfully odd bird."

Today Kroll resembles the actor Kirk Douglas. The only clues to his counterculture past are a mane of white hair pulled back into a ponytail and a "Legalize It!" flag that flickers over the front door of his home overlooking northern Lake Tahoe. In the fall of 1967, when he returned to Berkeley after a long hiatus in Europe and Africa, avoiding the draft in grand style—hitchhiking, cutting a record album and, ultimately, marrying a pretty Afrikaner named Joy—Kroll was a compact young man with a cute face framed by a thin beard and a passion for social justice. He had been raised in even more modest circumstances than Hillblom had; his elementary school was only one room. But there was an exoticism to him, a result both of his Jewish heritage and his world travels, that his friend lacked. Hillblom had not yet been outside the state of California. A shared sense of fearlessness that cemented the friendship. Hillblom had run for president of the cannery union, a quixotic quest to be sure but also an important protest against the old men who he thought ran the show for their own benefit more than for the workers like himself. Kroll had been an activist since the fifth grade, when he'd protested his school's policy of throwing away uneaten lunches rather than donating them to a food bank.

What struck Kroll immediately, as it would so many others, was Hillblom's physical oddness, which made his confidence that much more disarming. "He said he had had a car crash and you could see bumps in his forehead," Kroll recalls. "He told me he had a metal plate from a bad car accident and his face did look like it could have been reconstructed. He had an odd baby face." More idiosyncratic than his appearance were Hillblom's many tics. Parting his already parted hair with his pinkie and constantly shaking his legs are the two that his friends mention the most, but he was also germophobic. For a time, he carried his own bottles of Lysol and ketchup everywhere.

But most unusual of all was Hillblom's take on politics. Berkeley was then ground zero of virtually every countercultural scene, from the antiwar movement to the free speech movement to the percolating feminist and gay rights movements. Kroll's brother, a Berkeley undergrad, had been arrested for occupying the administration building a couple of years before, and Kroll himself would file a lawsuit on behalf of the student body when Governor Ronald Reagan took to the airwaves to chastise the students as a bunch of spoiled brats and their professors as a pack of overindulgent parents. Larry, however, found the notion of political activism beside the point—if mildly amusing. In endless debates that simmered from the library to Kroll's tiny house a few blocks from campus, Hillblom dismissed the tens of thousands of Americans being killed in Vietnam as irrelevant when compared to the number of those who died in highway accidents every year. He blasted sit-ins as a waste of time. But the brunt of his ridicule was reserved for the muses of the antiwar movement, Joan Baez and Jane Fonda. "Who cares what an actress thinks?" he would taunt Kroll and his fellow liberals. Right or wrong did not matter to the young man who still smelled of peaches. What counted was success. To achieve their goals, Hillblom chided, the anti-whatever activists would need to put down their guitars and their flowers and pick up the Little Red Book, the bible of the man that Hillblom considered the master of manipulation: the brutal Chinese dictator Mao Tse-tung.

"What he liked, I don't know," Kroll sighs, as an Italian speedboat attached to a water-skier slices across the glassy water beyond his deck. "You could say that perhaps he liked Chairman Mao's cold analysis and power, as an observer of history. He was always fascinated by power, as who wouldn't be? Kissinger always said it was an aphrodisiac." Hillblom seemed to embrace anyone's thinking as long as it was revolutionary. When he decided, unsuccessfully, to run for student president, he borrowed a slogan from the Black Panthers: *Burn, Baby, Burn!* "I think"— Kroll smiles—"he wanted to put forward that his answer was blow it up and start again, but he was talking more about beginning again than literally blowing something up. He was saying that the system was broke. How could anybody say that was wrong?"

But Hillblom's campaign for student president went nowhere, mainly because he was a terrible public speaker, incapable of holding even his own attention for more than a few minutes before branching off on a tangent—and then another, and another, until any vestige of the original argument was irretrievable. He was far more successful at being subversive in the classroom, where, sitting near the back of the room, he could throw off the entire class with a non sequitur. At Boalt, many classes were conducted as Socratic dialogues; students were respected as much as their professors. Hillblom's ideas veered so far from the mainstream, however, that he seemed to be reading from a different set of books. His corporations professor frequently kept the inscrutable farm boy after class to try to reason with him, even if Hillblom's unconventional thinking—and his stubbornness—made this impossible. For their part, his fellow students rolled their eyes as they waited for the discussion to veer back toward the familiar.

"They were interested in making money and pleasing their parents and being out there," Kroll recalls of their classmates with a sniff, "but they didn't really want to be at law school. Larry and I adored reading cases for what they said and what they didn't say, and the beauty of their logic. What made us special is that you couldn't ask us what kind of law we were interested in. We were interested in the law itself, as a way of thinking."

Kroll may have questioned his classmates' motives, but he won enough of their votes to become class president. And Kroll's grades earned him a place in the Order of the Coif, meaning that he was technically a notch above Hillblom academically. But when they studied at the library together, it was Hillblom, not Kroll, who would stroll over to the legendary professor Stefan Riesenfeld, a Holocaust survivor known for his legal tomes, and chat with him as though they were equals. As for grades and honor societies, Hillblom simply could not be bothered—being judged on such standards was beneath him. "It was always the argument that counted," Kroll remembers, "not the particular legal principle. He saw all the facets of the problem."

Hillblom did not dwell on hypotheticals; he had to work, too. By his second year, he'd accepted a full-time job as a courier for a small Los Angeles firm called MPA—short for Michaels, Poe & Associates. The firm's active partner, David Poe, was a former insurance man who had convinced his employer to fly him back and forth between offices to deliver important documents rather than use the post office, which was notoriously slow and unreliable. Poe had started a fledgling courier operation serving the Bay Area, Los Angeles, and Honolulu. Hillblom's route was Oakland to LAX and back. Every afternoon, after class, he would drive around the Bay Area to pick up documents from insurance companies, law firms, and banks. He then stuffed the documents into suitcases, boarded a Western Airlines 727 to Los Angeles, and handed them off to another courier, who would give him bags to take back north. Hillblom studied on the plane, slept in the airport, and boarded the early flight to Oakland, arriving at Berkeley just in time for class. The schedule explained his disheveled appearance in morning classes—and, sometimes, his absence—but it had two huge advantages: since he was willing to crash at Kroll's house or in his car on the weekends, Hillblom didn't have to spend money on an apartment; and he met a lot of pretty young stewardesses and secretaries.

Kroll had a job too, slinging hash at Si's Charbroiler on Ashby Avenue, Berkeley's main drag. They both lived on caffeine and speed, rarely getting more then a few hours' sleep. Hillblom appeared to be a nomad, his possessions fitting snugly inside a backpack, his hair perpetually dirty, his clothes always stained and frequently torn. For a while, he dyed his hair blond and he constantly fussed over both his weight and his beard, which he would trim whenever a pair of scissors ended up in his hands. He refused to buy a wardrobe befitting a law student because he had no intention of joining a law firm. With a prestigious degree in sight, Hillblom silently flipped another switch, set his sights on another goal unbeknownst even to his closest friend. By the time that Kroll assembled his small family for their move to Honolulu, where he had accepted an associate position in a corporate law firm after graduation, Hillblom would vanish amid the East Bay's fog. The rumor was that he was sleeping in his car and foraging meals from a Dumpster.

Two

The Courier

Larry was the unbusiest guy I ever met. He would sleep a lot and watch TV a lot, but he was very laid-back. Larry taught me one great thing: that you could ignore 99 percent of problems and that they would eventually go away.

—*Steven Kroll*

*H*e reappeared in the summer, materializing from a warm South Pacific trade wind at the front door of Kroll's condominium because he needed a place to crash. Hillblom returned on a regular basis, first sleeping on Kroll's patio; later, when Kroll's parents, Max and Blanche, moved to Hawaii after a stint in the Peace Corps, Hillblom claimed their living room couch.

In 1969, no city in the world was as sexy as Honolulu, the sun-drenched paradise where Elvis Presley had played the ukulele in *Blue Hawaii,* and where Jack Lord now hurtled across rooftops in a tight blue suit, behind the badge belonging to Detective Steve McGarrett, the coolest character on television's hottest series, *Hawaii Five-O.* Celebrities poured in to tape guest appearances, sip fruity cocktails out of coconut shells at Trader Vic's, and be seen at Henry J. Kaiser's Hawaiian Village Hotel. Shirtless young men dotted the surfline; tanned girls in bikinis awaited them on the beach under a perpetual sun. Within a year, brand-new Pan Am and United 747 jumbo jets stocked with prime rib and champagne would descend on the island's gleaming new outdoor airport every few hours, as would Presley's personal jet. The teenage Hillblom's idol shimmied "Burning Love" at the International Center in a white-and-gold jumpsuit—a performance that would be relayed via satellite around the world. That such a place existed under the American flag defied belief.

MPA was his ticket there. But flying the company's Oakland-Honolulu route, which he'd been unable to do during the school year, opened up more than the South Pacific. Secretaries who had turned the gangly courier down for dinner in San Francisco now jumped at the chance to spend a weekend in Honolulu. If Hillblom was traveling with enough documents, MPA bought two tickets rather than one, and he had an instant date. But Hillblom's weekend trysts didn't always pan out. Plenty of other couriers wanted to explore the land of Aloha. That he would have far more luck if he owned the company himself was obvious, but he had no experience starting a business and only a few thousand dollars left in the bank. More daunting, no major law firm or insurance company was likely to hand over their most important documents to a twenty-five-year-old in tight jeans and a torn Creedence Clearwater Revival T-shirt who slept in his car and was frequently jacked up on methamphetamines.

Yet Hillblom was not as out of synch with the corporate world as his appearance suggested. A year before, as tear gas from the antiwar protests had seeped into the hall where Hillblom and Kroll had taken their final exams, the rest of America was swinging back to the right. At the same moment that hippies were making their last stand in People's Park and amid the muddy fields of Woodstock, *Time* magazine was declaring the resurgence of what it called "Middle Americans," who could pass for today's Tea Partiers. "They feared," wrote *Time*'s editors, "that they were beginning to lose their grip on the country. Others seemed to be taking over—the liberals, the radicals, a communications industry that they often believed was lying to them. No one celebrated them: intellectuals dismissed their lore as banality. . . . But in 1969, they began to assert themselves. They were 'discovered' first by politicians and the press, and then they started to discover themselves . . . in a murmurous and pervasive discontent, they sought to reclaim their culture." The Middle Americans' game-changing accomplishment had been the election of Richard Nixon to the White House the previous November. Hillblom, according to his friends, admired Nixon, though it's doubtful that he actually took the time to vote for him. Nixon's pro-business, pro-trade, antiunion conservatism dovetailed nicely with Hillblom's emerging worldview. The young law school graduate could have had no idea that his new president's penchant for cronyism would soon present a formidable challenge to his own ambitions.

If DHL's official corporate history is to believed—and we really have no choice here, since only two men were there and both are long gone—the company was conceived during a chance encounter in a grocery store parking lot between Hillblom and MPA's salesman, a silver-haired, gray-suited fifty-eight-year-old bon vivant named Adrian Dalsey. Dalsey was the opposite of Hillblom—an impeccably groomed smooth talker who lived in a suburb northeast of San Francisco with his loyal wife of thirty years; by his mid-fifties, the silver fox had spent enough money on other women that none remained for his and Marge's golden years. Hillblom's conservative politics and his work ethic should have endeared him to a man of Dalsey's generation, but he lacked the older man's finesse, meaning that their encounter was probably more intense than respectful. Customers who happened to push their shopping carts by that fateful meeting might have mistaken them for a wealthy father tolerating a relentless son.

But they eventually agreed that their boss, Mr. Poe, had left a lot of low-hanging fruit unpicked. Insurers were not the only ones with time-sensitive documents. There was tremendous value to be captured if, for example, a shipping company could forward its bills of lading to customs in advance of a ship's arrival, saving days or even weeks in port. Ditto for banks, which could only begin collecting interest on deposits once the original canceled check was received by the Federal Reserve, or for a law firm that needed a physical signature in order to effect a contract. Sending these documents via the postal service might take two weeks, if they reached their destination at all. At a time of double-digit interest rates and looming postal strikes, both men knew that the market for a fast, reliable courier service was huge—and growing. They understood that their skills complemented one another almost perfectly. And they disliked each other immensely.

"Larry and Dalsey had a visible acrimony," Kroll tells me. "Dalsey liked to snipe and he had this, he was a bit unctuous, he had this—it wasn't a lisp, but an impediment—speech pattern that was distinctive and a little bit patrician. He was a distinguished-looking guy, a ladies' man, and thought himself so. He used to snipe at Larry in a scornful, patronizing way, and it annoyed you. So here you have these two people, with totally different worldviews and different functions within the company, at loggerheads, creating the nascent IBM—unknowingly." Kroll pauses for a moment and smiles. "Or maybe not."

Regardless of the natural tension between two very different people of two very different generations, Hillblom and Dalsey ultimately understood that they needed one another in order to make a go of it. Hillblom was overflowing with ideas and energy; he was willing to work twenty-hour days and could do a lot of the legal legwork. Plus, he had $6,000, which would become the company's seed capital. Dalsey had credit cards and client connections. They incorporated in September, using the initials of their last names and adding that of Robert Lynn, a real estate–investor friend of Dalsey's who had promised to help them raise capital. Lynn, however, dropped out of DHL almost immediately. He told them that the company could not succeed.

Dalsey quickly signed DHL's first client—the shipping giant Seatrain Lines, which needed to courier bills of lading between Los Angeles and Honolulu. Then he hit a wall. Hillblom and Dalsey had hoped that Lynn's financing would carry them through the lean months, but now they were forced to rely on a trickle of cash to survive. Marge, Dalsey's wife, became the corporate secretary and did the books on her dining room table. Hillblom was forced not only to travel with DHL's bags but also to pick them up at Seatrain before boarding the plane and drop them off after he arrived. During the few hours he was not working, he slept or studied for the bar exam. And waited for his supersalesman to sign one of their dream clients. But Dalsey, scouring the Bay Area in an old Plymouth Duster whose unmatched doors were salvaged from a junkyard, had stumbled on the first in a long line of catch-22s: DHL needed banking clients in order to become profitable, but they could not afford the expensive insurance that banks demanded. While the value of the checks that the banks were sending was, on its face, negligible—nothing more than paper and ink—if even a single large check became lost or delayed for more than a few days, the interest lost could be substantial. Nearly a year would pass before an insurance agent offered up a solution. In the meantime, Hillblom nearly starved to death in paradise.

"I was hired as an operator in 1969 at American Telephone Answering Service," she begins, sizing me up from behind a pair of square-framed schoolteacher's glasses. Her name is Marilyn Corral. Until her retirement two weeks before Hillblom's presumed death, Corral was the longest-serving employee in DHL history. Her last title was vice president of human resources. A woman with a cherubic face that belies a suspicious nature, Corral has retired to the tiny town of Mariposa, in the shadow of the great Sierra Nevada, not far from where the young Hillblom and his two brothers used to fish.

American Telephone Answering Service happens to be the company that Adrian Dalsey hired to answer DHL's phone calls—usually clients calling to schedule a pickup. Corral, then a new military wife, was in command of a turret wired with ten phone lines, each marked with a particular customer's name so that she would know how to answer the phone. This personalized "executive" service cost more, but Dalsey had decided it was worth paying for because callers were duped into believing that they were calling an actual DHL office. When Dalsey returned to San Francisco, Hillblom suddenly began to appear in Corral's office to pick up DHL's messages. "He'd always show up at mealtime"—Corral smiles—"and we felt guilty because he looked like he was starving to death and never had anything to eat. So we bought more than we normally did—Chinese food or whatever—and he would eat lunch with us."

Back then, women like Corral were "girlie" or "honey," and silver foxes like Dalsey were allowed to let their eyes wander and linger wherever they wished. But whereas Dalsey came across like a dirty old man—"sleazy," says Corral—Hillblom was charming. He would loiter around the office for a couple of hours, teasing Corral about everything from her constant dieting to the fact that American Telephone's office was on Hotel Street, where the hookers had solicited navy boys during the war. Not long after Hillblom started showing up, he hired her as DHL's first employee—albeit part-time.

Number 911 Alakea Street still stands, a narrow two-story colonial squeezed between two much taller office buildings in downtown Honolulu, only a few blocks from the ocean and two miles from the Honolulu International Airport. In 1970, it was occupied by two tenants: on the first floor, a Hawaiian restaurant with a rat problem; and, above it, the law offices of Curtis Carlsmith, a classmate of Kroll and Hillblom's. Larry had sublet the inside office from his friend Carlsmith; it was just large enough for a few desks. He'd hired a handyman to build a small loft space, where he eventually laid a mattress. Corral kept her day job at the answering service. But at night, she would drive over to 911 Alakea to schedule the courier calendars. And on the weekends, she would climb up into the loft, gather Hillblom's underwear, T-shirts, and bedsheets, and take them home to launder them because she knew that he never would.

"I would have all the filing done on Friday evening, and Monday morning the files would be all over the floor"—Corral sighs—"because he was looking for one document and couldn't find it. I wanted to kill him. He lived on the telephone. He looked like he was always nervous, and he was blind as a bat. Most people didn't like riding in the car with him."

Demand for DHL's service mushroomed. Although, on average, Dalsey was signing only two new accounts every month, existing customers wanted DHL to expand in order to service more offices. Growth was exponential and, considering the size of a few of DHL's early clients, such as Bank of America, limitless. Hillblom and Dalsey had tapped a vast well of demand that was just beginning to gush; their only obstacle was that they did their job too well for some. "People wouldn't believe that we could have their material on the mainland before the office opened," Corral recalls. "We had to give a lot of free service to get people to try us out. And once they tried it, they were sold."

DHL wasn't just faster and more reliable than the post office. It was far more elegant in its simplicity. Clients paid a flat rate for a nylon pouch that traveled between two destinations every business day. The smallest pouch was rated at four pounds, but customers were charged the same rate whether it carried nothing or whether they managed to stuff twelve pounds of documents in it. That the pouches expanded was, in fact, an unintended selling point. Mailroom workers who managed to "overstuff" their pouch thought they were getting the deal of a lifetime.

As DHL expanded to more destinations, the pouches were color-coded by city, then stuffed into bright green weatherproof duffel bags in a sorting area—sometimes a grocery store parking lot where the drivers would meet after finishing their rounds. The bags were then driven to the airport and loaded directly onto the airplane from the tarmac—last, so that they would be the first to arrive. A DHL representative would then meet the courier at the counter, hand him (or her) a plane ticket and a small pile of baggage claim receipts. Hillblom often drove to the airport to help load the planes, goofing off with the drivers as he had with Corral and her fellow operators at the answering service. Meanwhile, Corral scoured Honolulu for anyone willing to give up their baggage rights for a free ticket to the mainland or to Guam. She called schools and churches first. A few of Hillblom's old Boalt Hall professors became couriers, as did Steven Kroll and both of his parents. So did a good portion of the Mormon congregation in Honolulu. Hillblom and Dalsey both had a tendency to offer pretty young women jobs. And at one point, two FBI agents showed up at Alakea to investigate reports that DHL was giving people airline tickets for free, as long as they were willing to take only carry-on baggage. The fact that would-be couriers were instructed to meet a Mr. Monty Hall at 11:00 p.m. underneath a digital clock beside the Pan Am ticket counter did not help assuage suspicions that there was something nefarious going on. But by the time the FBI agents finished their investigation, Corral had convinced them to become couriers themselves.

So it was with DHL's customers. Once they understood the company, their trust seemed absolute. DHL's couriers accumulated large rings of keys that permitted them entry into banks, law offices, insurance companies, and the mailrooms of large shipping firms. Corral was amazed that anyone would give Hillblom and his minions, who were often even younger and more questionable-looking than himself, access to their inner sanctums.

Of course, expansion required more than just couriers. Every station, particularly one like Honolulu, where pouches were being forwarded east or west, needed a manager. Hillblom and Dalsey naturally turned to a couple of their former coworkers at MPA, Bill Robinson and Jack Atwood. To foster an entrepreneurial spirit—and to save cash—Hillblom decided that each station should be owned by its own managers under contract with DHL. Robinson ended up with Los Angeles. Atwood quickly left to open an office in Seattle. That freed up Dalsey and Hillblom to focus on Asia, where their big shipping clients already were and where their banking clients wanted to be. Dalsey did most of the traveling, making sales calls and chatting up potential station managers, often in hotel bars. Hillblom stayed in Honolulu, devising a network that could grow exponentially but still be controlled. In theory, moving documents around the globe was not unlike moving crates of peaches from a farmer's truck to a loading bay. The real challenge was building the network, which involved a number of thorny legal and logistical issues. Legally, for example, most countries required that a shipment's actual owner (or an employee of an owner) clear customs. DHL was a third party. If DHL was using a subcontractor in another country, its client was twice removed from the shipment's original owner. Then there was the question of payment. If the shipper was a DHL customer, and a DHL courier shipped the pouch from Hawaii to Guam, for example, but another company shipped it onward to Singapore or Tokyo, how much did each company get paid? And whose customer were they? Then there were technical issues. If you loaded a shipment at point A and picked it up at point B, the courier business was pretty straightforward. But the hub-and-spoke system envisioned by Hillblom meant that shipments could become delayed—or lost—at several points along the way to point D or E or F. How did you keep track of thousands of important documents that could be in dozens of places at any given time?

While Larry grappled with these issues at Honolulu's law library and his office, his partner, Dalsey, was jet-setting the Far East in gleaming new Pan Am 747s. The older man usually stopped in Honolulu just long enough to see his girlfriend there and have dinner and an argument with Hillblom. "I was never very impressed with him," Corral says. "Of course, I was probably biased because Larry didn't like him at all. He admired his sales ability and Dalsey could really talk the talk. But they were always fighting about stuff. They differed about how everything should be done. We eventually decided it was really because Adrian was fifty-five and Larry was twenty-six. Larry wanted to try it and see what worked; Dalsey wanted to do it the way it had always been done. They would have yelling matches on the phone. In front of the rest of us, they would be civil, but I knew what was going on. Larry always won, because he would convince all of us that he was right."

Alakea was far too small and too messy for company meetings, which were held a mile down the road at a diner called the Tasty Broiler—Hillblom's favorite restaurant because of its $5.99 prime rib special that included soup, salad, and a drink. Money was very tight. If Dalsey joined them for dinner, he and Hillblom would try to outsit each other at the end of the meal, waiting to see who would eventually pick up the bill. Once or twice, an unsuspecting employee was left picking up the tab when both men abruptly left. Corral was forced to take money out of her own savings account to make sure that her paycheck cleared, while Dalsey and his wife maxed out credit cards and took out a second mortgage to pay the bills. Corral remembers having to comfort her young boss frequently. "We're doomed!" was a favorite refrain of Hillblom's, she recalls. But at the same time he was playing Chicken Little at the office, he dialed up his old college roommate Dave Crass and bragged about how much money his company was losing.

"That's crazy," Crass told him. "You'd better get out while you can."

"Nope," Larry replied. "Pretty soon, we're gonna be making money. *A lot of money.*"

Three

Unwelcome Attention

*R*uss Sands will never forget his first visit to DHL's new offices at the dawn of the 1970s. The young insurance agent had circled the Honolulu airport parking lot five times in his steaming rental car before Larry Hillblom finally jumped out from behind a concrete column waving a stopwatch.

"What the fuck are you doing?" Sands growled as Hillblom, dressed in board shorts, led him into an oversized Quonset hut adjacent to Pan Am's giant hangar.

"I was timing how long it would take government agents to find this place," Hillblom replied matter-of-factly. Sands did not ask him to elaborate. He was drenched in sweat and fuming.

Once inside, the two men negotiated a maze of hallways and small rooms previously occupied by the U.S. Customs Service that appeared less corporate office than bunker (outside) and commune (within). There were no placards announcing DHL's corporate headquarters and the doors had been stripped bare of names and titles. They passed a huge floor where piles of color-coded pouches were being sorted by hand, finally reaching a large room filled with desks and office equipment where a dozen young employees dressed in jeans and T-shirts milled around in barely contained chaos. None seemed tethered to any particular desk or piece of equipment, maybe because none had a title. Sandy Brant, an ebullient young air force wife whom Hillblom had just recruited to fill the courier schedules, had burrowed into a tiny space underneath a staircase and was happily banging away at an IBM Selectric typewriter. "If you can find this room," Hillblom quipped to Sands, "you're hired."

The company that Bob Lynn declared would never succeed was now growing faster than any other start-up of its era. From 1969 to 1971, sales would increase nearly 1,000 percent—from $64,750 to $661,376. When Marge Dalsey tallied 1972's sales from the huge ledger books that buried her dining room table, DHL would undoubtedly be a million-dollar company in only its third full year in business. (Microsoft would need another full year of operations to reach this milestone after its launch several years later.) DHL controlled 70 percent of the courier market between San Francisco and Hawaii and 80 percent of the market between Los Angeles and Hawaii. In a little more than twenty-four months, Adrian Dalsey had talked the talk from San Francisco to the Far East, adding the Federal Reserve, IBM, Standard Oil, and others to an ever-expanding client list of law firms and technology companies. DHL stations opened in Guam, Tokyo, Hong Kong, Manila, Sydney, and Singapore. It was poised to become the fastest-growing global corporation in history.

Moreover, the network was growing organically. Bank of America considered DHL so essential to the development of its overseas business that the company offered to prepay their invoices; like a number of DHL's other clients, they were addicts. And Hillblom's company simply could not keep up with the demand, though not for lack of trying. If a few clients demanded that DHL open an office in a new city, Hillblom obliged, even if the "office" was nothing more than a hotel room with a newly hired local working next to a jet-lagged American attorney. Steven Kroll would be called upon to perform the latter role many times. He would fly into an unknown city, meet with the station manager—a glorified driver in many instances—and file the necessary papers, then pray for the best before flying on to the next city. The station manager's expenses were paid by DHL. Depending on the station's size and importance, the manager was either an employee or worked on a cost-plus basis as a franchisee and signed an exclusive agency agreement. (Kroll received a suit as payment.) Hillblom's elegant solution for maintaining control over an increasingly disparate empire did not always hold, but it did accomplish two important goals: it made the franchisee-owner work harder, and it kept DHL's workforce from unionizing. The agency agreements also enabled the company to grow very fast with little cash, a constant issue.

By the early 1970s, DHL was opening a new country every two months and a new city every eight days. Friends often worked for free, while Pan Am's cargo manager in Honolulu held the company's invoices until DHL was able to pay them.

Station managers had to possess a driver's license, but they also had to know how to work on a shoestring budget and talk themselves out of sticky situations. Customs agents were not used to seeing a single passenger walk through with twenty or so green duffel bags. In some countries, they demanded a little something extra for their trouble. A station manager who figured out how to grease the wheels did very well irrespective of his résumé—*if* he had one. Hillblom was more interested in whether someone knew how to work. "Larry was pretty hard on those of us who were closely working with him," Corral recalls. "He didn't want any of us to drink. He wanted us to be aboveboard because of the potential of the reputation of DHL being harmed. He really demanded a lot of the managers. Before he pulled out, he would come to the corporate office and go through people's expense reports because he thought we really should not be turning in expenses, and it irritated him that people would travel and turn in meals and things like that. He felt that people should be grateful."

And ambitious. The chairman of DHL-Philippines was a sugar farmer and gas station owner who'd struck up a conversation with Adrian Dalsey at a bar on Guam. The top guy in Australia was a relentless taxi driver named David Allen, who had been hired on a rugby field in Melbourne. Allen and his young lieutenants would develop much of DHL's overseas network over the next ten years; in Honolulu, they were known as the cowboys.

Stateside, Corral had hired more than fifty operations people to feed the beast—including Steve Kroll's father, Max, and Hillblom's half brother, Grant Anderson. At Hillblom's insistence, they all worked full-time. Hundreds of couriers also had to be located and scheduled every month.

"There was a great compensation in knowing that me and my family could go anywhere," Steven Kroll explains. "Knowing that I could fly anywhere in the world, for a poor kid, was like being rich for me. With the couriers, DHL got unpaid employees who felt rich. I think it's almost a human characteristic that people like to think that they've gotten something for free—even people of dignity."

It was all too good to be true, of course, and in January 1972, the impending doom that Larry Hillblom had constantly sensed suddenly clackety-clacked onto a white sheet of paper spitting out of a telex machine. Marilyn Corral read it aloud. The sender, she announced, was an attorney at the Enforcement Division of something in Washington, D.C., called the Civil Aeronautics Board. The missive—thirteen words printed in stark, black capital letters—could not have been more direct:

> DHL SHOULD IMMEDIATELY CEASE AIR FREIGHT FORWARDING OPERATIONS UNTIL PROPER AUTHORITY IS RECEIVED.

Hillblom had no choice but to disobey the order; shutting down DHL's operations for even one day would have been fatal to the network. Then he jumped into his station wagon and drove to the law library, where a cursory study of administrative law revealed that the CAB, as it was commonly known, claimed jurisdiction only over airlines. This, Hillblom thought initially, was a huge relief; DHL did not own, lease, or operate airplanes. By the time that Hillblom returned to the office, however, he'd decided to ask Corral to book him as the courier to Washington, D.C., that night; in an abundance of caution, he wanted meet with the author of the telex face to face.

Hillblom arrived at Honolulu Airport's John Rodgers Terminal a little after 11:00 p.m. clutching a ticket for Pan Am's midnight flight to LAX. A balmy evening gust tousled his hair as he climbed the steps to the 707's front door, where he was greeted by a smiling stewardess wearing a sky-blue hat and gloves. He looked forward to spreading out in the back row of the cabin and getting some sleep, as he'd done in law school. He wasn't particularly concerned. His professors had taught him that federal agencies existed to help entrepreneurs like himself, to foster young companies like DHL. After all, this was America.

Several months earlier, Hillblom had encountered his first real adversary. A vice president of Loomis Corporation, the large courier and armored car company based in Seattle, had called on Dalsey and himself at DHL's office near the San Francisco Airport. For nearly two years, Loomis's employees had flown in the same airplanes as DHL's couriers and double-parked their vans outside the same office buildings as they made their pickups and deliveries. Otherwise, the companies could not have been more different. Loomis proudly traced its heritage back to 1852, the days of the Pony Express, the California Gold Rush, and the development of the Alaska Territory. Its bespectacled founder, Lee Loomis, had driven the first armored car west of the Mississippi in 1925, and the company's literature boasted that its employees had included Wild Bill Hickok, Wyatt Earp, and Buffalo Bill Cody. The company was now run by Loomis's grandson Charles.

The Loomis executive who had called on Dalsey and Hillblom had begun the meeting in an appropriately gentlemanly fashion. DHL was clearly growing very fast, he'd noted; its customer list, as far as the executive could tell, was very impressive. And DHL was already active in the Far East, a market that Loomis had been eyeing for some time. The obvious solution, he'd remarked, was for the two companies to combine their efforts. And because Loomis was roughly fifty times DHL's size, that meant a buy-out of DHL's two shareholders. Dalsey had enthusiastically nodded in agreement. Hillblom had not. By the time he'd stood up to leave, the Loomis executive had resorted to threats. "If you don't accept our offer," he'd said before leaving, "we'll institute legal proceedings and drive you under. We've done it before."

Within days, DHL's couriers, including Steve Kroll's father and Hillblom's half brother, Grant, had reported being tailed; occasionally, the insides of their cars were photographed by mysterious men as they made their deliveries. Hillblom increasingly blamed Dalsey for attracting Loomis's attention, and he wondered if the older man was secretly egging Loomis on in order to convince him to sell out. Dalsey nagged at Hillblom to sell, pointing out that MPA, their former employer, had recently gone bankrupt because of the kind of litigation that Loomis had threatened. "I can easily see Dalsey trying to sell to Loomis," Kroll sighs. "Dalsey's tolerance for risk would have been considerably less than Larry's. He was of my parents' generation, but he was probably more motivated by fear of losing everything, and you don't criticize someone who lived through the Depression for feeling that way."

But now that Dalsey's worst fears had been realized, Hillblom dug in his heels even further. He ignored Loomis and refused the CAB's order to shut down, even as he called on their Washington, D.C., headquarters in an effort to placate them. While the CAB's bureaucrats dallied, apparently unsure what to make of his rebuke, Loomis lost its patience and filed an action against DHL for operating illegally without a freight forwarder permit. What they wanted was an injunction to stop DHL from doing business, the theory being that a cease and desist order from a federal court would be more effective than a telex from a constipated federal agency.

Elements of *Loomis Armored Car v. DHL Corporation* were laughable, including the pretense that allowed Loomis's attorneys to file it in the first place. Loomis claimed to be a "party of interest," legalese for innocent bystander. As an upstanding corporate citizen, the armored car giant was being unfairly forced to compete with a rogue operator. Or so said Loomis's polished attorneys. They did not mention that their client was at least equally roguish as DHL. Despite transporting similar goods on the same routes in exactly the same manner—sometimes for the same clients—Loomis had never filed for an operating certificate either.

Hillblom hired Kroll to draft DHL's response. Then they flew to the San Francisco courtroom of Judge Samuel Conti, a stern Nixon appointee, who had been assigned the case. Adrian Dalsey, ensconced in the gallery behind the bar that separates attorneys from observers, sensed trouble the moment that Loomis's attorneys strutted up to the plaintiffs' table in tailored suits. "It's like Huey and Dewey versus Perry Mason," he groaned to Marge within earshot of Hillblom, Kroll, and Marilyn Corral, who had stayed up all night typing DHL's reply brief.

When Conti entered the courtroom, Loomis's legal team, from the white-shoe firm of Pillsbury, Madison & Sutro, immediately zeroed in on DHL's operating without authorization. Conti nodded appreciatively, as Kroll, nearly hysterical, jumped up from the counsel's table to object, pointing out the glaring double standard of Loomis's action. Conti dismissed him in curt volleys. Kroll became argumentative and, after an exasperating back-and-forth, questioned the judge's motives. By the time Conti's gavel fell, the judge had made it clear that he considered DHL an illegal operator, though he would allow Kroll a chance to change his mind at trial rather than rule on summary judgment, as Loomis's lawyers asked. Hillblom and his company were left hanging.

"There was one night with the lights coming through the fog, dreariness," Kroll remembers. "We were in Burlingame, which is where DHL's San Francisco office was. We were deep in the Loomis case, but I'm just telling you it's strange because my memory is of the entire sense of it. Larry was crying; he was terrified of losing the case and losing his company. I do remember that because it was something so unlike Larry, the fear of losing, and that is when my maternal instincts kicked in to protect him. I vaguely remember him talking about being very concerned for the people who worked for DHL and that it was not just a dream of his that was at stake, but that there were human beings whose livelihoods depended on what was going to happen here. And that impressed me deeply. The pessimism surprised me. He was not a negative person. I'd never seen him think that he might lose before or since."

Kroll began preparing a countersuit accusing Loomis of anticompetitive behavior that would be filed in federal court in Honolulu, but it would take months, maybe years, to go to trial—much too long to save his company. And Kroll, maternal instincts aside, lacked the experience and gravitas to fight the kind of litigators they had just encountered. Hillblom's only hope was to throw himself at the mercy of the CAB and hope that they'd give him the operating certificate that he was still convinced he did not need, before December, only a few months away. So the next morning, he boarded a Pan Am jet bound for Washington. He was ready to play ball, still dangerously unaware of the forces conspiring against him.

Four

Courting

Of course he got nowhere. The CAB's monolithic cement-and-glass headquarters on Connecticut Avenue was even more of a fortress inside than out. "Larry," recalls Patrick Lupo, who would accompany him to Washington on future trips, "starts trying to see people. And they won't see him. And the classic is, Larry used to fly in from SFO [San Francisco International Airport]; he'd fly all night. He'd go into the CAB to see somebody and they wouldn't see him, so he'd sleep on their couch. He'd fall fast asleep on their couch—one hour, two hours, three hours—and then, finally, someone would see him. Or maybe not. I think there were a couple of times when he stayed there all day and they refused to see him. So, on the one hand, they didn't call the police to cart him out, but on the other hand, they ignored him. . . . He got absolutely nowhere."

Hillblom, Marilyn Corral remembers, once arrived at the CAB before the office was open. Exhausted from the red-eye, he pulled a bench up to the front doors and fell asleep, assuming that the first employees to arrive would wake him up. Instead, thinking that he was intentionally blocking them, they called security. Hillblom had finally met his match, an adversary even more stubborn and more ambivalent than himself: bureaucracy. He complained bitterly that his Boalt Hall professors had sold him a false version of America. "How can you be more patriotic than to believe that one of the branches of government will bring justice?" Kroll smiles.

Hillblom felt betrayed, but not defeated. He spent a good chunk of DHL's precious cash hiring a Washington, D.C., law firm. And on his way back from Washington, he decided to lay over in New York City, where a friend from law school named Jimmy Braziler had settled. Braziler was young and inexperienced, but he was practicing environmental law for the EPA, so he had some insight into how large government agencies like the CAB worked. Hillblom wanted to pick his brain about a legal term known as "compliance disposition." A CAB attorney had promised that, if DHL could prove that it had acted in good faith and was doing its best to be in compliance with the law—i.e., its compliance disposition—then the agency would issue the company its license and Conti would vacate his cease and desist order. Even if Hillblom's research, as well as common sense, strongly suggested that DHL did not need an airline license in the first place, DHL did not have the time (or the money) to fight a turf battle with a much larger competitor aligned with one of the federal government's most powerful agencies.

Braziler still lives in New York City. He's retired and prefers not to talk about Larry Hillblom in light of all the press attention. Given his age and lack of experience in the matters vexing his former classmate, one can assume that Braziler provided little more than a couch for Larry to crash on in his tiny basement apartment back then. But Braziler's wife, Alice, a vivacious Queens native with a ready smile, provided access to something equally important: a girl.

"I'm not positive when we met," Carla Summer tells me as she picks at a small bowl of cut watermelon with elegantly thin fingers. "He decided that he liked me when I had hardly met him." Summer is now a middle-aged grad student majoring in social work at nearby Yale University. In 1971, she was Carla Bostom, a nineteen-year-old psychology major at Queens College—a striking girl with jet-black hair, a dancer's body, and a penchant for both antiwar and civil rights activism. She was then in the midst of divorcing her husband. And she was Alice Braziler's best friend.

To say that Summer was different from the girlies—the stewardesses and the secretaries—that Hillblom was used to dating (his previous girlfriend's name was Peaches, if that's any indication) would be an understatement. Summer had been a member of the antiwar group SDS at Barnard College. In the spring of 1968, she'd participated in the takeover of the president's office at Columbia University, alongside members of the school's African-American alliance.

When Alice introduced her to Hillblom at an apartment party in Brooklyn, Summer ignored him—*not* because of his politics, which were diametrically opposed to her own. She didn't let the gangly weirdo with the blond hair get that far. Indeed, Summer found it hysterical that a guy who looked like Hillblom could believe that a girl who looked like her might be interested at all. But when he kept coming back to New York, he became harder to brush off. Finally he cornered her at another party. "I really want to get to know you and you're not letting me," he blurted. "Can we go somewhere else and be together?"

"Some other time," Summer replied. "And let's do something fun." In other words, she wasn't interested in a date; if they hung out, there would have to be a built-in distraction.

On their first non-date, a canoe outing to the Delaware Water Gap with Alice and Jimmy, Hillblom became infuriated when the current turned against him. Summer laughed hysterically as Larry stabbed the water with his paddle again and again until he finally allowed the canoe to move with the current. On subsequent encounters, he would show up at her mother's house in Queens with a caseload of grapefruit or cherries— grapefruit because he'd read that they dissolved fat and cherries because they caused your bowels to move, thereby increasing the flow of calories through the body. "He ate armloads of grapefruit and cherries," Summer laughs. "It was about him wanting to be attractive and thin."

But it wasn't enough for Hillblom to fixate on a particular food. "He would physically take the food and stuff it into my mouth," she recalls. "I couldn't die before him—he talked about that a lot. He had decided that I should be as healthy as he was going to be."

Another reason that Hillblom loved to shove cherries and grapefruit down her throat was that she didn't expect it. His unique way of relating to other people was to tease and torment them and become very overbearing. If they went to a dinner party hosted by liberal Jews, for example, Hillblom would loudly praise the writings of Ayn Rand, the objectivist author of *The Fountainhead* and *Atlas Shrugged*. But if he was surrounded by Republicans, Hillblom might suddenly espouse the genius of Chairman Mao. Summer began to think that he was incapable of relating to people except as a provocateur. But while those who didn't know him could be offended, Summer had never taken Larry seriously from the start.

"He was actually very fragile and very shy," she says. "He would get me to introduce him to other people. Then he would be able to start in. He enjoyed living but there were some ways in which he was inhibited that I was not that he really enjoyed, almost kid-like. For example, I loved to sing. Larry would say that everyone in Kingsburg told him that he looked and sounded like Elvis, but he wouldn't sing. He just didn't have that style of expressing his joy of living. He was living vicariously. He was very cautious. He liked to watch."

Summer grabs a cube of watermelon from the table and pops it into her mouth. "My grandmother would take me to the beach when I was very little," she says, "and I would insist that she take the first bite out of the peaches because I thought she would make it juicy for me. That was Larry: 'You make it juicy for me.'"

Hillblom had a harder time making it juicy for her. Summer was flattered, amused, even charmed by his attention, but seduced she was not. "I didn't find it endearing," she says of his initial attempts at courting her. "In hindsight, I probably hadn't met someone like him. I just didn't think of him as unique."

Like the uncooperative river, the more Hillblom tried to force her to his will, the faster she resisted. "In some ways"—she laughs—"it was the way I ended up treating my kids—laugh and know that I'm not going to get anywhere fighting it, distract him to move on to something else." But Hillblom was just as incapable of being distracted as he was of going with the flow. He had never really courted women; he'd *recruited* them with the promise of a job or a vacation. Carla would not make him change his tune, though Hillblom eventually realized that she required a variation on the same theme.

"I felt very responsible for the condition of the country and the condition of the world," Carla says with a smile. "At different times, there were things that became the most important. Larry wooed me by painting DHL as a civic duty. It was the rights of a small company up against this huge conglomerate and the Civil Aeronautics Board." She pauses. "I took the bait, with pleasure."

That May, she agreed to spend her short break before summer semester in Honolulu. Larry had bought a little house in Kaneohe, a small village on Oahu, which he shared with his half brother, Grant, and a high school friend, both of whom worked for DHL. He showed her off to Marilyn Corral at the bunker, but they spent most of their time canoodling in bed, frolicking in the pool, or lying under a clipped mango tree. He nicknamed her "Audie," short for "Arty-Farty," because he said she passed gas. Driving through the short tunnel that connects Kaneohe with Honolulu, Carla sang along to the radio at the top of her lungs as Larry turned up the volume, lips moving silently, hips shaking to the beat:

Delta Dawn, what's that flower you have on
Could it be a faded rose from days gone by

At night, tucked into bed, she whacked his head with a rolled-up newspaper to relieve his constant migraines. He told her that the metal plate in his forehead had saved him from going to Vietnam. He confided an intense desire to emulate Howard Hughes—running an empire from the background, pulling the strings from behind a curtain. He would stay up for hours after she'd dozed off, watching the preacher Jimmy Swaggart, sometimes manipulating the screen so that only Swaggart's lips were visible. He told her that he wanted to be an evangelist. As with Mao, he was fascinated with the almost psychic power that Swaggart held over millions of people.

Five days after she'd arrived, Carla called New York and asked her mother to take care of her cat and close down her apartment. She wasn't coming home; Larry had only bought her a one-way ticket anyway. Her mother was thrilled, but when she came to Honolulu herself, she found her daughter in the middle of a power struggle. Adrian Dalsey, Carla says, immediately cornered her mother to deliver his increasingly desperate pitch. "He knew how to speak to women of her generation," she recalls. "He would sit next to her and say, 'Your daughter's missing the boat. This is a now or never opportunity. If we sell to Loomis, she could be provided for,' and on and on."

But there was no driving a wedge between the two young lovers. "I liked Carla a lot," Corral tells me. "She was a sweet kid. I felt sorry for her because Larry would tease and prod her all the time, but I was impressed with how smart she was. They were inseparable, and hanging on each other. It was a big joke about the two of them because they were constantly clinging to each other. You learned to knock first. You were never sure what you might find." Carla helped Hillblom research his *Loomis* pleadings at the law library, scouring the stacks for law journals as he struggled with words. "He really agonized over whether something was done," she remembers. "He had to write a lot of first drafts. He was afraid of what Steven would have to say." She accompanied him on the grueling trips to the CAB, where, despite the fact that they seemed to be getting nowhere, Hillblom would act as though victory was just around the corner. "The CAB thing was totally frustrating," she remembers, "but Larry always portrayed it to me like he would win. He was kind of macho about it. But clearly, they didn't take two kids in jeans seriously."

When Judge Conti scheduled a second hearing on a Loomis motion for summary judgment, Carla flew to San Francisco to serve as a courier between Kroll and Hillblom, who drafted their response late into the night at Kroll's aunt's apartment above Ghirardelli Square, and Marilyn Corral, who was staying at a downtown hotel along with DHL's IBM typewriter. "Steven took it very seriously," Carla recalls, "He took it personally and he was a perfectionist [but] Larry's mind was always going faster than his ability to type. . . . He had the concepts, but had great difficulty putting them on paper. So Steven would get very upset and he was very hyper and God knows what drugs they had been on to get the work done. I think Larry just really had a fear of being called to task when he wasn't prepared."

Arriving at the courtroom the next morning with Corral, Carla, Kroll, and the response that they'd just finished—a novella that admonished the judge not to destroy an enterprise that "once had a place in the American Dream"—Hillblom was ambushed with an *amicus* brief written by the same CAB attorney who had promised a certificate if DHL improved its "compliance disposition." He was rereading it when Conti appeared, cast a disparaging glance at himself and Kroll, and quickly granted summary judgment in favor of Loomis—exactly what the CAB was requesting in its *amicus* brief. DHL, Conti ordered, was to cease and desist all operations by the end of 1973, only a few months away, unless the CAB explicitly authorized the company to continue.

Seated in the gallery, exhausted from crisscrossing Geary Street the night before, Carla knew how devastating a blow the ruling was—not just to DHL, but to Larry personally. "We were all feeling ourselves drowning." She sighs. "We were scared." They needed a savior, someone who knew his way around a federal courtroom, who'd taken on big corporations and huge bureaucracies and expensive law firms and won. Someone who was not a kid in blue jeans.

The Professor

The University of San Francisco School of Law occupies one of several three-story buildings clustered atop a modest hill that crowns a quiet neighborhood adjacent to Golden Gate Park. Founded as part of a Jesuit mission in 1912, USF has spent the better part of a century shrouded in fog, a not-so-subtle reminder of its relative obscurity. Reputation-wise, the school is eclipsed by Boalt Hall to the east and Stanford to the south, though USF consistently ranks in the nation's top 150 law schools and publishes a respected quarterly journal.

In the fall of 1973, constitutional law was taught by a middle-aged antitrust lawyer named Peter Donnici. Recently divorced, Donnici looked and acted like a favorite uncle: pudgy and cerebral but also patient and approachable. Outside of class, Donnici had for years worked beside the legendary San Francisco mayor, civil rights activist, and antitrust lawyer Joe Alioto. The son of Italian immigrants, Alioto had pioneered the private use of antitrust statutes, the laws passed by Congress in the 1920s to thwart the monopolistic ambitions of the robber barons. Alioto's strategy was revolutionary: instead of using the law like a hammer to shatter a corporate behemoth into smaller bits, as the Justice Department had done, he would sue on behalf of clients that had been harmed by their anticompetitive behavior. This market-driven application of antitrust law had made Alioto a legend in legal circles and a millionaire many times over. In the late sixties and early seventies, his junior partner, Pete Donnici, had helped him take on some of the largest corporations in the world, including the mother of all trusts, Standard Oil. Donnici had also argued a defamation case against *Look* magazine, after it published a salacious article linking his boss to the Mafia.

In early 1974, Donnici was preparing an appeal to the Ninth Circuit of a lawsuit that the Alioto firm had just lost—a dispute between International Harvester, the farm equipment giant, and one of its dealers—when a colleague who taught antitrust across the bay asked the professor if he would meet with a former student named Larry Hillblom, now the vice president of DHL, a small but rapidly growing courier company based in the Bay Area. Hillblom, he said, had evidence that one of his larger competitors was conspiring with a government agency to put him out of business. Donnici had never heard of Hillblom or of DHL, nor was he especially familiar with the courier industry. But Hillblom's predicament sounded like the classic antitrust case that Donnici had spent his professional career training for: six-hundred-pound gorilla beats the small guy into submission. If DHL's competitor was really in cahoots with a federal agency, that would certainly be an interesting twist, especially considering what the papers were just now uncovering about Richard Nixon's administration.

So Donnici told his colleague that yes, he would be interested in talking to Larry Hillblom.

Peter Donnici once referred to himself as "Darth Vader." The last writer to interview him received a twelve-page, twenty-one-point itemized letter threatening legal action after her story was published in *GQ* ten years ago. For months, I have been warned that he would either not talk to me at all or try to charm me. But the man presently holding court behind a polished conference table overlooking a quaint manmade marina in Petaluma, a small town one hour north of San Francisco that is now home to the Larry Lee Hillblom Foundation, is none of these things. Eased into one of those high-backed leather chairs that dominate most conference rooms, he simply looks apprehensive—and very tired. Here is a man on the far side of middle age: overweight, skin embalmed with nicotine, face hung slightly lopsided from the skull, someone who has voluntarily shrouded himself in dark suits for so long that his neck seems to slouch a bit without a tie to hold it in place. *Consigliere* is the word that comes to mind. On his desk in the adjoining office is a framed photo of himself and his second wife, Diane, formerly a DHL receptionist, on their wedding day. They are smiling in front of a white Rolls-Royce limousine.

"I don't know what you've heard but there's no way Larry's alive," the funereal Donnici begins in a very deep voice. "He wouldn't be able to stay out of the action this long." Then he ticks off a few random thoughts—how Larry might have regretted fighting for airline deregulation considering the perpetual nightmare that air travel has become; how Larry would have hated the yellow-and-red DHL color scheme; how he never would have sold out to Deutsche Post. When I ask him to recount the story of their first meeting, a smile emerges. "I was in my academic office at the University of San Francisco," Donnici says, "when a young man poked his head in the door. I assumed that he was one of my students because of the way he was dressed and the way he carried himself. I asked him to return a little later because I had a previously scheduled appointment. He kind of grunted or nodded. Then he walked back out into the hall.

"About twenty minutes later, he poked his head into my office again. 'I think I'm your appointment,' he mumbled. 'I'm Larry.' He had been waiting just outside the door the entire time!" Donnici chuckles. "'Well, okay,' I said. 'Come right on in.'"

Antitrust attorneys and college professors hear their share of sob stories on a daily basis, but I imagine that Larry Hillblom's came harder and faster than most. From the edge of his seat facing Donnici's, Hillblom launched into the background of *Loomis Armored Car v. DHL Corporation,* ending with Judge Conti's death sentence. Donnici did not need a calendar to know that, if he took the case, there would be almost no time to save Hillblom's company.

"After he finished," Donnici says, "I told him that he had a fascinating case, and that his enthusiasm was contagious. *But,* I also told him, 'One of the things that a lawyer takes into consideration when deciding whether or not to take a case is the fee involved.'"

"We don't have any money," Larry had interrupted. But, he'd promised, the judge would eventually award Donnici attorneys' fees—when they won the case. Not surprisingly, Donnici did not agree to take the case right away. He could not have believed that DHL would win, much less that a judge would award him a generous fee, but DHL held two trump cards: Steven Kroll had filed the antitrust lawsuit in Hono-lulu, and Hillblom could provide a limitless number of plane tickets there. "Donnici took the job," Marilyn Corral recalls, "because Larry told him he could have free flights to Hawaii. He had girlfriends, so he would take all of his girlfriends to Hawaii."

"The funny thing"—Donnici grins—"is that most of the people who started DHL came from humble backgrounds and they were just very energetic and had good ideas and were willing to sacrifice. They did not live the good life during those early days." Even senior manag-ers like Marilyn Corral were forced to travel as couriers, which meant flying at night and arriving with little or no clothes, often red-eyed and exhausted. Then they were expected to work a full day. After all, Hillblom had worked around the clock at Boalt Hall, and he was now involved in every facet of DHL's operations, including, of course, the *Loomis* case.

Despite the CAB's ambush, Hillblom still counted at least one friend in the bureau's legal department and he had made a huge compromise in the hopes of receiving an operating certificate. Hillblom had agreed that DHL was an air freight forwarder, an innocuous classification that should have entitled him to a certificate as a matter of course, much like a driver's license. Instead, the CAB had issued only a temporary authorization attached to a long list of recommendations—actions that its attorneys claimed were necessary to prove DHL's "compliance dispo-sition."

The first recommendation was that DHL fold all of the independent stations into DHL Corporation, meaning that the major station manag-ers would no longer be small business owners; they would be minority shareholders in Dalsey and Hillblom's company. Second, DHL would be forced to issue airbills and tariff schedules—voluminous lists of the prices that DHL charged per pound of freight; these schedules would have to be approved by the CAB at least three months in advance; finally, the agency had decided that Hillblom and Dalsey could not own any part of DHL's international stations because that would constitute an illegal "tie-up"—in other words, the exclusive agency agreements that Hillblom had envisioned as the glue of the DHL network were illegal.*

The CAB's recommendations would be expensive to implement and onerous—particularly the last one. But Hillblom felt he had no other choice. He had to play by their rules now because he wanted Donnici to argue that only the CAB—and not Conti or any other judge—had the authority to regulate a freight forwarder. Acknowledging the CAB's authority was an extremely risky strategy considering that the bureau had already issued a cease and desist order of its own and had sided with Loomis in its lawsuit. If Donnici succeeded in reversing Judge Conti's opinion using this argument, Hillblom would still have to convince the CAB to essentially reverse itself and look favorably on his company. He could not ignore them a second time. They were the lesser of his two evils.

At first, Hillblom's new strategy appeared to work. On December 19, two days before Judge Conti's deadline, the Civil Aeronautics Board suddenly issued an order authorizing DHL to operate on a probationary basis. Six months later, Hillblom and Peter Donnici appeared before the Ninth Circuit to argue that Conti had never had the authority to shut DHL down in the first place and that the CAB should have exclusive jurisdiction over DHL. Hillblom spoke first but was shot down after only a few minutes. "You understand that this is an appellate court," one of the judges interrupted, with the unctuous tone of Adrian Dalsey or Samuel Conti, "because you are arguing issues that a trial court decides."

Humiliated, Hillblom sat down and let Donnici deliver the arguments that they'd crafted, along with a few other defenses—that DHL had not been aware that a certificate was needed, for example, and that the company had worked tirelessly to prove its "compliance disposition" to the CAB, including manufacturing tariff sheets and airbills and divesting its founders' shares in DHL's international operations.

---

* Modern equivalents of illegal tie-ups would include code-sharing agreements between airlines that result in monopolies or near-monopolies of certain routes. Generally, such tie-ups are seen as reducing competition and allowing the partnerships to control pricing.

Unfortunately, Donnici does not remember much more, other than the rather obvious fact that his efforts eventually won what he calls "the good result." Unable to answer any of my requests for more specifics, he apologizes for his imperfect memory and then dismisses a few of my lame attempts to probe into other aspects of Hillblom's life—and death. Only as I am being led out of the conference room does Larry Hillblom's former consigliere touch on the controversial: "I know that you've been speaking to some of our enemies," he says. "You know that we were totally exonerated in a court case here in San Mateo."

"No," I said. "I did not know that." And we leave it at that, because neither one of us wants to go down that road, at least not quite yet.

Six

Interlopers

*A*drian Dalsey died less than a year before Hillblom's disappearance and only a few months after he reunited with his young partner to celebrate the twenty-fifth anniversary of their creation. He had almost become an octogenarian. Dalsey was survived by his second wife, Annie, whom he'd met while establishing DHL in the Philippines, and their young son, Jonathan. Dalsey's tiny obituary in the *New York Times* noted that the company he cofounded had grown to serve 223 countries and territories, employ 33,400 people, and have annual sales of approximately $3 billion. A DHL spokesperson contacted by the paper stated that neither Dalsey nor Hillblom had held a title at the company, which was not true. The last line of the obituary claimed that Dalsey had helped build the company until the mid-1980s, when he retired from day-to-day operations, which was also not true. Dalsey's ouster had come far before then, thanks partly to Larry Hillblom's long-held suspicions that his partner had conspired with Loomis but ultimately due to Peter Donnici's doggedness.

The smoking gun is buried among acres of court records stored in the federal archives in San Mateo, squeezed into a box filled with documents that Donnici had subpoenaed almost immediately upon taking the *Loomis* case. One of these documents was an internal memorandum from Loomis's Honolulu office based on the notes of an executive named George DeBon, who had attended a meeting in June 1973 between one of Loomis's vice presidents and Adrian Dalsey. Loomis and DHL were then knee-deep in very acrimonious litigation. DeBon's notes make it clear that Larry Hillblom was not present that day, as Adrian Dalsey paid a visit to a handful of Loomis executives. According to DeBon's notes, the silver fox had been very generous with information, sharing DHL's financials and details of his and Hillblom's compensation—including the curious fact that he received $400 more per month in salary than his equal partner. He'd revealed that DHL had bought an armored truck in Guam and was trying to diversify into Loomis's core business there. He had even taken some potshots at his stubborn younger partner. "Hillblom is a much more technically and operationally oriented person than a people-oriented person," he'd said euphemistically when asked about Larry's importance to DHL's success. Perhaps worried that that might be too subtle, Dalsey had added: "He probably wouldn't be someone we would seek to continue to employ because he is kind of an eccentric—good for only limited kinds of corporate things."

According to DeBon, Dalsey had then offered up his 50 percent of the company for $250,000, give or take, plus a five-year employment agreement that would float him until he was two years from retirement.

When Donnici unearthed what Dalsey had said about him, Hillblom went ballistic. But he did not confront his partner about the incident directly. Confrontation was not his thing. "He would get coldly explosive," Steven Kroll recalls. "His eyes, slits anyway, would close even further. He'd clench his jaw and he had a certain look when he was displeased—a set in his mouth. He had very full, lovely lips and the squint and the focus and that mouth, that was how he expressed his anger."

Carla's recollection is less dramatic: "He told me, 'Adrian has to go,'" she says. "That's when Larry saw the silver lining of being in a regulated industry. He used the computerized stuff to get the books moved out of Marge's hands."

Ever since Adrian Dalsey had signed Seatrain, his wife had handled DHL's accounting with the help of an elderly CPA. Even considering DHL's growth, Marge's job had not been difficult because clients were charged a single monthly fee depending on the size of the pouch (or pouches) they used. But now, as a licensed freight forwarder, DHL was required to publish quarterly tariff schedules and file them with the CAB. The company also had to generate airbills for every single shipment—i.e., no more four-pound pouch with twelve pounds of documents stuffed inside. Once Hillblom had classified DHL as a freight forwarder, the simple, self-regulating system he'd invented had suddenly become a data-intensive accounting nightmare. To generate the necessary paperwork, he rented time on an IBM mainframe above an aloha-shirt shop in Honolulu. From dusk until nearly dawn, Hillblom and Carla programmed the giant machine to create airbills and invoices for each DHL shipment—though they were mostly just backing out numbers based on what their clients were paying anyway.

By the time of DHL's board meeting in 1975, Marge Dalsey and her sharpened pencil could no longer keep up. It was then that Marilyn Corral received a long-distance phone call from the Dalseys' dining room; it was Hillblom, telling her that she had been appointed to replace Marge as treasurer because the company's headquarters were being moved to Honolulu. "What does a treasurer do?" Corral blurted. She was thirty-one years old and had no financial background. "You know," Larry replied, "you've got to set up an accounting office and do the books." Of course, Corral would have to get them first, and a few days later, a visibly distraught Marge Dalsey handed stacks of handwritten ledgers over in the middle of her dining room office, where she had spent the past six years holding DHL together on maxed-out credit cards and a second mortgage. "They got Adrian," Marge told one of the company's longtime vendors a few days later. She knew that power had shifted to her husband's socially inept young partner; the company she'd nurtured with such devotion and love had been spirited away to an island paradise halfway across the Pacific Ocean. She was bitter, and her husband had just returned home with a pregnant young Filipina. But she still, somehow, cared for Larry.

Now that Hillblom was in control, he expected total devotion to the cause. "Our families had to come to the office in order to see us," Marilyn Corral, who had a husband and young daughter at the time, recalls. Because Hillblom arrived at the office a little after 6:00 a.m. and the last batch of couriers didn't depart Honolulu until midnight, the office was dark for less than seven hours a day—seven days a week. The distribution center, where pouches were sorted, ran twenty-four hours a day, every day. On Friday night, Hillblom insisted that every package in the warehouse had to be either delivered or accounted for before anyone could leave.

Corral was expected to be available anytime Larry needed her. When she took a weekend beach day with her husband, Hillblom was furious and sent Grant Anderson to track her down. Working conditions were no less stressful than the hours. Hillblom prohibited signs in the office, making it nearly impossible for suppliers and new employees to find DHL. Advertising was also forbidden. So too were cameras. Paranoia sometimes seemed to be the only fuel that Hillblom—or DHL—ran on. Returning to the office from dinner with Carla and Marilyn, Larry saw a man holding a couple of garbage bags; he slammed on the brakes, jumped out of the driver's seat, and chased the guy down the alley until he dropped them. It wasn't the first time Larry had exploded over nothing. "He's doing it again," Marilyn whispered to Carla.

On the early side of 1975, two auditors from the CAB suddenly appeared at DHL's headquarters. "They just showed up," Marilyn recalls. "They were wearing suits. They walked into the warehouse area of this customs place where we were all working. The operations manager came and said, There's two guys from the CAB. Larry and Carla happened to be at the law library. When I got him on the phone over there, Larry freaked out: 'What are they there for?' 'I haven't even met them yet,' I said. 'I'm just alerting you that they're here.' "

Hillblom drove back to the office immediately, but he was too nervous to go in, so he sent Carla. He knew what the feds were after—they wanted to take a hatchet to DHL's "compliance disposition." But also he knew that they would not leave until they spoke to him, so, after Marilyn had taken them on a tour of the facility and Carla had chatted them up, Hillblom finally emerged from his hiding place and introduced himself. But he was so nervous that he pulled out the wrong business card, the international business card with his name imprinted over the title Vice President. He realized his mistake immediately. Turning white, Hillblom suddenly walked out as quickly as he'd walked in. Corral was close enough to see the card. But there was nothing anyone could do. Hillblom himself had just handed the CAB evidence that he had not divested the international company as promised—that he had not only misled the agency but, more important, that he was not behaving.

He drove to the airport that night without a good-bye. He boarded the flight to Guam, leaving his girlfriend and his number one employee to deal with the fallout from his monumental screw-up. "Carla felt threatened," Corral recalled. "And, of course, I felt threatened from the standpoint that they were trying to find us doing something wrong." When a hysterical Hillblom dialed in from Guam and, later, Hong Kong, demanding to be told what the auditors were up to, Corral told him to come back and see for himself.

"It was really scary," Carla says. "I was locked in the room with one of the auditors the entire time. The auditors kept me and Marilyn in different rooms and they made us explain the same things over and over again."

For two weeks, the CAB auditors tried to make sense of a hodgepodge of records and computer printouts, to no avail. Eventually, they summoned Corral into an office, declared DHL "unauditable," and left.

By the time Larry reappeared, Carla had moved into Corral's house. The woman he had wooed by painting DHL as a movement, who had become DHL's most devoted acolyte, had finally begun to question the man she was working for. When he asked Carla to marry him, she said no—twice. Though she would move back into the house at Kaneohe and continue to work for the company in various capacities for another decade, the intimate relationship was over—even if, for months after their breakup, Larry would sleep on the little couch in her bedroom. He claimed that he was unable to sleep without her nearby.

"Larry hated to be with himself," Carla would reminisce years later. "He was very lost."

Seven

The Fighter

"In the course of your research, has anyone ever mentioned Larry being autistic? No? I was just curious."

L. Patrick Lupo, DHL's third general counsel (after Steven Kroll and Hillblom himself), perches on the edge of a comfy chair in a solarium overlooking his estate one hour north of London—lush hills once home to the Beatles and now peppered, he says, with Russian billionaires. Lupo is a tall, confident man with thick hair and a groomed mustache. A native of Montana, he has lived in Europe for the past twenty-five years, most of that time as chairman and chief executive officer of DHL, International. More than anyone besides Hillblom himself, Lupo is responsible for DHL's $4 billion-plus in annual revenues. A dossier of press clippings on his coffee table attests to his stature among the leaders of global businesses; more than a few make note of his razor-sharp wit.

Lupo was a star pupil at the University of San Francisco School of Law when his constitutional law professor, Peter Donnici, asked him to work on an antitrust case he had just filed in federal court in Honolulu. Lupo had never heard of either DHL or Loomis Corp., but he was interested in regulatory law, and the prospect of frequent trips to Hawaii sold him. What he did not know at the time was that DHL was basically broke, so he would be flying back and forth as a courier, which meant always taking the red-eye, loitering around the Pan Am ticket counter near midnight, and receiving his ticket at the last moment—often with twenty-odd bag tags attached. "You'd really feel like you were doing something illegal!" he howls. Which, of course, is exactly what the CAB and Loomis were alleging—and what Lupo had been hired to disprove.

Meeting Hillblom did not inspire confidence. Although Lupo assures me that Peter Donnici would have warned him about the DHL founder's lack of social grace, their first meeting was a disaster. "He and I were going to Seattle to take depositions in the *Loomis* case," Lupo recalls. "And he went through this whole spiel about how Loomis had just about destroyed DHL and how it was populated with bad people and all that, immediately. He had a tendency to get intense right off the bat and you'd really feel like he was in your face."

Lupo decided to assume the role of objective observer—the role he'd been taught in law school. As such, he did not necessarily believe Hillblom's sob story. Settling into a chair in the plush conference room of Loomis's downtown Seattle offices the next morning, however, the young law school graduate, who had yet to pass the bar, found that keeping a lawyerly demeanor would be extraordinarily difficult in the presence of Larry Hillblom. With Donnici preoccupied researching the appeal of the San Francisco judge's cease and desist, and with whatever money DHL had for lawyers being spent in Washington, Hillblom had decided to conduct the depositions himself. First up was Charles Loomis, the company's chairman and the grandson of its founder. ("It was pretty clear that he would most likely have not gotten where he was if not for his surname," Lupo says sheepishly.) As Hillblom worked his way through a stack of Loomis's internal memos, the chairman's memory suddenly went blank. Hillblom produced a memo to which Loomis had signed his initials, but the older man shrugged his shoulders and denied any recollection of it. "I used to just write my initials on things," he explained. "Otherwise they'd just keep coming back to me."

When the two sides recessed, a frustrated and angry Hillblom took Lupo aside and ridiculed the office's pristine views of Seattle's Puget Sound. No wonder they couldn't compete with DHL on price, he sniffed. Charles Loomis and his cronies were manipulating the law to overcome an economic reality—that they were losing to a more efficient competitor. By the time he returned to the conference room, Hillblom was more agitated than ever.

Picking out a deposition from the pile of papers in front of him, Hillblom began to point it at Loomis, until William Swope, Loomis's attorney, had had enough. Unlike Hillblom, Swope was a trained litigator who knew the rules. When Swope excoriated Hillblom for not entering the deposition into evidence first, Hillblom ignored him. The argument escalated as Hillblom insisted that Loomis respond and the silver-haired Swope retorted that it was impossible to know what he was even referring to. "Larry's got all of these stupid stick 'em notes with all of his bloody questions on it," Lupo remembers, "and Larry's like, 'I wanna know! I have a right to know this!' And Swope says, 'Let me see it!' And Larry says, 'I'm not going to let you see this!' And Swope says, 'Give it to me!' And Larry goes, 'No! I'm not going to give it to you!' And they're going back and forth. And finally, half of it rips, and Larry goes, 'Let the record reflect that Mr. Swope ripped my deposition!'

"Larry," Lupo says, grinning, "would get very vexed and very intense and loud in that context."

He would also get destructive—maybe unwittingly. The month after taking Loomis's deposition, Hillblom left the coffee machine on during a night session in Honolulu, flooding Swope's law offices. The next week, he left a hot pot of coffee on the conference table of yet another law office during another round of depositions, causing $5,000 in damages. Donnici received the bill. ("Larry objected," Lupo recalls.) A few days later, having witnessed a couple of secretaries carrying boxes of documents to the trash, Hillblom surreptitiously raided the Dumpster behind Loomis's San Francisco offices; Lupo came in to work the next morning to find Hillblom knee deep in a mass of damp paper, half-eaten sandwiches, and rotten eggs, searching for a smoking gun, which he didn't find. "I can just imagine him inside the bin, bent over, basically stealing all of their documents and running back to the DHL office," Lupo roars. "It was hilarious. It was typical him."

· Lupo was still not convinced of a conspiracy. On the surface, *Loomis v. DHL* seemed like little more than legal hardball. But he was convinced several months later when the judge in DHL's countersuit ordered the CAB to release its internal correspondence, which included a telling memo from the bureau's chairman, a Nixon appointee named Robert Timm, to the head of his enforcement division. "Timm said, 'I had a call from an old fraternity friend of mine, Charles Loomis, and he's telling me about this unauthorized courier operating as a freight forwarder and blah-blah,'" Lupo recalls. "'Will you investigate this company?' I think he says something like, 'If warranted, take action as appropriate.' Well, when you get that mandate from the head guy—a political appointee and all-powerful at that time, with authority over all the airlines, all air freight forwarders, everything. He's a seriously powerful individual."

On August 7, 1975, the Ninth Circuit reversed Judge Conti's cease and desist order. Loomis, the three-judge panel ruled, had had no standing as a "party of interest" to sue DHL in the first place. Furthermore, DHL was not required to have the certificate that the CAB claimed was needed to operate as a certified freight forwarder. The appellate court acknowledged that the CAB could exercise some authority over DHL and other indirect air carriers without stating exactly what that authority might be. DHL's fate was therefore bounced back to the CAB, which promptly announced that it would conduct a final review of DHL's application for a freight forwarder's certificate—even though the court acknowledged that the certificate might not be needed. Convoluted as it was, the reversal was a clear victory for Peter Donnici and a stunning defeat for both Charles Loomis and his expensive attorneys.

Hillblom, however, had no time to relax or to celebrate. After months of surveillance, the Hong Kong Postal Department had invaded DHL's Asia headquarters on a muggy afternoon. Pushing past a modest green door* in Hong Kong's rancorous Wan Chai District, uniformed officers had detained the station manager as postal inspectors swarmed the warehouse, impounding hundreds of DHL pouches, tearing them open, and combing their contents for evidence that DHL was violating the postal monopoly. By the time Hillblom spread his lanky frame across four seats in the back of a Hong Kong–bound Pan Am 747, DHL had been indicted for the criminal offense of transporting letters, a violation of the Postal Department's monopoly on carrying mail. If the magistracy court agreed with the Postmaster General's definition of a letter, he knew, the entire express courier business would be a criminal enterprise—and so, of course, would DHL.

Steve Kroll would follow Hillblom across the Pacific a few days later, but the stakes were too high for them to even consider writing DHL's response themselves. What they needed was an advocate who exuded a quality that Hillblom terminally lacked—gravitas—but who could also be relentless as hell.

---

* According to the ancient Chinese discipline of feng shui, green is the color of money or growth.

Eight

Hong Kong

"He was charming, endearing," purrs the elegant Eurasian man in the tailored suit sitting across from me. "Always in blue jeans. He felt that the day he wore a suit would be the day he quit the business."

In 1975, Sir Henry Litton was one of the youngest members of the British Empire to have attained the title Queen's Counsel, a sovereign appointment reserved for solicitors of a certain experience and reputation. Like barristers, the English equivalent of attorneys, QCs are allowed within the bar that separates practitioners of the law from the public, and sometimes wear distinctive silk gowns and powdered wigs, but QCs do not typically interact with clients directly. Instructed by the clients' solicitors instead, QCs focus exclusively on the law itself, practicing the law as scholars more than as advocates.

I had wanted to meet Litton from the moment that Steven Kroll told me how proud Hillblom had been of *his* QC—prouder, in fact, than of anything else he'd accomplished up to that point. And Litton is famous himself—not only as a jurist but as a survivor. In 1973, the high-rise in which Litton and his girlfriend lived buckled during a typhoon. Litton's legs were trapped by wreckage. As the rains poured and the water level began rising up the side of the hill where his building had once stood, he sang Beatles songs so that rescuers could find him. Which they did, but by then his girlfriend, who had been trapped just below him, had already drowned. Litton refused to allow them to amputate his legs, enduring hours of pain before being set free.

So, on a very hot and very humid day in late July, having endured a fifteen-hour flight from Los Angeles, I find myself walking up a short path through the narrow park in downtown Hong Kong that leads to the island's Court of Final Appeal, where I have an appointment to meet with the court's eminent chief justice.

Sir Henry's office is absurdly large and quiet for a city as hectic as Hong Kong, yet spare enough to remind you that the only thing of real value here is the man sitting behind the desk. *Regal* is an adjective that immediately comes to mind. "Larry really did not need a Queen's Counsel," Litton says with a hint of annoyance. And Sir Henry was then involved in something far more prestigious—the historic negotiations for China's repossession of Hong Kong. But Litton had been charmed enough by Hillblom's unique brand of charisma to argue his case. How could one resist an ambitious young man who crisscrossed Asia dressed like a hippie? Even the Beatles had worn suits when they'd come to Hong Kong!

DHL's problems were "huge," Litton recalls. After all, the Royal Mail, of which the Hong Kong Postal Department was part, was not only more established than Loomis, it was more than twice as old as the United States itself, having been founded by Henry VIII in 1516. The mail had first been made available to the public 120 years later by Charles I, and the postal monopoly had been invented by Charles's overthrower, Oliver Cromwell, in 1654. Cromwell, who ruled England for five years as Lord Protector, literally stole the mail out of the hands of the private sector, mainly London coffeehouses that had formed a network to deliver letters. He then installed his spymaster as overseer of the mail.

The principle of a government-owned postal monopoly eventually survived Cromwell, as it did the end of the British monarchy and the British Empire itself, based on an academic theory known as economies of scale. According to this theory, private mail couriers would cherry-pick the most profitable routes, leaving the government-run service with the most undesirable and most expensive ones, thereby creating an inefficient and prohibitively expensive public postal system. The only alternative would be for people in rural areas, for example, to pay more for mail service or else go without. So embedded was this theory that the United States had adopted the concept of a postal monopoly from the beginning, meting out the occasional exemption to private carriers, like the Pony Express, who were willing to go where postal workers were not. Hillblom, however, having witnessed how DHL's service had enabled companies to grow and trade across borders, suspected that the modern postal monopoly had survived more to protect the jobs of hundreds of thousands of unionized workers than in deference to some corn farmer deep in the heartland who deserved to get his *Reader's Digest* as fast and as cheaply as his banker in Wichita. But Loomis had taught him that crafting the most compelling legal argument would not be enough to win.

Indeed, Litton says, the core of the legal issue was almost absurd in its simplicity: What was a "letter"? Was a "letter" of credit really a letter? What about a contract? Or a canceled check? Or a computer tape that happened to contain correspondence? What about an intercompany memo? He did his best to take such arcane questions seriously. And in Magistracy Court, before an audience that included Hillblom, Carla, and Steven Kroll, the overqualified QC made quick work of the Postal Department's contention that the documents carried by DHL were covered by its monopoly. The Crown quickly ruled in DHL's favor. Rather than appeal, the postmaster general decided on another tack.

"The postmaster general realized there was a loophole at that point," Litton remembers, "and tried to stop it with a law expanding the postal monopoly to include business correspondence. Larry wanted me to work on the larger political argument, but I must have told him to get someone with PR expertise. I'm a forensic lawyer, not a politician. But he wouldn't give up with me."

Litton and his barrister flew from Hong Kong to San Francisco, laying over one day in Honolulu so that the QC could have a tour of DHL's offices. ("All they had was a great big hangar, like a very large Quonset hut. I was amused by the great democracy of the company.") At the San Francisco airport, Litton and his barrister were greeted by Hillblom and DHL's twenty-four-year-old general counsel, Pat Lupo—maybe the first general counsel of a multimillion-dollar corporation who had not yet passed the bar exam. Hillblom drove them across the Bay Bridge to Berkeley, where the four men spent a week holed up in the stacks of Boalt Hall's law library, researching postal statutes from all over the world during the day and trying out possible arguments on one another at night. "We would go hell-bent for leather for the research," Lupo recalled. "Then we'd adjourn at night and go for a meal and talk about various things." Hillblom's food fixation of the moment was fish, so they met at Spenger's, a popular fish market and tourist trap just off-campus. It was a terrible place to conduct a serious dialogue because the restaurant was always crowded and very loud. But the chaos seemed to energize the perpetually distracted Hillblom. As Litton tried to carry on a conversation with Lupo or his barrister, Hillblom would lean back in his chair, twist off squares of sourdough from the bread basket, and bean the eminent QC, who was not always amused.

"I remember Litton said, 'I have represented the richest tycoons in Hong Kong, and the poorest buggers you could ever imagine,'" Lupo tells me. "'But I've never represented an *enfant terrible.*'"

By the time Litton and his barrister returned to Hong Kong, the postmaster general's bill expanding the definition of *letter* (and outlawing DHL) had passed its second reading in the Legislative Council. Hillblom finally took Litton's advice to launch a public relations offensive. "So Larry got ahold of Ted Thomas," Litton says, "a Brit PR guy who'd worked in radio, and he organized a campaign mobilizing big business." Like Hillblom, Thomas was young and a little precocious. He had already handled PR for much larger multinationals like Otis Elevator, Matson Navigation, and Cathay Pacific Airways—Hong Kong's flag carrier. DHL would be a unique addition to his client portfolio: a small company with a big problem.

"I met Larry at DHL's office in Wan Chai, on Fenwick Street," Thomas trills over the phone from Asia. "It was a street of bars. Wan Chai was the sailor's playground, where all the whorehouses and massage parlors are located. The British [Royal] Navy put out an out-of-bounds south of Johnston Road, which blocked off most of Wan Chai."

Thomas first brought Hillblom to one of Hong Kong's legendary tailors for a proper suit and shoes. Only then was he presented to the island's political elite at Government House in order to argue his case. By that time, the postmaster general's bill was one reading away from becoming law. The consequences for DHL would have been disastrous; not only was China an increasingly important market (Nixon had lifted the embargo just four years earlier) but the Hong Kong station was the major entry point for shipments from the United States to anywhere in Asia. Finally, DHL's station manager in Hong Kong was secretly holding Hillblom's shares in the company's international operations; if the network's center suddenly shifted, Hillblom might have to conjure up another sleight of hand in order to maintain control of the network.

Thomas booked the ballroom of the elegant Furama Hotel downtown. He then contacted all of the important business leaders on the island, particularly the bankers and the big shippers, who had come to rely on DHL's service and who, according to the PR man, "run Hong Kong," to extend an invitation to what he called a meeting but what was really a performance—a debate between Henry Litton and the postmaster general. "On the evening of the event, the ballroom was literally spilling over," Thomas crows. "Henry gave a presentation about the effect that expanding the postal monopoly would have, though he refused to speak Chinese, which I wanted him to. He wanted to remain more upmarket." There was only one problem: the postmaster general had pointedly declined to attend. So Thomas placed an empty chair on the stage, and Litton proceeded to debate the empty chair, using the arguments that he and Hillblom and Lupo had crafted in the stacks of the Boalt Hall law library.

"The DHL guys and Larry and the PR company did a great job of whipping up the community," Lupo says. "And Litton gave a very impassioned speech because he said, 'I've done all this research and this law must change.' His speech was great."

"It was all over after that." Thomas guffaws. "Everybody revolted!"

The PR guru cannot remember whether Hillblom attended the meeting at the Furama. If he had, DHL's founder must have hidden himself in the crowd and slipped out before anyone noticed him. It is also possible that he tried to get in but that hotel security refused to allow such a strange individual into their ballroom. As Thomas concludes in his glib British accent: "He seemed to go a bit off the beam later in life, didn't he?"

The Messiah

I heard Larry say many times that if he couldn't be an
entrepreneur, he'd be a criminal.

—Jim Campbell

*H*illblom disappeared soon after the triumph in Hong Kong. Until
then, only Carla had been allowed to penetrate every aspect of his
life; now, no one was. Peter Donnici stopped by a DHL-owned apartment in San Francisco to find Hillblom crawling on the floor in the midst
of hundreds of computer components, attempting to build a word processor that he'd christened the DHL-1000. Pat Lupo received a call from
the Middle East that Hillblom had been in a motorcycle accident; twelve
hours later, his boss emerged from customs at SFO in a wheelchair, his
jaw wired shut. Russ Sands, DHL's insurance agent, fielded a request to
insure a Hatteras yacht parked near Bahrain, amid rumors of coke-fueled
parties with sheikhs and high-end prostitutes flown in from London.
When Helen and Andy flew into Honolulu, they received an audience;
a close family friend, however, was declined. Even Marilyn Corral, the
self-described "Larry girl," was shut out. "I knew he was taking flying
lessons," she remembers, "which was like, 'Oh my God! Heaven help all
of us!'"

The problem was that Hillblom did not want to run a company. Not
really. He wanted to control a revolutionary enterprise and, in the process,
he wanted to be a reclusive billionaire like his idol, Howard Hughes. "He
wanted to be able to dabble," Carla recalls. "He couldn't necessarily do the
ho-hum stuff ad infinitum. As the president of the company, he would
have had to deal with all of it, but otherwise he could pick and choose.

He wanted someone else to be the front person and methodically take care of the needs that an organization has, but in terms of making policy decisions, he still wanted to do that." Pat Lupo is more measured. "I guess you'd accuse him of flitting in and making all of these pronouncements and then jumping on an airplane," he offers. "But somebody had to live with that. Somebody had to execute."

Not everyone at DHL was so philosophical. A few of the original station-agents-turned-shareholders were beginning to grouse that Hillblom was running away—not only from his enemies at the CAB and Loomis, but from them. After all, he had convinced them to exchange their franchises for stock in DHL Corporation that they could not sell—because, he'd said, the CAB had demanded it. Then he had snatched DHL's fast-growing international division off the table just as it was taking off, once again blaming the CAB. Yet DHL still had no operating certificate, and it was an open secret that Hillblom and Dalsey still owned their shares in the international stations. Hillblom had left them with the scraps and then hired a handful of MBAs to run the international division. The guys who'd built the original stations in L.A., Seattle, San Francisco, Houston, and even Honolulu didn't know whether they'd been left behind or forced out.

No debate inspired more acrimony than whether the U.S. company should even expand at all. Most of the international executives, hired hands who had not been there from the beginning, felt that the money-losing domestic operation should be whittled down to a few stations in major cities capable of feeding the overseas profit machine, causing even the stoic Marilyn Corral to become resentful of Hillblom's sudden indifference to what she and others had worked so hard to build. It didn't help that, at the same time the U.S. company was starving for cash, Hillblom went on a buying spree, scooping up an interisland airline in Hawaii, a printing company in the Midwest, and a real estate management corporation. Or that, while the U.S. unit languished without a leader, Hillblom was devoting a great deal of time and money to ensure that his DHL-1000 word processor would be fluent in Arabic. But there was little that DHL's stockholders could do. Only one person was in a position to know how the network's money was being spent: Larry Hillblom.

In late 1974, Hillblom devised his boldest scheme yet. Once again, the bogeyman would be the CAB. The purpose, theoretically at least, was twofold: one, get rid of Adrian Dalsey, and, in doing so, disabuse Loomis of any delusions that they would be able to buy DHL, thereby forcing a settlement; and, two, provide DHL's domestic operations with a strong leader. The means would be DHL's first landlord and Hillblom and Kroll's former Boalt Hall classmate Curt Carlsmith.

"Curt's the only one who could come up with the money," Marilyn Corral explains during our second phone conversation. What Larry needed was two or three hundred thousand dollars—the amount that Loomis's vice president had offered Dalsey during their first meeting two years earlier. Even though DHL had grown substantially by then, the Loomis litigation was dragging on with no end in sight and Adrian Dalsey, tired from years of stress and having fallen in love with a young Filipina, wanted out. The other shareholders, Corral says, all wanted to buy him out but none of them had any cash—they'd invested it all starting their own stations, which were now owned by DHL. So Hillblom had reached out to Curt, whose father had started the largest law practice in the South Pacific. The Carlsmiths were also major landholders on Oahu and Curt had bragged of his family's connections in the insurance and financial spheres. Although they were opposites—Carlsmith wore pin-striped suits and would not have been caught dead at the Tasty Broiler—the two law school classmates had developed a friendship from the time Hillblom had rented out his loft at 911 Alakea. Carlsmith had even done some work for DHL vis-à-vis the *Loomis* lawsuit. What he had not done up to that point was show any interest in working for the company itself. "Curt was a good-looking guy, kind of an Ivy League–looking guy—blond hair, blue-eyed," Corral continues. "He was a surfer. He wasn't real tall, maybe five-eleven. He was almost embarrassed or afraid of the rest of us, kind of shy. What I recall was that I would walk into a room and he would leave."

The two-page agreement that Carlsmith drafted between himself, Hillblom, and the Dalseys was doomed from the start. One clause required that DHL obtain CAB certification before Carlsmith had to pay for the shares (he would, however, post collateral in the form of some family land on Oahu) while another called for Dalsey to turn over his shares in DHL's international business—shares that he, like Hillblom, had supposedly given up in order to satisfy the CAB. Hillblom signed it anyway. And for a time, DHL's managers were constantly told of the great things that Curt was going to do for the company, leading some to grumble that Larry had found the Messiah.

"They were really close at first," Corral continues. "They'd spend a lot of time together when they were sharing the office. We'd gotten a big cargo warehouse at the airport and we had to modify it with walls for offices, but Curt dictated that he had to have the biggest office, and he would send out dictatorial memos of how things had to be. Keep in mind that the managers he was dictating to had become shareholders, so here's this attorney who doesn't know anything about how DHL operates but what he's seen, telling them how to do their jobs. They were all in an uproar about it."

Oddly, Hillblom himself quickly became the loudest member of the chorus ridiculing Carlsmith's high-handedness—though never to his face, of course. "Right from the start, Curt was destined to fail." Corral sighs. "Larry started riling everyone about Curt—about the dictatorial memos he felt that Curt was sending. Once it started it just didn't stop. Larry sabotaged him. Finally, Curt just didn't show up to the office one day. He kind of disappeared into the sunset."

Hillblom abolished the office of the president, effective immediately. He told Corral that the title had gone to Curt's head. Then he assigned Carlsmith's side of the contract with Dalsey to DHL, effectively erasing his classmate from the company and making himself its dominant shareholder. Hillblom hadn't spent a penny and, most important, his stroke of genius was someone else's fault.

Ten

Washington, D.C.

I think when Congress considers the problem [of regulation] it
should say: To what extent can we protect the consumer while
still allowing the guy to get out of school, who has spent 4, 6
or 8 years paying for his education and whose parents are not
going to support him for another 10 years to get an airfreight
forwarding license or other license? And it just seems like this is
a forgotten aspect in legislation whether it be tax legislation or
whatever, that we are building a society of economic classes not
unlike India and not unlike Britain and not unlike Italy. We are
telling our youth, look, go to school and you can make it here
but when they get out that is the end of the opportunity. And
that seems to be in both our policies in treating our minorities
and others that until we open economic opportunity in those
areas that are feasible, that we in fact are having an education
that turns out to be a lie. And that tends to be a discouraging
process and causes the disillusionment that I think occurred in
the 1960s and 1970s and will even occur more in the 1980s.
>   —*Larry Hillblom, in testimony to Congress, 1975*

*I*n August 1975, a visibly frustrated Hillblom once again hopped the red-
eye to Washington, D.C. Even though the CAB's authority had been
severely weakened by the Ninth Circuit's decision, the agency had still
not authorized DHL as a freight forwarder. Worse, Hillblom had recently
found out that the CAB was conducting a secret review of his company,
led by one of Loomis's former attorneys.

Then Hillblom had gotten word that Senator Ted Kennedy was holding hearings on airline deregulation. Kennedy was a possible Democratic presidential candidate and JFK's younger brother was eager to show Americans that he was not only a serious legislator but that he was pro-business as well. The hearing was to examine abuses of power at regulatory agencies, including the Civil Aeronautics Board. Several airline executives had accused the CAB of shaking them down for campaign contributions to the Committee to Re-Elect the President, aka CREEP. Its chairman and Charlie Loomis's fraternity brother, Robert Timm, had also traveled on expensive golf junkets as a guest of a company under his agency's purview. Timm had been forced to resign and the head of his enforcement bureau had just committed suicide. The rumor was that the CAB's reputation was so sullied that it might be sunsetted, i.e., phased out or swallowed by another federal agency. After five years of flying hat in hand to the CAB's headquarters on Connecticut Avenue and having spent half a million dollars in legal fees, wiping out his company's profits, Hillblom had decided that the only solution was to kill the beast. *Burn, Baby, Burn!*

When his cab stopped at the curb in front of the vast Dirksen Senate Office Building early the next morning, Hillblom bounded over the hot pavement, onto the polished marble of the nearly empty foyer. He made a beeline for the gilded elevators, exited on the third floor, and found the door augustly marked:

ADMINISTRATIVE PRACTICE AND PROCEDURES SUBCOMMITTEE
OF THE COMMITTEE ON THE JUDICIARY

Hillblom did not have an appointment and, because Congress was on recess, there was no receptionist to announce him. As always, he was too shy to introduce himself, but an amiable young man in slacks and shirtsleeves eventually peeked in from the office hallway. The young man introduced himself as Jim Campbell, a staff researcher.

"I was the only one in the office," Campbell tells me over the phone from his home in suburban Virginia. "He started mumbling about the conspiracy—they're out to get him and all this other stuff, which didn't make any sense."

Campbell walked Hillblom across the street to the Senate cafeteria and bought him a cup of coffee. As Hillblom methodically led the staffer through *Loomis v. DHL,* Campbell found himself rapt. He already knew that the CAB was corrupt, but individual cases were not something that Congress intervened in, so he steered the conversation beyond *Loomis v. DHL.* As Hillblom emptied his coffee in sporadic gulps, Campbell explained that he was setting up a panel on the anticompetitive consequences of regulatory activities in the transportation sector. Hillblom offered up his view that the government should always promote competition—the philosophy that he'd espoused since law school. Campbell heard echoes of Kennedy's campaign rhetoric. He thought that DHL's story illustrated a not so well known and very anticompetitive effect of airline regulation, so he invited Hillblom to testify in an upcoming hearing.

But Hillblom hedged. "What about the possibility of retribution?" he asked. After all, DHL still didn't have its operating certificate.

Campbell shrugged his shoulders. That was Larry's call.

Several months later, Hillblom, Carla, Steve Kroll, Marilyn Corral, and Bill Robinson, the cofounder of DHL's Los Angeles station, who had become a key player in its international growth, flew into Washington from Honolulu—as couriers, naturally. In preparation, Hillblom had spent a huge amount of time at the law library, poring over case records. His opening remarks alone came to thirty pages of single-spaced text. "I said, 'Hillblom, what's that?' " Campbell laughs. "He says: 'That's my testimony.' I said: 'You can't read that! This is a United States Senate hearing. You have to cut it by 75 percent!' "

When Hillblom returned to Campbell's office later that night, the remarks still ran to nearly twenty pages. The young staffer immediately blacked out the case names. Hillblom objected but Campbell cut him off. "Ted Kennedy doesn't care what the law is," he admonished. "We make the law."

At 9:30 the following morning, Senator Edward M. Kennedy entered a paneled fifth-floor hearing room in a navy blue blazer and striped tie, waves of chestnut hair curling just below the neck, a little long for someone of his age and stature. He was surprisingly tan, tall, and athletic. As he assumed the chairman's seat and raised the ceremonial gavel, Kennedy flashed his family's famous smile toward the gallery. He'd just appeared on the cover of *People* magazine a few months earlier, at the wheel of a sail-boat beside his handicapped son, smiling and looking skyward. Kennedy's celebrity easily overpowered the others on the dais, even the famously conservative Southern bulldog, Senator Strom Thurmond of South Carolina.

Hillblom was listed as the morning's fourth witness, behind an assistant attorney general, an independent trucker, and the owner of a moving and storage company—and before the actor Warren Beatty, representing the Hollywood studios. His statement had undergone two major edits the night before—once by himself and then again by Campbell, who had deleted so much that it could have passed for the redacted version of a classified memo.

As soon as testimony began, Hillblom understood why Campbell had censored him so mercilessly. Witnesses were lucky to get off more than a few sentences before Kennedy interjected. Just as Campbell had warned, the senator was interested in changing the law, not analyzing it. But even with Kennedy's interruptions, the witnesses were moved in and out of their chairs with Japanese efficiency.

Hillblom's panel was called forward inside of an hour. He waited for the first two witnesses to finish, then pulled his chair slightly forward, adjusted the microphone, and began his opening statement. He was wading into the Loomis-CAB conspiracy when Kennedy suddenly leaned forward.

"In what way are you under the jurisdiction of the CAB?" the senator queried.

"The CAB," Hillblom replied, "suddenly decided that courier operations were freight forwarding operations; prior to that time the only decision on record indicated they had no jurisdiction."

"Does the DHL Corp. fly a plane?" Kennedy asked.

"No," Hillblom replied.

"Does the corporation own one?"

"No," Hillblom replied again.

"Are you leasing a plane?" Kennedy asked.

"No," Larry said a third time.

"How, then," asked Kennedy, "is the CAB connected with your corporation?"

Hillblom tried to explain the CAB's reasoning that made DHL an "indirect air carrier," but that seemed to confuse the senator even further.

"Do you understand this policy?" Kennedy interrupted.

"No," Hillblom said. "But"—he smiled—"we didn't believe it was intended to make much sense for us."

The gallery erupted in laughter. Even some of the senators chuckled. Seated behind his star witness, Campbell thought to himself that Larry had nailed it, just as he'd hoped—maybe better. A few seconds later, Hillblom found his place in the prepared remarks and resumed his statement with a new confidence. He had finally put the CAB on the defensive. With a joke, not a pleading or an appeal! DHL's problems in Washington were going to be solved.

Eleven

The Operator

"**I**'ll put it this way," Jim Campbell says. "Larry had a much better idea of how things are done than most people and how change happens."

That fall, a newly focused Hillblom was invited to recount his side of DHL's battle with the CAB to yet another Congressional committee. He estimated that nearly a quarter of his company's revenue was being spent to comply with regulatory costs and admitted that he had considered giving up. "We don't wish to continue our operation subject to the present type of policies," he warned the assembled congressmen, one of whom was taking a nap. But he soon went off topic, urging Congress to abolish regulations for companies smaller than DHL.

On the topic of deregulation, Hillblom was now a player. He understood the direction that the country was headed. Five years before the Reagan Revolution would sweep the capital, Hillblom was already spreading the gospel that government was the problem—not the solution. At Boalt Hall, his professors had found his economic rationale of the law inscrutable and his classmates had scoffed at his apathy to social issues. But now, age thirty-two and barely six years out of law school, he was interacting with Washington's boldface names and receiving public kudos from the scion of America's political dynasty. And he had become a public speaker! He'd found his voice. He bragged to his friend Steven Kroll that he'd taught himself to cry on the stand. When the tour ended, Hillblom boarded a jumbo jet back to paradise, convinced that he had vanquished his most powerful foe. He could not have been more wrong.

William Bolger was of Hillblom's stepfather's generation—lean, hard-working, and proud. Like Andy Anderson, Bolger had learned the value of loyalty during World War II, where he'd served as an air force bombardier. After the Japanese surrender, Bolger had gone back to work for his former employer, the U.S. Post Office Department, where he'd risen up the ranks with military certainty, eventually trading in his postal worker's uniform for dark suits, solid ties, and polished leather shoes. As postmaster general of the U.S. Postal Service, the graying septuagenarian's most exciting moment may have been the unveiling of a Harry S. Truman stamp, but his perfect posture and still chiseled features belied a fighter. He presided over hundreds of thousands of troops—none of whose jobs he intended to surrender.

Technically, Bolger did not report to the government but to a nine-member board of governors. That's because, five years earlier, President Richard Nixon had abolished the Post Office Department after an illegal postal strike had crippled the nation for two weeks. The new Postal Service, known by its acronym, USPS, was an independent federal agency— a structure that was supposed to make the post office more efficient, more businesslike, and, ultimately, more profitable. Instead, USPS had lost a record amount of taxpayer money and raised the cost of sending a letter by 50 percent. Bolger found a scapegoat in DHL and its compatriots in the burgeoning courier industry. While he readily admitted that express carriers might be wonderful for business and even for the economy, the postmaster general argued that they were "cream-skimming," i.e., taking the most profitable mail routes and ignoring the more expensive ones— precisely the market failure that the postal monopoly was supposed to protect against. Bolger warned that the onslaught of private courier operations like DHL would have to be driven back to protect the greater good: the jobs of USPS's more than half a million employees.

He'd already possessed a sledgehammer known as Section 601 of the postal code, which allowed private carriage of letters only if the correct amount of U.S. postage was affixed—as though they were being sent via the mail. But in late 1973, Bolger had gone one step further and defined a letter as "a message directed to a specific person or address and recorded in or on a tangible object." After howls of protest from businesses and the Interstate Commerce Commission, he announced that USPS would "suspend" its monopoly over letters in a few very limited instances—for computer tape that was delivered within twelve hours, for example. But private carriers like DHL, even those carrying materials covered by the suspensions, would now have to register with USPS and allow postal inspectors access to their delivery records. If the inspectors decided that a particular company was not compliant, Bolger could withdraw its suspension on a case-by-case basis. Couriers like DHL would now formally exist at the whim of both CAB and USPS edicts.

No private company could afford to launch a preemptive strike against the Postal Service, so the entire industry, including DHL, ignored the new regulations. Within a year, however, Bolger launched the first wave of troops. Platoons of postal inspectors, exposed pistols strapped to their belts, began to appear at the mailrooms of known express company customers. They would demand access to the mailroom's shipping logs, especially noting destinations and weights. Occasionally, on their way out, they would grab the pile of outgoing correspondence intended for DHL or another express company and drop it in a USPS mailbox. The next day a Postal Service salesman would show up in the same mailroom, reminding its manager of Section 601. Then the salesman would make a pitch for the postal service's express mail product by posing the obvious question: Why pay twice?

Having thus struck fear into the hearts of both the express companies and their clients, Bolger then opened up a second front. At the request of his postal inspectors, customs agents confiscated a large shipment of inbound DHL traffic. When DHL managers, including Pat Lupo, showed up to claim their clients' shipments, arguments ensued over what and what was not a letter. "They went through it," Lupo recalls, "and they found interoffice memos and they found invoices and things like that and they said, 'See, this is a letter!' And I remember arguing with these guys. It was stupid. They kept them for forty-eight hours and then they released them, and because they released them, it was almost impossible to go to court."

Lupo raced to assure his most important clients that the company he himself had once felt sheepish working for was, in fact, legal. He also tried to maintain his sense of humor in the face of Bolger's attack. "Because a blueprint has some words on it," he would deadpan, "then under the Post

Office's definition of letter, it has to go via USPS." Engineering giants like Bechtel and Brown & Root were then developing the massive oil fields of the Middle East, and using DHL to send blueprints back and forth on a daily basis. DHL could not afford to lose them any more than they could afford to lose DHL. The Postal Service would have added two to three weeks to the delivery time of every shipment and even then, delivery was far from assured. How ingrained DHL had become in the global economy hit Lupo during a courtesy call on a client's shipping manager. "I'm getting ready to go," Lupo recalls, "and this guy says, 'What do you think we should do with these?' And we go over to this massive filing cabinet about as big as this sofa and about eight feet high and it rolls out. For two years, they had weighed up the blueprints and calculated what it would cost to send them by first-class mail to Saudi Arabia and then bought the stamps. And there was, in this thing, I want to say hundreds of thousands of dollars of stamps. They'd been buying stamps so that they could then send it by DHL—and DHL would charge plenty!"

Based on the research they'd already done with Henry Litton, Hillblom and Lupo penned a fifty-six-page treatise asserting the rights of private carriers to exist. Donnici, credited as a coauthor, submitted it to the *University of San Francisco Law Review,* where it was published. Bolger's attorneys countered with a 200-page piece that appeared in the *Texas Law Review.* Donnici used the letterhead from his law firm, in which Lupo was now a partner, to draft opinions stating that DHL was a legal enterprise and that its customers did not need to pay postage on shipments that were not, in fact, letters. (Lupo wanted it to appear that an objective party had made the judgment, although the firm of Donnici & Lupo was little more than DHL's outsourced legal department.) To gain credibility in Washington, where Bolger was a familiar figure, Hillblom joined the National Association of Manufacturers, a pro-business lobbying group. Then he hired Jim Campbell and flew him out to Donnici & Lupo's downtown San Francisco offices to brainstorm. Hillblom's first proposal was a winner-takes-all volleyball match against the Postal Service. Campbell joked that Bolger knew he would lose. Instead, Campbell got to work on a postal "notebook" for shippers that explained their rights while questioning the Postal Service's most basic assertions of its monopoly as overreaching. But with customs now routinely confiscating DHL's shipments, legal arguments would be inadequate. More than manuals or law articles (or jokes), Hillblom needed allies. Many of DHL's loyal clients testified to the need for its service and, in his prepared testimony, Hillblom had often quoted a letter from Matson, the shipping giant, that read in part: "Until the inception of DHL, Matson's use of the U.S. mail and/or air freight and other alternatives proved to be a miserable failure." But as well connected as Matson and other customers might have been, there was only one organization in the United States that could come close to matching the Postal Service job for job and vote for vote. So Hillblom hopped back on the red-eye to Washington, this time taking his favorite lieutenant with him.

"Bloody Hillblom," Lupo recalls, "who always had issues with organized labor, the first place he takes us is the Teamsters. The national office in Washington, D.C.! So Larry and I go to the Teamsters and Larry starts arguing on behalf of UPS of all people! Because UPS had 100,000 workers organized by the Teamsters. Larry's saying, If the U.S. enforces the private express statutes, it will put UPS out of business. And the more we argued—mostly him—they picked up that this could be serious. And finally we ended up talking to somebody who was like the number two guy in the Teamsters and Larry is just passionately arguing that the post office can't compete: they're inept, and they'll put UPS out of business. And Larry got so fired up that we used to walk out of these meetings onto the street, and I swear, Larry used to go up to people on the street and start arguing with them. And I'm like, 'Larry, relax!'"

Lupo's voice betrays the exasperation he felt back then—maybe some resentment as well. His boss had no interest in the mechanics of running a company, the minutiae that Lupo estimates to be 95 percent of a business. While his minions—Lupo and Donnici in the San Francisco law office, Campbell in a rented suite in Washington—dealt with the CAB, the *Loomis* lawsuit, the postal inspectors, and belligerent customs agents, Hillblom was usually jetting 30,000 feet over the Pacific Ocean, his jeans pockets stuffed with news clippings torn from the magazines and newspapers he devoured with a pathological intensity. One article in particular engrossed his imagination—and amplified his paranoia. It was published in a science magazine. The author described a new machine that would make DHL obsolete.

> In the future, communications satellites will be used to facilitate an automatic mailing for every organization and every family or individual. You may visualize that it will be possible to subscribe to a service, similar to the telephone service, whereby the customers will be issued an instrument that will transmit and receive letters via satellite.
>
> You write or type a letter, insert it in a slot (almost like a copying machine), dial the recipient's code number (perhaps his Social Security number) and push the "transmit" button. Within seconds the recipient's machine will print out the letter, like a photocopy, and drop it in a "mail box" attached to the machine.

The inevitability of satellite mail would haunt Hillblom in the years ahead, but developing that kind of technology was out of the question for what was still a fledgling hodgepodge of courier stations. Still, Hillblom now insisted that his DHL-1000 send and receive data. He filed the more ambitious notion of electronic mail away in his brain somewhere and kept flying west, to explore his latest conquest.

Cocos

Cocos Island is so tiny that, after living in Micronesia for months, I had no clue of its existence. To reach it, you must first fly into Guam. Twelve hundred miles south of Tokyo, Guam is familiar to members of the U.S. armed forces as home to two huge bases and a bayside resort district that reminds one of Honolulu's Waikiki Beach with its veneer of Las Vegas–style glitz superimposed on a mass of rusting apartment buildings, poker dens, massage parlors, strip clubs, and meth dens. Tamuning Bay is a popular destination among jarheads because nubile young women in tight jeans tend to emerge from opaque glass doors at all hours of the day like *The Odyssey's* sirens.

By the time I reach the village of Merizo to board a small ferry that is the only means of accessing Cocos, more than half of the island's beaches have been swallowed by typhoons, and U.S. military operations have injected enough PCBs into the surrounding waters to scare off most of the thousands of scuba divers and fishermen who used to come here every week. The ferry is nearly empty, as are the narrow, sun-drenched beaches and the tiny buffet restaurant. A local wearing a monogrammed Cocos Island polo shirt informs me that the present owner is an American video game tycoon; his strategy for reinventing Cocos as a profitable enterprise remains as mysterious as the tropical storms that descend in sudden bursts of wind and rain, only to leave as quickly as they've arrived.

The island that Larry Hillblom, Steven Kroll, and Curt Carlsmith bought on a whim in the mid-1970s has vanished. Then, hundreds of young Japanese honeymooners canoodled on its white-sand beaches or beneath its scores of coconut trees, snorkeled around its edges, and dove down to a shipwreck just off its long pier, as jumbo jets connecting the United States with Asia roared overhead. In the late 1970s, Hillblom rented a house across the bay, in Merizo, a charming village of Quonset huts whose Spanish-built bridge had somehow survived the American bombing campaign of '45. In the lush hills that separate Merizo from the more populated parts of Guam, the islanders still hunt deer by burning fires to attract their prey. There is no easy or quick way to reach Merizo; it would take government agents—or anyone else—at least an hour to get there.

Steven Kroll was one of Hillblom's only regular visitors there. "We would go over to Cocos Island," Kroll remembered warmly. "It's not a big island, obviously, but you could walk through the jungle, and we came upon a Quonset hut and concrete bunker, which I was told was a LORAN* station. The vines and the jungle had eaten everything. Larry and I were fantasizing about what had happened in the war, like one of those flashback scenes in *Titanic*. We were making plans for a railway. He was looking at this in the way that people building casinos in Las Vegas look at their thing—like something more than a beautiful spot is needed here if you want to make money. So the ideas were a little railroad and a water park—things that were cheap to do that would make money! We had all these Japanese tourists, honeymooners. It was popular!"

Kroll fondly remembers showing Hillblom the parks in Guam where he cruised navy boys and locals for gay sex. Hillblom seemed to be experiencing a delayed, maybe permanent, adolescence. At one point he invited Kroll into bed with a girlfriend, though the threesome was not successful. "Larry was promiscuously into heterosexual sex the way I was into homosexual sex." Kroll shrugs. "If he could've been gay, he would've been gay. He was fascinated at the idea of going to a park and getting it on and getting on with your business."

In the winter of 1976, as Hillblom explored, the CAB suddenly released DHL's operating certificate. Then, on October 24, 1978, a press release from Postmaster General Bolger's office announced the suspension

---

* LORAN stands for Long Range Navigation and was a land-based navigation system using low-frequency radio transmitters in multiple deployment to determine the location and speed. LORAN was once used by the United States Navy and Coast Guard.

of the postal monopoly for urgent letters—an urgent letter being defined as any piece of mail sent for a cost of at least twice the first-class mail rate or three dollars, whichever was higher. The policy was calculated to prevent Congress from passing a bill sponsored by Trent Lott, a pro-business junior senator from Mississippi who had met with both Hillblom and Lupo, that would have explicitly limited the postal monopoly. The government had surrendered. Loomis capitulated a short time later, agreeing to pay DHL more than a million dollars in damages. Any hope of acquiring Hillblom's company had long since passed; during the litigation, DHL had leapfrogged its storied competitor and was now many times larger.

Hillblom began to feel invincible. The Pacific Ocean, he realized, was the impenetrable curtain behind which he could pull the strings. It empowered him, shielded him from confrontation, and even made him more effective. When Pan Am, DHL's only carrier to Latin America and Asia, threatened to limit the amount of bags that its couriers could carry— probably a greater threat to the network than either Loomis or the CAB— Hillblom did not bother to make a personal appearance, as he always had in past crises. Instead, he instructed Patrick Lupo to spend all of DHL's available cash—approximately $10 million at that moment—to buy Pan Am stock and then request an audience at the airline's annual meeting in Boston. The plan was that Lupo would make an impassioned plea to the airline's gathered shareholders and directors, noting how much business they stood to lose if their management followed through on its threats; by acquiring that much stock, DHL simply guaranteed Lupo some time on the floor. But Pan Am's CEO, unable to see behind Hillblom's curtain, assumed that DHL was launching a hostile takeover bid and capitulated before the meeting ever took place.

By the end of the decade, in fact, only one enemy remained tenacious enough to roust Hillblom from his island paradise. That enemy was a friend.

Curt

*O*ne afternoon between DHL's victories against the CAB and the Postal Service, the company's former president, Curt Carlsmith, walked into the clerk's office of Honolulu's District Court armed with a thick complaint alleging that DHL Corporation, Adrian Dalsey, and Hillblom had all committed fraud by inducing him to purchase Dalsey's shares in the company. Attached was the doomed "letter of understanding" that he, Larry Hillblom, and Dalsey had signed three years earlier—and that DHL had since assumed on Carlsmith's behalf without his knowledge. The complaint did not mention that Carlsmith had not paid for the shares, nor did it elucidate what, if anything, he had lost on the transaction. In fact, the document was little more than a character assassination—a detailed portrait of Larry Hillblom as criminal mastermind and insecure prick.

A photocopy of the complaint was made and time-stamped. Carlsmith, a familiar face in the clerk's office, walked out with his receipt. Thanks to DHL, it would take less than twenty-four hours for a copy of his allegations to reach Hillblom's legal office in San Francisco and another day or two to reach Hillblom himself, depending on where he happened to be at the moment.

My copy of Carlsmith's complaint, edges frayed but otherwise unchanged, resides at the federal archives facility in Burlingame, not far from DHL's former headquarters. It is an extraordinary document, both in terms of the viciousness of its tone and the seriousness of its allegations. For starters, Carlsmith alleges that a substantial portion of DHL's revenues came from "illegal operations"—an allusion to the company's failure to be certified by the CAB and to long-standing rumors that DHL couriers were smuggling drugs and pornography across international borders. He claims that both Hillblom and Dalsey routinely bribed foreign officials for special treatment. The company was also, he claims, violating a host of federal statutes, securities laws, and CAB regulations. And Hillblom secretly controlled DHL, International via a sham nominee. The CAB's attorneys had suspected as much ever since Hillblom had turned over the wrong business card to its auditors, but here Carlsmith fingers Po Chung, DHL's diminutive Hong Kong station agent, as the straw man. According to Carlsmith, Po received just two hundred shares of the international company's twenty thousand shares—a one percent bribe for pretending that Hillblom's company was an independent enterprise in compliance with CAB regulations. Not only did the arrangement allow Hillblom to thumb his nose at regulators; he was, according to Carlsmith, using it to evade income taxes.

But Carlsmith's most damaging claim is that Hillblom conspired to keep DHL Corporation operating at a loss or, at best, a break even, by siphoning money to the international division, which he operated as a tax-free slush fund. Though Carlsmith's complaint lacks hard evidence, DHL's cash-starved franchisees-turned-shareholders now had a legal record of their long-standing suspicions.

But the last paragraph of Carlsmith's complaint makes it clear that he has not filed the lawsuit for their benefit. He demands that DHL pay him $6 million, including $750,000 in punitive damages—twenty-four times the original value of the contract.

Hillblom's reaction was immediate. He flew back to the States and huddled with his consigliere and general counsel at the San Francisco law office. They were not sympathetic. Lupo felt that his boss had only himself to blame, that he should have confronted Carlsmith years before and worked out an amicable settlement. Instead, by undermining Curt's presidency and assuming the contract unilaterally, Hillblom had left the entire DHL network open to assault and himself exposed to a fishing expedition. Lupo was pretty confident that he could win the case, but Carlsmith had made some compelling points; worse, Adrian Dalsey, Hillblom's codefendant, would make a terrible witness. After all, Dalsey too had been effectively forced out of the company by Larry. Negotiating a settlement was the obvious solution. Otherwise Larry's brilliant end run around Dalsey and his shareholders was stymied, with him exposed and surrounded by enemies too big to run through.

But Hillblom was adamant: Carlsmith could not own any shares in DHL, and he wasn't getting $6 million. So Donnici & Lupo fired back with a lawsuit of their own, accusing Curt and his family of stealing airplane tickets and failing to deliver on promises to make his family's connections available to DHL, among other things. Carlsmith then warned that he had taped his phone conversations with Hillblom and others at DHL. "It was nasty," Lupo moans.

Discovery dragged on for three years, filling up several boxes in the clerk's office in Honolulu but otherwise accomplishing nothing. Depositions sometimes devolved into shouting and threats. It was Steven Kroll, Hillblom's and Carlsmith's partner in Cocos Island, who finally convinced Hillblom that he would have to broker a settlement himself, as he should have done in the first place. He would have to confront Curt.

A meeting was scheduled for a spring weekend in 1980 at Kroll's modest condo overlooking North Lake Tahoe. Hillblom flew in from Guam, Carlsmith from Honolulu. When they arrived, Kroll ushered them to his deck overlooking the water and the snow-drenched mountains that cradle the pristine lake. For three days, the preppy rich kid and the peach farmer's stepson disagreed about Carlsmith's agreement with Dalsey and his brief tenure as DHL's president while Kroll brought them homemade snacks and mediated.

The scene was tense, occasionally theatrical. Carlsmith was prone to storming off while Hillblom literally dug his heels into the deck. By the end of their last day in Lake Tahoe, they had gotten nowhere. Carlsmith still refused to withdraw his lawsuit and Hillblom would not allow any of the allegations in his lawsuit to stand unchallenged. But at two o'clock that morning, amid cool evening air, Kroll proposed an ingenious solution that would sidestep Carlsmith's accusations while still making him a multimillionaire: DHL would purchase Carlsmith's share of Cocos Island for just under $4 million and Carlsmith would simultaneously withdraw his legal actions. There would be no more depositions, no trial, no evaluation of whether or not DHL had acted illegally or whether or not Hillblom had deceived the CAB—or his fellow shareholders—by secretly holding on to his stake in the international operations.

They shook hands. Kroll drafted a brief memorandum of understanding on his IBM Selectric. Hillblom called Lupo immediately and told him to draw up the contracts. After three years of inaction, Hillblom was suddenly panicked. "This is it!" he shouted over the phone. "This deal *has* to get done!"

"If Larry saw problems with it he wasn't saying anything," Lupo recalls. Then he raises an eyebrow. "Of course he saw problems with it! I'm sure that I tried to defend myself and explain the problems to him but he wouldn't listen. I started to question, 'Well, wait a minute, if they're paying all this money to Curt and they're telling me there's nothing in his case, maybe there's more to the case than they let on in the first place, right?' So anyway, I had some great intellectual problems with this settlement, and Larry was just furious."

By the time Lupo convinced a federal judge to bless the settlement agreement, he knew that DHL's other shareholders were not all convinced that Curt Carlsmith's exit was in their own best interests, because the effect was to hand a supermajority of DHL to Larry Hillblom. Maybe, several of them mused, there was a lot more truth to Carlsmith's allegations than they'd been led to believe. Maybe Hillblom had used the CAB and Carlsmith to take over the company. Maybe he'd lied outright. But there was only one person who knew for sure, and he was slipping farther and farther away from them, toward yet another island paradise, where he would build his next empire: Saipan.

Part II

The Island

The Trust Territory of the Pacific, often referred to as Micronesia, whose stretch of 2,041 islands in the Western Pacific sparkle with such jewels as Majuro, Ponapei, Koror and Saipan, is doing its best to remain a virgin Lorelei. It will take all the persistence of the early American pioneer to penetrate either as an immigrant or as an investor.

—The New York Times, *December 26, 1971*

In the land of the blind, the one-eyed man is king.

—*Erasmus*

The ethos is that if you can afford it, you can do it. That is Hillblom's legacy on Saipan.

—*Professor Samuel MacPhetres, Northern Marianas College*

The Island of Thieves

"**M**r. James?" The voice pierces a muggy darkness; it is female, dreamlike, and vaguely familiar. More than a little salacious. The digital clock radio, a relic of the eighties, reads 3:01 a.m. Besides those three red numbers, the room is utterly black. The air is hot and nearly silent, excepting the whir of an elderly air-conditioning unit that is not doing its job nearly well enough.

"I think you have the wrong number," I say when the voice repeats my name.

"It's *Joy!*" she says. *Giggle giggle.*

"Who?" I reply, groping the air for a moment and choking the neck of a lamp with my left fist, searching for a switch . . .

"*Joy!* From downstairs."

"Downstairs?" Right. I am in a hotel room, second floor. I remember checking in not long ago after a twenty-hour, three-flight marathon; my eyes took a snapshot of the room before turning off the lamp: spare, dormlike, cement walls painted off-white . . .

"Joy from the front desk!"

"Okay . . ." I squint in order to re-create Joy: petite; Filipina; thirty-something; big, toothy grin. Was she flirting with me? I wonder. I am normally oblivious to come-ons—particularly ones that are not welcome. My friends call it "pulling a Scurlock." Did I encourage her unknowingly?

"How are you doing?" Joy purrs.

"Is there a problem with the credit card?" I ask, rotating my jet-lagged feet out of a thin, sweat-soaked sheet to the edge of the bed and onto a thin, fuzzy floor. Worn carpet is what you get for thirty-nine bucks a night, for being on a writer's budget, though when I reserved the room I remember congratulating myself that this was the type of hotel that Hillblom himself would have patronized.

"No!" Joy giggles. "How *are* you, James?" she asks, as though reading from a script.

"I'm tired."

"You need to relax. Would you like massagee?"

"What?"

"I give very good massagee."

"No. No, thank you."

"You sure?" she asks.

"Yes. Thank you."

"Okay. Good night." Joy does not hang up.

"Good night."

So goes my first conversation on Saipan, the largest and most important of the islands that comprise the Northern Mariana Archipelago. It will take several months to acclimate to the constant offering of sex that, as a white man, seems to be my birthright in much of Asia. My internal clock is still set to Los Angeles, where it is midafternoon, meaning that any chance of returning to sleep will be futile. And because nearly all of the flights into Saipan arrive between midnight and 3:00 a.m., I must wait several more hours to actually see my surroundings, though I have no doubt that beneath the darkness outside my window lies the island paradise I've been reading about for months: lush tropical foliage atop a massive reef that hovers just below the Western Pacific Ocean, 120 miles due north of Guam, 1,200 miles southwest of Tokyo and a slightly longer distance east of Manila. Discovered by the great Spanish explorer Ferdinand Magellan in the early sixteenth century and known among the Spaniards as La Isla de las Ladrones (translation: Island of Thieves),* Saipan is one-half the size of Manhattan and shaped like a giant monkey wrench. An interior of thick pea-green jungle ascends in three distinct peaks while the

---

* The name refers to an unfortunate incident aboard Magellan's ship that left several of his sailors dead and Magellan gravely wounded. At first friendly, a group of islanders who had boarded the ship uninvited attacked the Spaniards when they tried to prevent them from taking the ship's lifeboats, among other things.

perimeter forms a series of pencil-thin beaches and two massive bluffs to the north: Suicide Cliff and Banzai Cliff.* Knee-deep coral lagoons sandwich the eastern and western shorelines, transforming the deep blue swells of the Pacific and Indian Oceans into placid sheets of aquamarine. On the northern shore lies a beautiful grotto popular with Japanese scuba divers—or so I have read—and dotting the western coast a dozen world-class resorts, each with its own sparkling beach. A short drive over Navy Hill is a championship golf course designed by Greg Norman that overlooks pristine Lao Lao Bay. Not to mention the botanical gardens, the charming restaurants, the historic Paseo in Little Ginza, and the recently expanded jewel of Saipan: the Duty Free Stores mall, an edifice of pink marble and black lacquer emblazoned with the logos of Hermès, Prada, Louis Vuitton, and Chanel.

But Sunrise illuminates another island—a beautiful landscape littered with hideous structures, many unfinished. There is the massive concrete skeleton of what was to be a luxury hotel, occupied only by already hot, humid air and ubiquitous jungle. There are empty apartment buildings by the dozen and strip malls, some with rebar creeping skyward; later, I will be told how the Asian financial crisis of 2006 pulled the rug out from under everything in this part of the world. Occasionally I am reminded that my shoes are touching American soil: a military recruiting station that is the sole tenant of a large shopping center; four mammoth military ships anchored just off the reef, waiting; several gas stations; many more video poker shops, some advertised with hand-painted signs, all with the windows blacked out so that the gamblers inside are not distracted by the passage of time; a McDonald's and the carcass of a Wendy's; a Costco; a Ford dealership; Marianas High School—established in 1969 and home of the Dolphins, a mobile marquee announcing a UFC-style mixed martial arts fight this weekend.

---

* Suicide Cliff is so named for thousands of Japanese civilians who voluntarily, or coerced by Japanese soldiers, leapt to their deaths upon being told that the invading U.S. soldiers would rape them; Banzai Cliff was the starting point of the Japanese army's disastrous final charge.

A glance seaward reveals the satellite island of Managaha, the Cocos of Saipan as well as the northern bluffs of Tinian, not quite a mile distant and home to several airfields that, for a few years in the 1940s, were the world's busiest—a massive cement grid that launched hundreds of Japan-bound B-29 Superfortress bombers, including *Enola Gay* and *Bockscar*. Although the twin bomb pits that held their atomic payloads are commemorated by a dwindling clique of World War II buffs every year, Tinian has since rebranded itself as the CNMI's Reno; it is home to the Tinian Dynasty Hotel & Casino—described in the travel magazines as a gleaming five-story seaside resort featuring a Vegas-style flashing sign, dancing fountains, a world-class Chinese restaurant, a private club staffed by at least two dozen young Chinese girls, and rooms painted the color of Pepto-Bismol.

Beach Road ends abruptly at a war memorial, necessitating a U-turn. Polished monuments to the 55,000 or so lives cut short over a few terrible weeks in 1945 ring the island like a charm bracelet, but in 1976 the U.S. State Department dropped an explosive that has molded Saipan's landscape far more than dynamite: $16 million in cash. The money was to be divided among 7,000 islanders as war reparations for the losses they'd sustained during the American bombing of their island—everything from papaya trees to relatives.

"It was gone in a week," Samuel MacPhetres tells me over coffee in a small café across from the war memorial. The elderly MacPhetres is a professor at Northern Marianas College and Saipan's unofficial historian. "I had one student who sold a piece of family land and bought all of his aunts brand-new Mercedes sedans," he continues, raising a thick gray eyebrow. "But then people began to lose faith in the United States because they lacked citizenship, even though the Covenant with the United States had already been adopted."

He is referring to the Covenant to Establish a Commonwealth of the Northern Mariana Islands in Political Union with the United States of America, ratified by a 78.8 percent majority in the same year that the massive money drop occurred—not a coincidence, according to its critics. By then, the citizens of the Northern Marianas—Saipan, Tinian, Rota, and a smattering of sparsely populated islands that constellate north in a crescent, the last lying just south of Japan—had been subjects of four separate empires over more than three centuries. By most accounts, they were extremely eager to become American citizens, in part because the United States had finally liberated them, more so because an American passport guaranteed freedom, but the Covenant's passage had also been a clear victory for the U.S. military. By creating what is known as the Commonwealth of the Northern Mariana Islands (CNMI), the plebiscite had denied Communist China and the Soviet Union any influence in a strategically important region.

But the Covenant was also a humiliating rebuke to the islands' minority Carolinians, who had been brought to Saipan more than a hundred years earlier by the Spanish, who'd developed a habit of consolidating natives in order to convert them more efficiently. Carolinian leaders had helped draft the CNMI's constitution in the early 1970s. Like their neighbors, the majority Chamorros, they had been treated like second- or third-class citizens by their American occupiers, who fed them navy rations like Spam and corned beef, then rushed them into a relationship with America to fit some kind of secret, predetermined schedule. The Carolinians had an even better reason to resent the Covenant: the State Department had never bothered to print it in their language.

President Jimmy Carter issued a proclamation that the United States would implement most of the terms of the Covenant anyhow and the CNMI's constitution became effective on December 8, 1976. Thirteen months later, the Commonwealth seated its first elected governor and legislature, becoming the world's newest self-governing nation. There was one final catch according to the United Nations mandate, under which the United States administered Micronesia as a Trust Territory. The United States could not fully implement the Covenant without approval of the United Nations Security Council; nor could the U.S. terminate the Trust Territory with regard to just a single archipelago, like the northern Marianas chain. If any of the islands of the Trust Territory were to be removed from UN oversight, they would all have to declare independence at the same time. But the archipelagos of Palau, Yap, Truk, and Phonopei had yet to make a deal with the United States. The Northern Marianas had jumped the gun.

When Larry Hillblom arrived on Saipan in the early 1980s, he found a beautiful island bustling with flame trees and legal ambiguity. Despite the Covenant, hundreds of islanders had been denied American passports because they lacked birth certificates or for other technicalities; countries in Europe refused to recognize the CNMI because of the dubious way in which the Commonwealth had come into being; even islanders who had been told they were now American citizens did not possess the right to vote, while it was not entirely clear which constitution—the CNMI's or the United States's—ruled. Hillblom had grooved on legal conundrums since his days at Boalt Hall, and he would soon inject himself into the nucleus of Micronesian politics, but in his first few years on the island, the issue of citizenship obsessed him for reasons that were not at all academic.

For seven dollars (and approximately forty-five minutes' stewing in a humid government office alongside a dozen or so guest workers) the Commonwealth of the Northern Mariana Islands will issue you a driver's license. While mine more closely resembles the student ID I received at college—the spelling is incorrect, the address is a post office box that does not belong to me, and the lamination began peeling off immediately—it entitles me to the locals' rate at a name-brand hotel with clean carpeting where I won't be woken up at 3:00 a.m. by an insistent Filipina prostitute.

Those who establish that they are truly local, however, receive something far more valuable than a better room rate at the Hyatt: a 91 percent rebate of their federal income taxes under a special "mirror tax" provision of the Covenant. When Hillblom arrived, the rebate was an even more mouthwatering 95 percent. Better yet was a "fresh start" clause, whereby the cost basis used to calculate capital gains would be assessed at the time that the islands became a commonwealth rather than at the time the assets were acquired. In other words, Hillblom, who had started DHL with a few thousand dollars in 1969, could theoretically recalculate the cost basis for his shares as of 1982—when their worth was in the tens of millions. But it got even better. Because the CNMI theoretically retained sovereignty over its own affairs, it was unclear whether or not its citizens were required to submit tax returns to the Internal Revenue Service at all. Instead, they might be able to take their rebate in advance and submit the reduced amount due *and* their return directly to the Commonwealth's Department of Finance, bypassing the feds entirely. The U.S. government would thus be denied any right to audit Hillblom's tax returns—even as he maintained his U.S. passport. All Hillblom had to do was establish himself as a citizen of the CNMI. Which he did with typical fervor.

"The thing about Larry"—the professor smiles with a tinge of admiration—"is that he didn't let anything stand in his way. Hillblom wanted his own telephone system because he was afraid that the feds were bugging his, so my friend Bud White installed two mainframes for him at his office. When Hillblom wanted first-run movies, he opened his own theater, and then he created the Supreme Court when he wanted an appellate court on the island. He bought the Bank of Saipan because he didn't want FDIC-insured banks on-island. He gave a friend of mine a Bank of Bahrain Visa card with no limit and told him to open up a computer company." MacPhetres takes a breath. "He was like a kid in a sandbox."

But two of the first things that Hillblom did when he came to Saipan—after securing a driver's license, naturally—were to purchase a bank and buy real estate. These were things that only a citizen of the CNMI could do.

Fifteen

The Great Bird

A great bird sailed into the Port of Saipan in the spring of 1982, spread a pair of shimmering stainless steel wings, and took off down Beach Road toward Garapan, where it banked left before settling in the carport of a modest cement home.

By now everyone on Saipan who mattered knew that Larry Hillblom was the *H* in DHL and therefore a very important man, but the arrival of the brand-new DeLorean DMC-12, the most talked-about vehicle of its time and the star of the hugely popular Hollywood film *Back to the Future*, was an event in and of itself, a coming-out ritual for someone who had thus far preferred to operate under the radar. Word that the exotic automobile was a gift from Prince Naif bin Abdul-Aziz Al Saud, a member of Saudi Arabia's royal family and DHL's partner in the Middle East, circled the island faster than the supercar itself. And while Larry Hillblom's new toy may have inspired more than a few jealous stares from the expats up on Navy Hill, it conferred a certain kind of cultural legitimacy upon a people who were not yet considered American enough to have a McDonald's; the Saipanese would have to wait another several years for the Golden Arches to arrive.

Hillblom hated the car—not because of its many quirks, but because the prince had not covered the import duties. Hillblom was forced to pay more than the entire price of his trusty Honda Civic just to take delivery. But the DMC-12 would become far more useful than he imagined. When he was off-island—which was often—he loaned it to the politicians and businessmen whom he hoped to befriend. And the DeLorean, with its tinted windows and futuristic digital display, was a perfect foil for the way

90

that Hillblom dressed and carried himself. Already he had endured a few disconcerting episodes where people simply refused to believe that he was who he said he was. When told that the scraggly guy in the T-shirt was his boss, a DHL courier had shot back, "And my dad's the president of the United States!"; on Saipan, a local photographer, upon being introduced to Hillblom in the customary fashion ("Meet the *H* in DHL") had looked Larry up and down and, convinced that he was on the receiving end of a practical joke, growled: "Fuck you and the horse you rode in on."

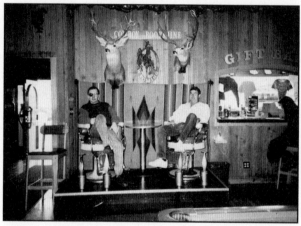

Relaxing in the lobby of the ill-fated Cowtown, not long after the Cessna accident (Courtesy of Michael W. Dotts)

"Larry was larger than life!" Roger Gridley crows over the phone from Florida. Gridley arrived in Saipan in the sixties, one of hundreds of young Americans who came to serve the island in the Peace Corps, which was an inexpensive way for the U.S. government to appear that it was educating the locals. At the end of his term, he stayed on as a contract teacher and indulged in the local hobbies: fishing and drinking. He also dabbled in a number of business ventures, but none of them came close to making money. By the time Hillblom's DeLorean arrived, however, Gridley had set up a fledgling realty company with a Texas attorney named Jack Layne. Layne, who had come to Micronesia to serve as attorney general, had figured out a way for nonnatives to lease—and sometimes even buy—land: partnerships where locals legally owned a majority of the shares, even if they did not maintain control. Given Saipan's close proximity to Japan, its

shimmering beaches, and its unusually temperate weather, Layne's innovation provoked a speculative tsunami. The Asian Bahamas.

"By the time Hillblom approached me," Gridley recalls, "people were making fortunes overnight. Lao Lao Bay was bought by one investor for five dollars per square meter and flipped for eighty."

Hillblom bought several parcels of land from Gridley, forming corporations that were technically owned by his local friends or employees. Then he created a venture called Saipan Cattle Corporation, which took over the lease of the northern tip of the island, already envisioned by another businessman as a kind of Wild West Disneyland. "Cow Town!" Gridley laughs. "It was originally going to be a dude ranch for the Japanese businessmen as well as a brothel. They imported some cowboys from Montana but they caused too many fights. Then they got some Mormons from Utah, but it just never worked. Larry ended up showing films there, installed some bleachers in the cow field, and then it kind of died."

Hillblom's most important venture in Micronesia remained Cocos Island, however, where he was determined to build a miniature Las Vegas. Here he had a very different problem. Since the Spanish invasion, virtually all of the Micronesian islands had become devoutly Catholic. While politicians were tasked with running the government, the bishops called the shots on social issues. And the bishop of Guam was not inclined to allow gambling anywhere in his diocese. His churches were dealing with enough problems from two other American imports: beer and fast food. Gridley recalls an undaunted Hillblom rushing into his office after trips to Guam, bragging that he was converting the bishop. The plan was to allow slot machines on Cocos but nowhere else on Guam, effectively restricting gaming to Japanese tourists.

"But at the same time," Gridley recalls, "Jack and I had introduced ten slot machines at the Hyatt Regency in Saipan. Larry was angry—rightfully so, I guess. He saw that was really going to screw up his deal on Cocos Island if it got bad press." Which is exactly what happened. Gridley and Layne sold their modest operation to a couple of mobster-looking businessmen from Las Vegas, who started building video poker dens under a loophole in the law that allowed machines as long as they were not imported. Since

they were technically coming from the Hyatt Regency, the hotel could import the machines and resell them elsewhere. Video poker dens became as ubiquitous as sugarcane, a phenomenon that did not go unnoticed in the bishop's sermons.

Gridley tells me that he and Hillblom had a second—and final—falling-out after he was asked to sell Cocos Island in the mid-1980s. When the sale to Japan Airlines took longer than Hillblom wanted, Gridley discovered that Larry had gone behind his back. By then, Cocos had become a liability and a huge embarrassment. Pat Lupo still recalls the hotel's disastrous grand opening—with fireworks shooting into the crowd of dignitaries Hillblom assembled, followed a short time later by the discovery that Cocos's management had neglected to pay the IRS.

Saipan energized him. Hillblom was at his happiest and most adolescent crawling its handful of paved roads in his gull-winged DeLorean, imagining future golf courses, hotels, and apartment complexes and checking in on his hobbies. "Isn't this great? It's just like college!" he would crow to visiting friends, as though he'd found a place in which to remain forever young. He bartended at a local beachside restaurant, where he was known less for the quality of his drinks than for his proclivity to throw people out—even his friends—if he didn't think that they were spending money fast enough.

Peter Donnici became a frequent guest; Bill Robinson, one of the few original DHL shareholders who remained friendly with Hillblom, lived there briefly. When Hillblom was not entertaining statesiders or racing his cigarette boat—another gift from the Saudi prince—in the lagoon, he could usually be found in one of his three offices. He kept desks at the Bank of Saipan's only branch, Saipan Computer Services, and the Nauru Building—each of which became a clone of 911 Alakea, with papers strewn everywhere. Visitors arrived to find Hillblom crouched on his hands and knees, searching for whatever paper he was interested in at that particular moment. They came away impressed by his enthusiasm and almost child-like insouciance, but the truth was very different.

On Saipan, Hillblom often awoke before dawn to desperate faxes from DHL's new headquarters south of San Francisco. The U.S. company had rarely posted a profit; now it was building its own airline in a last-ditch attempt to compete with Federal Express, which had ironically entered the document business after the USPS victory. The increased debt and the lease payments on airplanes put further pressure on the company's finances. Worse, DHL-US did not have an experienced leader. Thousands of miles away, Hillblom was trying to pull the strings, but nothing was working.

Overseas was the opposite. DHL's operations in the Middle East, where the company enjoyed a monopoly on express shipments, were pouring untold millions of dollars into DHL's coffers. The region had even embraced the DHL-1000. Runoff from DHL's Middle Eastern cash cow was stuffed into nylon DHL packs in bricks of pristine $100 bills and invested in residential property on Maui, as well as a 1,200-acre ranch in Half Moon Bay, where Hillblom envisioned a fog-shrouded Xanadu that would include a disco and a huge lake stocked with bass. Maybe he assumed that International's success would overwhelm the problems in America. Or maybe he thought his problems would simply disappear, as they always had. Either way, Hillblom had a new focus: He was determined to build an empire in Micronesia.

"Has anyone mentioned a company called UMDA?" Roger Gridley asks suddenly.

"No, " I reply.

UMDA, he explains, is an acronym for United Micronesia Development Association. The conglomerate was founded in the mid-sixties by a civil servant named Russ Curtis. "Curtis was a true pioneer," Gridley says. "He was a fascinating man. He had been in Micronesia as a civil servant during the McCarthy era. He was stationed in Yap for a long time. He helped a lot of local businessmen start their businesses and grow their businesses." But Curtis also happened to be a Quaker—something that did not sit well with Senator Joseph McCarthy. When Curtis refused to sign a loyalty oath, he was fired. So he stayed in Micronesia and started UMDA in the mid-1960s in order to bring in sugar, cement, and rebar. UMDA was the first corporation owned by Micronesians to service the few Micronesian businessmen who were starting their own companies. Curtis embedded UMDA's purpose in the charter: at least 60 percent of its shares had to be owned by islanders.

Curtis traveled from island to island on his ship, selling shares to islanders around Micronesia, sometimes just one share at a time. In those days, a little more than a decade after the American invasion, there was only one local with a large enough business to be a major shareholder: Joe Tenorio, aka "Joeten." Joeten, Gridley remembers, "was the guy." A slight, gentle islander of partly Japanese heritage, Tenorio would build a conglomerate that included hardware stores, shopping centers, a hotel, and car dealerships, among other things. "I think Joeten and Larry were friends," Gridley says. "They were very similar in that they befriended people that could expedite their interests . . . but I would wager it was Larry who would seek him out for his agenda." He adds that Joeten passed away many years ago, but there is someone more important whom I should talk to, and he is still on-island.

Sixteen

Picking a Fight

*J*oe Lifoifoi, the chairman of UMDA, emerges from a sliding glass door, lumbers forward to shake my hand, apologizes gruffly for the dogs ("My security, because of the frequent power outages . . .") and sets up a few plastic chairs next to the pool. His face is the color of chestnuts; his teeth are stained red with the residue of betel nut, a mild narcotic sold at the gas stations here and chewed with lime and salt to induce a pleasant buzz. His nose is wide, almost Polynesian. There is no trace of the Japanese or Spanish lineage that distinguishes so many islanders here, whose parents or grandparents mated with their occupiers. (I am told that the last pure Chamorro or Carolinian died in the late nineteenth century.) Lifoifoi apologizes for his broken English, making fun of the education he received from the American occupiers when he was a boy.

A Carolinian whose father was active in Micronesian politics, Lifoifoi is the consummate insider here. He attended the University of Guam in the early 1960s, where he mingled with the children of other prominent Micronesians from Palau, Yap, Phonopei, Truk, and the Marshalls. After school, Lifoifoi returned to Saipan and became a politician, eventually rising to the position Speaker of the House. Many of his friends did the same. Local government is by far the largest industry in Micronesia; for years, it employed 80 percent of the adult population here. The second-largest is tourism.

Lifoifoi was a representative in the CNMI Legislature when Continental Airlines was awarded an exclusive contract to provide air service to Micronesia, in large part by creating a new airline that would be majority-owned by Micronesians themselves. Air Micronesia, or Air Mike, as it was known, was 60 percent owned by United Micronesia Development Association, aka UMDA, and 36 percent by Continental. (The balance belonged to the Hawaiian carrier Aloha Airlines.) Continental provided the planes, the personnel, the operational expertise, and even the cocktail napkins and agreed to pay UMDA a percentage of profits after it recouped its investment. In exchange, Air Mike allowed Continental to use its route authorities, as well as its gates in Honolulu, Guam, and Tokyo. Because airports rationed gates by nationality, Air Mike's foreign ownership provided Continental with a valuable back door to Asia.

So the creation of Air Mike made UMDA a major player in Micronesia but at a steep price: UMDA was no longer a vehicle for empowering the islanders to control their destiny, as its founder Russ Curtis had imagined; now its most important division was a legal sleight of hand that appeared to empower the islanders while a cadre of executives quietly ran the show from Continental's headquarters in Houston. The principle of outside control was memorialized in Air Mike's operating certificate, which stated that it could fly only under the control of Continental Airlines. The result of such a lopsided "partnership" was inevitable: by 1983, UMDA had yet to receive a dime of profit sharing and, despite repeated requests from its board of directors, Continental had never even provided the islanders with a simple accounting. Whether there were profits or not became the subject of public debate. The *New York Times* reported that Air Mike had made money as far back as 1971, while Continental claimed that its joint venture in the islands had accumulated more than $20 million of losses. At a special board meeting in August 1983, Air Mike called Continental's bluff, repudiating their profit-sharing agreement and contesting Continental's right to use the Air Micronesia name. Less than a month later, DHL filed an application with the Civil Aeronautics Board to replace Continental Airlines as Air Mike's operating partner.

Continental, however, was already plotting a hostile takeover of UMDA. The airline's lawyers at the Carlsmith firm first approached UMDA's president, a friendly expat named Garrick Utley. Utley agreed to sell his stock to Continental for $400,000; more important, he agreed to help Continental acquire director proxies to vote at the next UMDA board meeting, where the airline planned to amend UMDA's articles of incorporation so that there would be no 60 percent local ownership requirement and no accounting requirement. Meanwhile, an attorney from the Carl-smith firm was sent to cajole Joseph "Joeten" Tenorio, UMDA's chairman and the largest shareholder, to cooperate. Joeten, however, had no inten-tion of selling. If Continental wanted to acquire a majority of UMDA, he told them, they'd have to get their shares elsewhere. Carlsmith's attorneys refused to back down. The pressure became so intense that Joeten col-lapsed during one particularly contentious meeting and had to be removed on a stretcher; at around the same time, UMDA's counsel returned to the States. (The rumor, according to a current UMDA director, is that the man had suffered a nervous breakdown.)

Joeten, Lifoifoi tells me, sought out Hillblom's counsel in a very unusual meeting. The old man invited Hillblom to his office and then asked him to hide in his private bathroom so he could listen in on a meet-ing that Joeten was about to have with one of Continental's attorneys. Hillblom obliged; he sat on the toilet seat, ear pressed against the door, as the attorney cajoled and threatened Joeten to support his client's take-over of Air Mike. Meanwhile, Hillblom made up his mind: he would buy UMDA himself.

Of course, that was more easily said than done. Carlsmith had already signed option agreements with every large shareholder except Joeten. The rest of UMDA's shares were spread all over the islands, in such small amounts that acquiring them seemed like more trouble than it might be worth. Hillblom thought otherwise, though he would need connections. Joeten immediately thought of his friend Lifoifoi.

"When I met Larry," Lifoifoi grumbles, "he said what he wanted to do was better for the people of Micronesia than what Continental was plan-ning; was for the good of Micronesia. And I said, 'Okay, I'll go.' But Larry didn't know me then. I'd heard about him being Larry Hillblom, being rich, but I didn't care about that. If his intention is good for the people in this region, I will volunteer. I'm not looking for a salary. So we started traveling, and I started opening up the doors for him to meet the president of FSM [Federated States of Micronesia], the presidents of Micronesia, Republic of the Marshalls, Republic of Palau, and all that."

Lifoifoi and Hillblom scoured Micronesia for shares of UMDA. They flew in small planes, stayed in small hotels, and drank a lot of beer. Although Hillblom was younger and, in theory, the less politically experienced of the two, he lectured the islander on how to read people. "This guy's phony," he would whisper to Lifoifoi during a meeting. Or, "This guy's real." One of Hillblom's greatest insults was "This guy's a dime a dozen."

The more time they spent together, the more bizarre Larry became. Lifoifoi noticed that he had an aversion to talking on the phone with anyone, particularly his executives at DHL. "Sometimes they have to call me to talk to Larry to please call," he remembers. "I relayed that message, and Larry would say, 'You know, they're getting good pay to think and now they want my answer, they want to know what I'm thinking? No. I'm paying them a good salary for them to think.' So he would never answer the telephone. Never!" There was only one exception: if locals called, Hillblom would answer the phone right away. Only one DHL employee, Po Chung, met with Larry on a regular basis, flying in from Hong Kong whenever he needed an audience.

When Lifoifoi dropped in at Hillblom's office on Beach Road, he was surprised to find the *H* in DHL sitting at the computer, typing rapidly. He was even more shocked by the hours his new friend kept. Hillblom ordered a cot delivered to the office so that he could work all night and take short naps to recharge. Meals were often nothing more than a piece of fruit and some coffee. While the locals were terrified of Continental Airlines, which was, after all, the great bird that delivered them—and nearly everything else—to their islands, Hillblom seemed to relish having such a powerful adversary .

"Larry loves to go to court," Lifoifoi says with a grin. "He loves you to sue him! I mean, Larry loves to sue, but he'd prefer that you sue him first. And he countersues, and he stays on you until you collapse. You know, it's just like that boonie dog who bites you," he continues, referring to the ubiquitous stray dogs that wander Saipan in lascivious packs. "And he stays and stays for five or ten years until you go broke."

Seventeen

Under Attack

*H*illblom's latest opponent was no silver-spooned heir like Charlie Loomis, nor a golf club–swinging bureaucrat like Robert Timm. A ruthless strategist and self-made multimillionaire whose youthful face was appearing on the covers of magazines, including *BusinessWeek* and *Time,* Continental Airlines chairman Frank Lorenzo would soon be described by Barbara Walters as the "most hated man in America." Handsome, tan, impeccably dressed, and prematurely gray, he remains a poster child of the "decade of greed," a hero to an emerging breed of financiers who would make vast fortunes slashing jobs and destroying companies. By the time Hillblom purchased his first share of UMDA, Continental was already in bankruptcy—less than two years after Lorenzo had acquired it. (A few years later, he would take over Eastern Airlines and drive it out of existence entirely.) Lorenzo would become so hated that he and his executives required a security detail to walk through their own hangars. So, on the surface at least, Lorenzo and Hillblom could not have appeared more different. Yet they shared more than outsize ambition: a middle-class upbringing, success in a highly competitive industry, an almost pathological fear of unions, and a fascination with bankruptcy laws. (In fact, Lorenzo had just become infamous by using bankruptcy to void his pilots' expensive contracts.)

By the winter of 1984, Frank Lorenzo and Larry Hillblom shared something else: each owned roughly 25,000 shares of UMDA. Equal, however, they were not. Lorenzo had dozens of corporate attorneys at his disposal. And by placing the airline in Chapter 11, Lorenzo had made himself the beneficiary of the law of unintended consequences. Because all litigation involving a bankrupt company or individual is automatically stayed and removed to that company's bankruptcy court, Continental's bankruptcy guaranteed Lorenzo a home court advantage. But Hillblom had an ace up his sleeve, too.

Continental Airlines v. People of Micronesia* et al. was filed in FSM Superior Court on October 9, 1984. As expected, the complaint was immediately removed 8,000 miles west, to a federal bankruptcy court in downtown Houston (only a few blocks from Lorenzo's skyscraper office), where a cherubic Mississippi native named T. Glover Roberts and a phalanx of corporate attorneys now awaited Hillblom's response. So did the FSM's young counsel, a brilliant legal wunderkind who hoped to stem what appeared to be Micronesia's biggest battle in four decades.

"I started as a lawyer with Clifford & Warnke in 1975," the attorney Barry Israel begins, referring to the legendary firm founded by Washington power broker Clark Clifford. Ensconced at a table in an elegant restaurant of a colonial hotel that he owns, Israel is a pudgy man of middle age who wears a boyish haircut and wire-rimmed glasses, and clutches a Black-Berry. In the late 1970s, his firm was representing the Federated States of Micronesia—a nation that the UN had just created out of a few stray archipelagos in the Western Pacific. Clifford & Warnke also had a close relationship with the CAB and represented Continental Airlines; Israel himself had appeared before the CAB in support of Continental Airlines.

Israel eventually left Clifford & Warnke, but he managed to keep both Continental and the FSM as clients. "In 1983 or 1984," he recalls, "Continental's attorney called me and said that the Air Mike situation was untenable. I think that they were making a play for control." Israel called on his two clients: Tosiwo Nakayama, the president of the FSM, and Frank Lorenzo and Barry Simon, Continental's general counsel. A deal was brokered: Continental would own 55 percent of Air Mike, with

---

*In typical fashion, Hillblom incorporated a holding company to acquire his shares in UMDA. The name, which resulted in the appearance that Continental was suing the islanders rather than Hill-blom, was clearly not an accident.

45 percent owned by the governments of Micronesia. In addition, Continental would agree to continue servicing all the Micronesian archipelagos. But at the same time that Israel was putting together a compromise, Continental's law firm on Saipan, Carlsmith, was optioning UMDA shares on behalf of Continental. That's when Israel found out that the infamous Larry Hillblom was also trying to buy UMDA.

"I had first met Larry in 1982," Israel says, "and then I'd run into him on airplanes. Larry thought that he was a territorial law expert. He liked to discuss his ideas with me, but I couldn't understand what he was talking about. Larry had a brilliant but complex mind. We were approached by FBI agents thinking that he was a drug dealer because of his own drug problem and the cigarette boat. A lot of people thought he was CIA."

Hillblom at a settlement meeting in San Francisco with Judge T. Glover Roberts, Continental's bankruptcy judge, as Ted Mitchell looks on (Courtesy of Barry Israel)

The next time Israel flew to Micronesia, he got word that Hillblom wanted to meet him. The multimillionaire picked him up at the Hyatt on Saipan in his DeLorean and drove to Lao Lao Bay for a round of golf. As it turned out, Hillblom wanted to talk about his vision for Micronesia—a subject with which Israel was already somewhat familiar. He had heard about Hillblom's lawsuits, and how he planned to embarrass the United States at the UN for its hypocrisy vis-à-vis its colonies in the Western Pacific. In fact, Hillblom's well-known legal theory that the Territorial

Clause did not apply to the CNMI was causing Israel's client, the FSM, some concern. "As a lobbyist," he says, "I knew that it could interfere with the compacts we wanted."

As they traversed Saipan's most beautiful golf course, Israel paced himself to beat Hillblom by one stroke, and Hillblom reiterated his views on the CNMI's sovereignty. "He mentioned that he'd bought the Bank of Saipan and didn't want FDIC oversight," Israel says. "He said he was interested in telecommunications. He talked about the lawsuits that he'd filed against the federal government." Israel thought that Hillblom wanted to make Micronesia more independent from the United States because it was to his benefit as a tax haven.

When Israel asked Hillblom how he viewed himself working with a government, he replied that he didn't have any intention of working with a government and if he had to pay people off, he would—though, he added a little sheepishly, he would not do anything directly. When they strolled off of the eighteenth green, the Philippine Sea shimmering in the distance, Israel tallied his score: one under Hillblom. Then he turned to his opponent. "There's no way that either I or the FSM can work with you," he blurted. One month later, Continental fired Israel's firm. A short time after that, Joe Lifoifoi and Hillblom showed up at President Nakigawa's office and threatened to keep his country in litigation for a decade if they consummated Israel's deal.

Continental's bankruptcy judge was not amused that a single individual could hold the airline's plans hostage from 7,500 miles and fifteen time zones away. Hillblom and representatives of all four of Micronesia's nations were promptly summoned to a settlement conference at a posh San Francisco hotel.

Nearly a decade and a half had passed since the *Loomis* battle, but when Hillblom peered out at the Golden Gate Bridge from his airplane window, his mind must have processed the similarities. Instead of Loomis, he was fighting a much larger rival: Continental Airlines. Instead of the hostile Nixon appointee Samuel Conti, he would face the hostile Reagan appointee Roberts. Instead of the Pillsbury law firm, he would be going toe-to-toe with attorneys from a downtown Houston outfit. Instead of Perry Mason v.

Huey and Dewey, it was Perry Mason v. the Professor (Peter Donnici), the islander (betel nut–chewing Joe Lifoifoi, sitting next to him), and UMDA's new general counsel, a bombastic expat named Ted Mitchell.

Mitchell, a middle-aged Harvard Law School graduate who was fond of Hawaiian shirts and groomed facial hair, was probably the most prominent attorney on Saipan and was fast becoming Hillblom's favorite. Despite the Ivy League pedigree, Mitchell was scrappy, like him. Other attorneys would describe "Ted" as brilliant but psychotic—the latter due to alcoholism, perhaps. Mitchell had been hired by the Congress of Micronesia to start the islands' first legal services corporation in the 1970s after founding a similar outfit on the Navajo reservation in the States. His most famous victory had prevented the U.S. Air Force from testing high explosives in a delicate coral reef—a case that had prompted a State Department official to sniff to the *New York Times* of Mitchell and his fellow attorneys, "They consistently project an image of hostility to the United States." He could be a tireless advocate for the powerless islanders, then become violent with family and friends when he drank. Mitchell would become infamous for shoving a fellow attorney into a jukebox during an argument at a Saipan bar—with such force that the man suffered permanent brain damage and died a short while later.

Hillblom, Mitchell, and Lifoifoi stayed overnight at the DHL ranch in Half Moon Bay. The next day, Hillblom drove back to SFO to meet the members of the Marshallese delegation. "He had two cronies with him," Israel, who had gone to the airport with the same idea but got there a little too late, remembers. "I walked around a corner as one of the Marshallese said to Larry: 'If you want us to do this, you need to pay us more.'"

The settlement conference percolated for two days. As usual, Hillblom stuck to his position—that the Continental takeover of United Micronesia Development Association was unlawful—while Donnici talked to Judge Roberts and Lifoifoi sat silently, arms crossed, chewing betel nut and gawking at the two dozen–plus corporate lawyers on the other side of the table. "Finally," Israel remembers, "Judge Roberts said, 'I've had it. This is going nowhere.' He ordered us all to come back together and come to an agreement. We went back and forth and came to the San Francisco Accords. Everyone signed off, including the governments. I have a picture of Larry looking at the agreement and smiling."

Hillblom would have plenty of time on the plane ride home to contemplate the deal brokered by Israel and Judge Roberts, and he would not like its end result. He would be forced to give up all of the shares of UMDA that his People of Micronesia had accumulated so far—shares that he knew were worth far more than he'd paid. Meanwhile, Continental and the governments of the CNMI, Palau, the FSM, and the Marshalls would split UMDA and its cash cow, Air Mike. Whether Hillblom really intended to be cut out and return his shares is doubtful. What is certain is that his mind was racing every bit as fast as the Continental jet whisking him back to Saipan. He was not retreating. He was plotting his next move.

Eighteen

War

"**I** created Potawatomie for Larry!" Bob O'Connor exclaims at the mention of the unusual name that Hillblom used for a condominium complex he built near the top of Mount Tapochau—Saipan's highest point. "The Potawatomie are the Indians in my little island in Michigan where I went to camp as a kid."

O'Connor, UMDA's attorney and Larry Hillblom's former law partner, sinks back into his leather chair, the crows'-feet on both temples creasing tanned skin. He has been coming to this office for the better part of two decades, having arrived on-island only a few years after Larry himself, whose former office across the hall now belongs to the island cable television company. Directly above us, on the third floor, lie the remains of the old federal courthouse, now located a mile north in a newer building, and several floors above that, an abandoned Chinese restaurant that once occupied the building's crown: a circular space with a revolving floor that features 180-degree views of the western side of the island, as well as Tinian and Managaha. A marquee in the parking lot announces the Marianas Business Plaza, but everyone still calls it the Nauru Building, a sentimental nod to the glory days, when the building was full and its owner, the Republic of Nauru, boasted the highest per capita income in the world.* I am told that there is still an empty ten-

---

* The Republic of Nauru—once known as Pleasant Island—which lies in the southern reaches of Micronesia, due east of Papua New Guinea, equidistant between the Marshalls to the north and the Solomons to the south, is the world's smallest island nation. Its landmass covers just 21 square

room suite on the seventh floor reserved for Nauru's king, though he has never slept there.

"When I arrived," O'Connor remembers, "there were only two hundred to four hundred alien workers on the island, mostly Korean construction workers. . . . There were no apartment buildings and no streetlights. There was one KFC. The governor's salary was $8,000 a year. One year later, the last patrol car broke down. Prisoners showed up in casual clothes with no handcuffs. Once, I got a job prosecuting a drunk ax-murderer/sailor. I ended up taking the guy to lunch when he showed up early to my office for a deposition! Prisoners would often sneak out of the jail and get a drink at a bar. There were no laws on incest or cruelty to animals. The culture also had a system of apology: if a perpetrator apologized and the family accepted, then there would be no prosecution. At the time, eighty percent of children were born out of wedlock, so kids got traded around a lot. For example, if you accidentally killed a kid, then you gave that family one of your own children, or you gave yourself."

O'Connor had almost exhausted his sabbatical from the Ventura County DA's consumer fraud unit when he encountered Saipan's most famous resident by chance in a local snack bar. He and his girlfriend were celebrating his passage of the CNMI bar exam—what he assumed would be a pointless achievement—with a cheap breakfast. Hillblom and his girlfriend of the moment were seated at a nearby table. ("We were both cheapskates.") When she heard that O'Connor had passed the bar, Hillblom's girlfriend turned to Larry and said, "You should hire Bob."

Hillblom didn't skip a beat. "Yeah," he replied, sipping a mug of coffee, "I've got a big case against Frank Lorenzo coming up. I'll pay you five thousand dollars a month for half of your time and give you a free office."

---

kilometers (8.1 square miles)—less than one-fifth the size of Saipan. Nauru is also the world's smallest republican state and the least populous member of the United Nations. In the late 1970s, thanks to the discovery of large phosphate deposits, its suddenly wealthy king binged on all kinds of ill-considered investments, including the eponymous eight-story office building in Saipan capped by the revolving restaurant. By the mid-1990s, the king was broke and his island's once beautiful landscape had been ruined by overmining. Desperate for cash, the king contracted with the government of Australia to run an off-site detention center for its most dangerous prisoners and dumped his overseas investments, including the building on Saipan.

O'Connor was shocked. He had just been offered a job in the most cavalier way imaginable—and that job was to sue Frank Lorenzo, one of the most feared businessmen in the world. The next day, he drove to Hillblom's modest house across from the beach, where Larry plied him with coffee and fed him the details. O'Connor left discombobulated. "I couldn't get it," he recalls, "I just couldn't understand how Hillblom intended to beat the Goliath."

Larry had told him not to worry, that he never lost a case, but O'Connor wondered how that could be true. Hillblom clearly wasn't a good writer or a good speaker—he might even be dyslexic. Hillblom, he realized, couldn't even spell the word *maybe*.

Yet, the next month, O'Connor found himself calling his boss at the DA's office in Ventura and hearing the words depart his lips as soon as his boss answered the phone: "I'm staying." By the time he hung up, the security of his life was gone. No paycheck. No career path. No bureaucracy. Just Larry Hillblom.

Their first office was a tiny house buried in jungle, not far from Saipan's only quarry. As O'Connor remembers, it had a tin roof, no air-conditioning, no water, no telephone, and an electric typewriter. "Clients would have to find us, we were so hidden." He didn't know that hiding was an essential part of Hillblom's MO. At first, Joe Lifoifoi's wife typed up their briefs. Within forty-five days, however, O'Connor had hired an assistant. Two months after that, they opened an office on Olopai Beach, not far from the Nauru Building. In addition to the Continental suit, O'Connor and Hillblom filed numerous actions against the State Department on behalf of CNMI citizens who had been refused U.S. passports. A typical case was Joeten's wife, who had been born on Fiji. When the federal judge on Saipan, Alfred Laureta, issued a blistering opinion ordering the State Department to treat the islanders as citizens rather than subjects, Hillblom printed T-shirts emblazoned with the judge's order and distributed them among the locals. He was now like a rock star on Saipan. His biggest fan may have been his law partner.

As O'Connor spent more time with Hillblom, his boss's confidence seemed less like arrogance and more like the natural by-product of a relentless work ethic combined with the most formidable intellect that O'Connor had ever encountered. "When he'd walk out of the room, I couldn't figure out, 'How could anybody be so smart?'" O'Connor gushes. "As a lawyer, I would ask his advice on cases, but before I'd ask it, I'd have a pad and a pen ready, so that I could write down, as fast as I could, the ideas that he would give me. Because if I didn't write them down, he would forget what he told me."

O'Connor's praise of Hillblom is as limitless as a groupie's. He tells me how Larry could listen to a piece of music, sit down at a piano, and play it note for note—like Mozart, I guess—how he had an encyclopedic knowledge of any given subject despite the fact that he never seemed to read. But he also admits that his friend was often inaccessible. He distrusted people's motives. He made sure that no one saw the whole picture. He kept you guessing.

The Bachelor

Continental is currently engaged in a massive unlawful scheme to permanently take control over Air Mike. The sinister nature of this scheme is of the same magnitude of the white missionaries: exploitation of the Hawaiian. We implore this court to learn from history and prevent Continental's duplicitous scheme to permanently deprive Micronesia of this most valuable economic entity.

—*From* People of Micronesia v. Frank Lorenzo et al.

"Larry sounded like he was calling from the moon and he spoke very fast," the litigator Parker Folse recalls of the phone call that changed his life and launched a career that most lawyers would envy—a career that has led up to this corner office in a posh downtown high-rise overlooking Seattle's Puget Sound. "I had to really struggle to understand what he was saying. Typically, a client in his shoes would have handed the task to an underling, who would have researched the case and found an attorney who knew the judge involved or at least who had distinguished himself or herself in the kind of case at issue. I still don't know why he cold-called me, why he didn't go the normal route.

"In fact, the receptionist had only forwarded the call to me because she liked me and she knew that I needed the work. I believe I was the youngest and least experienced of the attorneys in our office, and we were really just a boutique litigation firm in downtown Houston. I don't even know how he got our number.

"I warned Hillblom that I had no experience in bankruptcy court and little experience at all as a litigator, but Hillblom wanted me anyway—

probably because I was enthusiastic. I also offered up an idea that would allow us to bypass Roberts: a RICO* lawsuit. RICO is a criminal statute. Because it is typically filed against individual defendants and not enterprises, and because only Continental was in bankruptcy, I thought that such a lawsuit would be easier to remove from Roberts' bankruptcy court.[†] Larry loved the idea, but he wanted to pile on four more counts: breaches of fiduciary duty; violations of the Securities & Exchange Act; the Foreign Corrupt Practices Act; and fraud. He also insisted that we file the lawsuit in federal district court on Saipan.

"I didn't even know there was a district court out there! Larry told me that he knew the judge real well. That if we could get the case removed to Saipan, we'd squash them. So the only other question was, 'How much are we suing for?' We finally ended up with—or Larry came up with—$149 million."

One of the named defendants in Hillblom's RICO case was Barry Israel, who happened to be in the FSM when President Nakigawa and one of his most important advisers, Andon Amarich, were served. "Amarich," Israel remembers, "the man who had led the country to independence from the United Nations and the United States, had a heart attack because he was so upset by the lawsuit. President Nakigawa was beside himself." That night, an Air Mike jet flew Amarich to Hawaii for medical treatment. Meanwhile, Israel, knowing that Hillblom would be traveling to the FSM, prepared a lawsuit against his new adversary. "We found out that Larry was at the airport." Israel laughs. "We found him hiding under a counter and served him with a lawsuit to counteract his lawsuit. We alleged fraud, among other things."

If the irony of being sued by Micronesians—the very people he had promised Joe Lifoifoi that he would protect—stung, Hillblom never showed it. His law office became a war room where he and Bob O'Connor trolled thick law books for cases that might be relevant. Peter Donnici and his office in San Francisco were enlisted to create arguments also. But the

---

* Racketeer Influenced and Corrupt Organizations Act.

† Technically, only actions involving Continental Airlines as a party would be subject to the bankruptcy court's purview.

bulk of the work fell on Parker Folse's desk in Houston, where Hillblom's calls began to arrive from every corner of the globe.

"He called nearly every day." Folse smiles. "And Larry always made me feel like kind of a wuss. I never knew where he was calling me from, but he'd always start out with 'What about this?' or 'This is what we should do.' Then he'd wait for me to poke holes in his argument. If I couldn't convince him otherwise, he expected me to execute. 'Don't stop too soon in your thinking,' he would tell me constantly. 'And don't tell me what can't be done. Convince me that I'm wrong.'"

The one thing that Folse could tell Hillblom for certain was that his lawsuit was doomed in Judge Roberts's court. But an enraged Roberts was demanding that Hillblom come to Houston and explain the RICO lawsuit, which the judge clearly found not only meritless but deeply offensive. Hillblom ignored him. Instead, he sent Folse and Peter Donnici as his surrogates, where they soon found themselves being knocked around Roberts's courtroom on a regular basis. When more threats, delivered in an increasingly agitated if syrupy Mississippi drawl, failed to elicit Hillblom's attention, Roberts issued an injunction for Hillblom to cease and desist suing Continental; then he entered a contempt order, fining Hillblom an eye-popping $25,000 for each day he refused to withdraw his lawsuit. But over Folse and Donnici's pleas, Hillblom once again ignored the Houston judge. The cease and desist order, he pointed out, simply gave them an opportunity to appeal and perhaps even to have Roberts kicked off the case. (Even a federal judge cannot order a private citizen *not* to seek justice, after all.) But Hillblom was not so patient that he would wait for Roberts's ouster and risk being arrested when he flew back to the States. He needed to bring Frank Lorenzo to Saipan.

"I think we're here."

Three boonie dogs bark expletives as Bob O'Connor suddenly U-turns the SUV around a hedge that we have passed several times in the last forty-five minutes, revealing a rusted aluminum fence camouflaged by vines. By the time he has unlocked the gate and led me into the front door of the modest cement home behind it, melancholy has softened the chiseled features just a bit. "Sad" is the only word that escapes his mouth for several minutes.

The media referred to Hillblom's home as a "mansion," but even if one ignores the mildewed carpets, the smashed windows, and the truncated wires poking out of huge tears in the walls (the theft of copper wire is epidemic here, as it is in most depressed parts of the United States), it is clear that this house was never deserving of such a grandiose label. The front door doubles as the kitchen door. One steps down into a small living room and ducks below an oddly placed concrete beam to reach the slightly larger den, which had been Larry's favorite room for meetings. Just past the den, on the right, is a tiny, windowless room walled with shelves that once held Hillblom's law books—where he crafted most of his lawsuits against the federal government. Upstairs is a modest master bedroom and bath. On the floor below is an uncomfortably small guest bedroom and en suite shower. From the top deck, reached by a rusted-out spiral staircase and home to an orphaned Jacuzzi, one can gaze at the Western Pacific Ocean, unobstructed to the horizon, or at Mount Tapochau, or the bishop's residence, which sits just a bit higher than the governor's mansion.

Larry and Josephine (Courtesy of Michael W. Dotts)

Directly below, overlooking the Pacific, is a giant cluster of tangantangan vines that eventually slopes downward and disappears into the bluff. Saipan's landscape was re-created in the late 1950s by Navy Seabees after one of the most relentless bombing campaigns of the war wiped out the island's vegetation, leaving its soil defenseless against frequent tropical storms. Navy engineers imported tens of thousands of the tenacious tangan-tangan, half tree, half vine, the only plant capable of growing faster than it could be washed away, in order to anchor the soil. Most of the island is now covered in the unsightly tangan-tangan, whose only asset has become a liability. Left unchecked, it can overgrow roads and just about anything else in a matter of days. While the gigantic castor bean may have saved Saipan's soil, it has also compromised the growing of anything useful besides cucumbers, tomatoes, watery avocados, and the increasingly rare taro.

After a short tour of the house, O'Connor walks down the winding paved driveway to the garage, which turns out to be empty save for a smattering of moldy pleadings guarded by a family of freakily muscular black arachnids. Maybe a hundred feet away is the swimming pool, covered with a thick veneer of algae, where O'Connor and Hillblom used to retire at night with a six-pack of Budweiser and discuss the Continental case, among other things.

"You know," the attorney begins, "there's a couple things I remember him telling me. He said, 'The first seven million is the hardest seven million to make. After that, it's easy.' And he also said that there was a time, when he first made money, that he started spending it. He bought a fancy car and a house and all that, and then it wasn't any fun. He said, 'I've already been through that stage and there's nothing to it. It's just a waste of time, a waste of energy. There's nothing fun about it.' He didn't get any enjoyment out of buying cars and houses and stuff."

What Hillblom enjoyed would soon become very clear to O'Connor: young girls. Dabbling in the local waters had been a favored pastime of colonists for centuries, of course. Many of O'Connor's friends would marry young Asian women, including O'Connor himself. But there was something more aggressive and strategic about Hillblom's approach to dating. Roger Gridley, the Peace Corps volunteer turned real estate magnate, noticed that Larry only dated women he ended up hiring; he now theorizes that Hillblom could not afford a wife. O'Connor guessed that Hillblom had lacked experience with girls in high school; he sighs, "His idea of a girlfriend was someone to talk nonsense with, to have fun with, wrestle with—not to be intellectual with. The relationships he formed out here were more compatible with his personality."

So on a sweltering summer evening at the height of the *Continental* case, Larry, O'Connor, and Sid Blair, an Oklahoman two decades Hillblom's senior whom he had hired to manage the Bank of Saipan, entered one of the bars that were spreading on Saipan like brothels in a boomtown. Poppy's Nightclub was small and less than a block from the beach. The owner, an ambitious Korean, treated Hillblom and his entourage like VIPs, even though Hillblom was never a big drinker. He complained that liquor gave him migraines; his typical limit was two beers. (When he did get drunk, friends noticed that he became unreasonable, nasty even.) Hillblom had come to Poppy's for something else: young dancers flown over from the Philippine provinces, perks of Saipan's lenient immigration policies. In fact, one of the bar's waitresses was then living with him. Tonight, however, he had left her behind.

As Hillblom and his companions discussed Cowtown, the rodeo-brothel on the northern tip of the island that Blair had started and Hillblom intended to finish (he had already promised Joeten the enviable job of recruiting long-legged cowgirls from Brazil*), the bar owner summoned a couple of pretty waitresses to their table. Although he was notoriously cheap, Hillblom was known around the bars as a generous tipper, meaning that he had an unwritten first-look deal with respect to new arrivals. Tonight, a shy, slight eighteen-year-old Filipina with big black eyes, smooth skin, and full lips caught the intense gaze behind the oversize plastic sunglasses. Like all of the women who work at such establishments, euphemistically known around Asia as waitresses, dancers, models, or GROs (guest relations officers), the girl could be taken on a "date" outside of the bar for an additional fee, called a "bar fine." Provided that she was amenable, of course. But before negotiating the bar fine with Poppy's owner, protocol required that Hillblom signal his interest by buying her the requisite "lady drink"—tonight, grape juice poured into a wineglass but costing about the same as a premium cocktail. When he signaled for it, the shy Filipina then introduced herself as Josephine and sat down next to him.

---

* Hillblom's theory was that Japanese men preferred blond women with long legs and would pay more for them.

She was pretty if not stunning. Saipan did not get its pick of dancers, even back then. The A list were sent to Tokyo, the B list to larger vacation spots popular with wealthy Japanese and Russians; Saipan, and other, lesser-known destinations got whatever was left. But Josephine was pretty. And despite her shyness, she was, like most of her compatriots, ambitious. She had come on a worker's visa to support her family back in the Philippine provinces, to make money with her body though she did not consider herself a prostitute any more than the bar owner considered himself a pimp. Josephine lived in barracks attached to the restaurant and was paid a small percentage of the lady drinks that her customers bought. To make serious cash she would have to incur plenty of bar fines and perhaps even a "cherry fee" if she was willing—or still able—to lose her virginity. But in order for Larry to "table" her ("table" being the unlikely euphemism for taking a girl out of the establishment), Josephine would have to consent.

But every time Hillblom asked, Josephine's answer was no. Nor did she make eye contact. Her stubbornness captivated him, hinted at a kindred spirit, a strong will. She made him work for her affection. Finally, Hillblom got to the point, offering her a better life if she came home with him. When she asked what that meant, he lamely replied, "Better food." Eventually, she agreed to go.

"He was just instantly smitten with Josephine," O'Connor recalls of the first meeting. "I couldn't see why, because Josephine didn't speak much English, and all she said was 'no, no, no.' Every question: 'No!' And I thought, 'Geez, Larry, why are you wasting your time with this girl? She's not very interesting and she just says no . . .' But there was something about her that just struck him and there was something about him that struck her, and they were inseparable from the moment they met, and he just took her into his life without telling his previous girlfriend that he was going to do it. She just had to sort of notice it, because, when you come home from dinner tonight, there's Josephine sitting at the table. She just sort of had to figure out that this was the way it was going to be and she had to just leave without there being any discussion about it."

O'Connor thought Larry was being cruel, but eventually he would come around to like Josephine. He even became convinced that Larry might have opened up the narrow compartment he'd reserved for women into something much broader, perhaps even love—if it was possible for

Larry to be in love, of course. But Hillblom was incapable of monogamy, and he had no plans to remain faithful to her outside of the island. A few years before, on a visit to Palau, Peter Donnici had watched Hillblom table a young islander after a long night of partying and dancing to the Police's "Every Breath You Take"—Hillblom's favorite song. Walking on Fifth Avenue after a session at the UN, Professor Sam MacPhetres had seen Hillblom climb into the back of a limousine with two strippers—or, as he calls them, "lovelies." Once Josephine got her CNMI driver's license and Hillblom bought her a sporty lipstick-red Toyota MR2, Josephine would search the bar parking lots for his tiny Honda. If she found it, Hillblom's entourage learned to expect a scene.

But Hillblom was just as jealous. He recruited his friend Sid Blair to collect Josephine from Poppy's after work and bring her to his house, making certain that she was not "tabled" by anyone else. Then he hired her as his maid, which removed her from Poppy's entirely. He also hired her brother, Bautista, as a handyman. In time, she would bring him to visit her family in the provinces south of Manila; she would convince him to buy her several cars and a couple of pieces of land there; she would try several times to make him change his will; she would also try to make him her husband, but Larry Hillblom had extended that invitation to only one woman in his life. He would not do so again.

Twenty

The Legislator

All peoples have the right to self-determination; by virtue of that right they freely determine their political status and freely pursue their economic, social and cultural development. . . . Immediate steps shall be taken, in Trust and Non-Self-Governing Territories or all other territories which have not yet attained independence, to transfer all power so the peoples of those territories, without any conditions or reservations, in accordance with their freely expressed will and desire, without any distinction as to race, creed or colour, in order to enable them to enjoy complete independence and freedom.

—*United Nations General Assembly Resolution 1514XV*

*W*hen Hillblom decided to run for the CNMI Congress in the fall of 1984, he shrouded himself in the same David-versus-Goliath persona that he'd adopted for his ongoing fight against Continental Airlines. The locals thought it was hilarious.

"He was giving a speech one night on the beach," O'Connor remembers, "and he stood up with the microphone. He was speaking in English and he had a man standing next to him with a microphone interpreting what he was saying into the vernacular. Of course, I could hear the English of what he was saying. When people started laughing I asked my friend, 'Why are people laughing?' And he said, 'Well, because the guy who is interpreting is just saying, 'Well, I don't understand what this guy's saying but you all know Larry, he's a nice guy and he's rich, so vote for him!' ' "

One local who failed to see the humor in Hillblom's political ambitions was a crusty former marine named Lee Holmes, who'd moved to

Guam with his wealthy wife after the war. The Colonel, as he liked to be called, owned the cable television stations in most of Micronesia, including Saipan. Although he had never run for office himself, Holmes had become one of the region's most influential residents by virtue of weekly video editorials broadcast at the tail end of his local news shows. The editorials were known both for the personal nature of their attacks and for their effectiveness. Holmes considered himself something of a crusader against corruption, and there were plenty of crooked deals in an area where hundreds of millions of federal dollars flowed through a small number of local agencies staffed by a handful of families.

Maybe Holmes saw Hillblom as competition. Maybe he suspected that Hillblom was using his wealth to exert undue political influence. Regardless, as soon as Hillblom ran for office, the Colonel nicknamed him "King Larry" and recorded a series of broadsides. Hillblom countered that Holmes's TV stations were guilty of a number of insidious practices, not least of which was jumbling showtimes so locals would be forced to buy his weekly calendar of the listings; Hillblom even threatened to start a rival network.

Unbowed, a few weeks before the election, Holmes flew to Saipan to sabotage King Larry's candidacy. "Mr. Larry Hillblom," he bellowed, "is a Democratic candidate, a founder of DHL Courier Services, one of the wealthiest men in the Marianas. We oppose him for his arrogant behavior. . . . We should warn everyone that he is not fit for public office. He [has] proposed to start his own cable TV system, which is fine with us because we will beat him."

Hillblom was furious. He sent his law partner, O'Connor, across the street to file a fair use claim based on the Equal Time law, which mandated that opposing political views be given equal time on news shows. "I went to Judge Hefner at the CNMI Superior Court," O'Connor recalls, "basically arguing that Larry had the right to respond in kind. Hefner declined to hear the case so I went to District Court, where Hefner was also the judge that day because the acting judge was off-island. So after Superior Court Judge Hefner had tossed me out, District Court Judge Hefner granted my temporary restraining order. Larry and I rushed to Holmes's TV station and filmed the rebuttal that night."

After that, however, while Hillblom and O'Connor remained in the studio, the Colonel suddenly appeared, reclaimed Hillblom's still-warm seat, and filmed a rebuttal to Hillblom's rebuttal. "There was nothing we could do," O'Connor sighs. A week later, the results were in: Hillblom had placed fifth in a field of nine. Had he garnered a few hundred more votes, he would have been elected.

While O'Connor fretted, however, Hillblom celebrated with his friends. "He told me that he had no expectation of winning," remembers Roger Gridley, "but when the time came to sell DHL, he wanted it to be absolutely clear that the IRS could not challenge his residency status because he'd run for Congress. Larry's political stuff was simply business. He had no desire to be in office."

And for good reason: Hillblom was already the most influential legislator in Micronesia. As Holmes may have suspected, Hillblom had secretly rewritten the CNMI's banking laws two years earlier and was advising governments in Palau and the Marshalls in their negotiations with the United States. When Bill Millard, a reputed billionaire who relocated to Saipan in 1985, invoked the wrath of the U.S. Congress, almost causing a clampdown on the CNMI's tax policies by announcing that he planned to claim the 95 percent tax rebate on the sale of his hugely successful company, Computerland, Hillblom penned an amendment to the CNMI tax code overnight that abolished the rebate for anyone with an income over several million dollars. He sent it up to the Legislature the following morning (via Bob O'Connor), then personally took the signed bill, along with a six-pack of Budweiser, to the governor's mansion for his signature the same afternoon. Hillblom could accomplish such feats because, Bob O'Connor tells me with a straight face, he was known to be "philanthropical."

King Larry he was. But, like the European monarchs who had once controlled the mails, he sat uneasy on his throne, mainly because the Covenant to Establish a Commonwealth of the Northern Mariana Islands in Political Union with the United States of America still provided for a much cozier relationship with the U.S. government than Hillblom would have liked. Among other things, the Covenant provided for the feds to ultimately control the CNMI's immigration and minimum wage policies.

Far worse, both the U.S. Congress and the majority of local politicians believed that the Commonwealth fell under the powers of the Territorial Clause, meaning that the Congress could legislate over the islanders, who did not have the right to vote for them or even for the president. Most foreboding of all, California Congressman Philip Burton, the chairman of the House committee that oversaw Micronesia, had made it publicly known that he did not agree with Hillblom's income tax theories. According to Burton, the Covenant called for the full amount of federal income tax due under the "mirror code" to be paid *before* any rebates; moreover, said the congressman, local tax records could be inspected and even audited by the IRS.

So even as dozens of little pink slips containing messages from his investors and DHL executives around the world piled up on his various desks around Saipan, Hillblom obsessed over the wording of the Covenant, the Trust Territory mandate, and both the CNMI and U.S. constitutions. The more Hillblom studied, the more he became convinced that his leverage resided at the UN, and, in particular, at the UN Security Council, where Russia and China could still veto the Covenant, postponing America's absorption of the CNMI indefinitely.

Since, as an American citizen, Hillblom's interpretation of the Covenant was irrelevant, he ceased to see himself as such. Rather than live in one of the Navy Hill developments where the other expats cocooned themselves, for example, Hillblom rented a beachside cottage from a local politician and patronized local bars, where, occasionally drunk, he expounded his views of the Covenant with the same evangelical fervor that had driven his crusade against the imperialistic postal monopolies. "He believed that the Covenant gave the CNMI more power than it says it does," one of his Chamorro friends tells me, echoing a sentiment I will hear over and over again. Hillblom, many of the locals thought, wanted to "reinvent" a done deal.

From his hot-tub perch high above the Western North Pacific, Hillblom looked wistfully toward the three other Micronesian archipelagos. The FSM and the Marshalls had both opted for more independence under so-called free association arrangements that gave them absolute sovereignty over their internal affairs while ceding only issues of foreign policy and security to the Americans. Palau remained locked in an extraordinarily contentious—and violent—internal debate but was also headed for free association. For a decade, the CNMI technically remained in limbo, awaiting a UN Security Council vote that would end Trust Territory oversight and trigger full implementation of the Covenant. But President Ronald Reagan was losing patience now. The word from Hillblom's contacts in Washington was that Reagan would soon execute a Gipper-like end run around both the Trust Territory mandate and the UN Security Council.

Sensing a critical moment, Hillblom convinced his friend CNMI governor Larry Guerrero to create a task force in order to assert the islanders' views of what the Covenant meant—naturally, they would assert that the Territorial Clause did not apply to the CNMI. As with the Covenant, the task force's findings would be put to a plebiscite and then presented to the UN Territorial Committee.

Those who served with Hillblom on the task force tend to brush it off with a laugh nowadays. Back then, most local politicians *wanted* their Commonwealth to be included under the Territorial Clause for a simple reason: they wanted to keep their U.S. passports! But Hillblom managed to build a consensus for his theories anyway. He wrapped them up in an aspirational catchphrase found in the Trust Territory Mandate itself: *Self-Determination Realized*. And when "Self-Determination Realized" was put to a plebiscite toward the end of 1986, it sailed through with almost three-quarters of the popular vote—nearly the same percentage as the Covenant itself. Ecstatic, Hillblom stuffed a copy in his briefcase and hitched a ride with a skeptical delegation of local politicians bound for New York.

"At the United Nations," remembers Professor Sam MacPhetres, a member of the UN Territorial Committee in the mid-1980s, "Hillblom drove up in a limousine to the delegate's entrance in a T-shirt and shorts, carrying a wardrobe bag over his shoulder, then changed in the restroom into a suit." Armed with "Self-Determination Realized," Hillblom took a seat at the witness table before the Territorial Committee.

He had not been subtle in his drafting. Where the Covenant stated, "The people of the CNMI will have the right of local self-government and will govern themselves with respect to internal affairs in accordance with a Constitution of their own adoption," Hillblom's manifesto went much further: "Neither Congress nor any other branch or agency of the United States Government may utilize the Territorial Clause or any other source of power, for that matter, to supersede the sovereign power of the CNMI to control and regulate matters of local concern."

"Hillblom's bottom line," MacPhetres recalls, "was that as long as the Northern Marianas remained a Trust Territory, then federal law didn't apply."

What was much less clear to his audience at the UN was who, exactly, Larry Hillblom was and why they were listening to him rather than an actual islander. As Hillblom expounded his theory of internal sovereignty, a flustered Russian committee member turned to MacPhetres and asked, "Who is he representing?"

One year later, Hillblom returned to the UN along with thirty-two Chamorros. They planned to take turns reading "Self-Determination Realized" into the permanent record. "He was really relentless," MacPhetres says with more than a hint of annoyance, "and he did have a couple of supporters: Sue Rabbit Roff and Roger Clark—a New Zealand human rights activist who was on the committee. I found them both kind of obnoxious and grating."

Twenty-One

Brinksmanship

Larry just had a formidable intellect. I don't think that he
necessarily wanted people to know how smart he was. He just
wanted them to know how stupid they were.

—*David "Grizz" Grizzle, EVP, Continental Airlines*

He was certainly a pain in the neck. He was obviously rich and
on top of that, he was obviously smart. Loony. He was a strange
person. Not your average guy but very intelligent. I had a high
regard for him. That's not to say I'd want to spend hours and hours
with him. He was a very narcissistic person. He could be very
boring because he talked about himself a lot, but he was also a
sweet person. I didn't think he had bad motives. I thought he was
an adversary, and very creative and very determined. Formidable.
As I recall, I tended to view him with respect and accept his
motives as genuine. . . . I thought he was acting on principle.

—*Barry Simon, general counsel, Continental Airlines*

While Hillblom warned the international community of an illegal
invasion by the U.S. Congress, there was one federal official whose
power on Saipan he very much wanted to expand: Alfred Laureta. The
judge who had written the passport opinion emblazoned on Hillblom's
favorite T-shirt was known as something of a maverick. Hawaiian-born,
he was the first Filipino-American to be appointed as a federal district
judge. Short and dark-skinned, he looked more like an islander than a
statesider, and his opinions reflected an empathy for the locals. Indeed,
Hillblom had bragged to his lead attorney, Parker Folse, that if they could

just move *People of Micronesia v. Frank Lorenzo et al.* to Laureta's tiny courtroom on the third floor of the Nauru Building, Continental Airlines would be brought to its knees.

The trick, of course, was somehow removing the lawsuit from bankruptcy court in Houston to Laureta's sanctuary on Saipan. Hillblom still had no doubt that it could be done. Folse and Peter Donnici, however, thought otherwise. So Hillblom ultimately did what he had always done when a legal conundrum presented itself: he went back to school.

Waiting for him at the Boalt Hall law library was a familiar face—the elderly professor and author Stefan Riesenfeld. Hillblom and Kroll had taken Riesenfeld's real property course in law school and both practically worshipped him. "Riesenfeld was a famous figure at Berkeley," Kroll recalls. "He was small and Jewish-looking. He had a hooked nose, he was thin and wore glasses. We would see him in the library writing, surrounded by stacks of casebooks. He was like a piece of performance art!" Thanks to one of the books he'd researched at Boalt Hall, Riesenfeld was also one of the world's foremost experts on bankruptcy law. When Hillblom presented himself at Riesenfeld's office on a gloomy day in 1985, explained his situation with Judge Roberts—including the likely possibility that he would be sent to jail if the standoff went on much longer—the old professor shook his head. "No student of mine is going to prison!" he declared. After some consideration, the professor came up with an elegant solution: Hillblom should declare bankruptcy himself.

Larry fell in love with the idea immediately and called Saipan, where Riesenfeld's bold gambit fell to Bob O'Connor to execute. O'Connor would have to convince Laureta that Hillblom's People of Micronesia was, indeed, bankrupt. Since the company had no debts, he had to be creative. He was. Continental, O'Connor soon argued, was a huge corporation attacking a tiny one in multijurisdictional litigation. Therefore, since POM's only assets were the UMDA shares, it would inevitably run out of funds with which to fight. "We filed bankruptcy on People of Micronesia in the U.S. District Court on Saipan," O'Connor explains, "causing an automatic stay of all actions and orders against People of Micronesia. So the Houston Court's order to cease and desist was stayed." In other words, by declaring bankruptcy himself, Hillblom had canceled out Continental's bankruptcy and removed his original lawsuit back to Saipan. O'Connor then returned to Laureta's courtroom and entered default judgments in the full amount of the complaint, $149 million, against Lorenzo, Barry Israel, President Nakigawa, and the others when they failed to respond to *People of Micronesia v. Lorenzo et al.* (Their lawyers at Carlsmith, believing them all to be protected under the bankruptcy law's safe harbor provision, had advised them not to.) Instead of responding to Hillblom, they had simply waited around Houston for Hillblom to appear. How, they figured, facing huge fines and possible jail time, could he not?

By the time that Frank Lorenzo and his codefendants realized that Roberts's cease and desist order did not protect them from an order issued by another federal court, no matter how small the jurisdiction, it was too late. When their expensive attorneys finally flew to Saipan to have the default judgments tossed out, Hillblom was waiting. O'Connor explains, "Larry found a case that essentially said, 'If you allow your default to be entered for strategic reasons, you're stuck with it.'" He flew Peter Donnici in from San Francisco to argue the motion. Donnici prevailed. "The settlement negotiations with Continental," O'Connor recalls, "began immediately after that."

"When I told Larry that Barry Simon, Continental's general counsel, had called me wanting to settle," Parker Folse tells me, "Larry was ecstatic. 'I'm not going to make this easy for them!' he warned me over the phone. 'They're going to have to meet me on my ground!' he said, 'and I've got some things planned for Barry!'"

Folse suppresses a laugh. He too was ecstatic, but more than that, he was *relieved*. The young attorney had pleaded with Larry to come to Houston and been rebuffed. Then he had tried to convince him not to file the default judgments, fearing they might send Judge Roberts over the edge (and that such a flagrant disregard for a federal bankruptcy judge might have ramifications for his own fledgling career). Now, not only had Hillblom gotten his default judgments, Folse's appeal of Roberts's contempt order had also been reversed. Larry's confidence, which had seemed arrogant just a few weeks ago, now looked prophetic.

When Folse, accompanied by Barry Simon, touched down at SFO several days later, Hillblom emerged, Houdini-like, out of the fog and escorted them to a dirt-splattered Range Rover. He had a mischievous smile on his face as he helped them with their bags. Then he started to ramble, but Simon was not in a conversational mood; Continental's general counsel was still stunned by the appellate judge's reversal of Judge Roberts's injunction. Not only had this judge scolded Roberts for improperly issuing the sanctions against Hillblom, he'd excoriated Continental and its attorneys for improperly using the bankruptcy court as a sanctuary from which to launch hostile takeovers. He had also reminded Simon and his boss, Frank Lorenzo, that a federal judge in Saipan did not take orders from a bankruptcy judge in Texas. From now on, it was clear that Continental was to have no refuge in Judge Roberts's bankruptcy court, nor would Hillblom's lawsuit be litigated in Houston.

Fifteen minutes later, Hillblom turned his SUV onto the long, rough driveway that led from Highway 1 to his ranch in Half Moon Bay. Then he hit the accelerator, transforming hundreds of ponderosa pines into a green blur. They passed an American sedan with a smashed windshield overturned in a deep ravine, which Larry casually mentioned he'd crashed a couple of weeks earlier—on the way to his fortieth birthday party. Every time Folse sensed the back wheels fishtailing, his teeth clenched and his eyelids slammed shut. He realized that his right fist had melded with the plastic grip bar above the glove compartment.

A few feet behind him, he could feel Simon gripping the back of his seat as the forest flew by and Larry blathered on about how he'd acquired the ranch and excavated the road himself. When the Range Rover finally came to rest in front of a series of Mission-style structures anchored by a modest two-story house, Folse and Simon descended from the SUV, knees buckling beneath them as their feet touched pavement. Folse took a deep breath.*

Inside the main house, Pete Donnici awaited. When the four attorneys finally sat down in the living room, Folse stole an empathetic glance at Simon. The man had probably never been subjected to such disrespect in his life—at least not in his years as general counsel of a Fortune 100 corporation. The executive must have been furious but he maintained a poker face as Larry recited a long list of demands, capped by Frank Lorenzo's PS-1 pass, the CEO perk that allowed him a first-class seat anytime, on

* Simon says that he does not remember this incident.

any flight, even if a paying passenger had to be bumped to accommodate him. Not only that, however. Hillblom demanded that Lorenzo personally hand the pass over to him.

"Let me get this straight," Simon interjected angrily. "You want Frank Lorenzo's pass?"

Hillblom nodded. "If there's only one seat on the plane, and it's between me and Frank," he said, "then I have to come first."

That night, Hillblom, Folse, Simon, and Donnici dined at the posh Beau Rivage Inn on Skyline Boulevard, where waiters in crisp tuxedos treated Hillblom like royalty. Simon and Hillblom both ordered abalone, a rare agreement. Continental's general counsel was impressed with Hillblom's balls—that anyone would ignore a federal judge's contempt order was, he thought, unbelievable—and he was even more impressed with the young litigator who had won the stinging reversal of Judge Roberts's contempt order. But Hillblom's demand that he take Lorenzo's PS-1 pass grated— proof, he thought, that big cases often turn on idiotic issues. The next morning, Simon flew back to Houston without even the seeds of a deal.

Nevertheless, negotiations continued sporadically on Saipan and elsewhere for months. There was too much at stake not to settle. "Lorenzo finally asked if I would go out and provide a second opinion as to whether we should settle because the lawyers were recommending that we settle," says a Continental executive who had dutifully flown to Honolulu and sat through a day of tense discussions before Hillblom finally arrived in typical attire: dirty blue jeans, a San Diego Surfing Association T-shirt, and Keds. "Without a great deal of effort," the executive remembers, "he takes command of the conversation. He's so on top of the facts and the law, and I called Lorenzo immediately and said, 'Frank, I don't know the facts, but I've met our adversary, and based on that, I think we should settle.'"

Not long after, Frank Lorenzo entered a Houston conference room and deposited his PS-1 pass into Hillblom's outstretched palm (Larry remained facing the boardroom table so that the two never actually had to face one another). His lifetime dream of owning an airline—a feat achieved by Howard Hughes in his early thirties—had been accomplished at forty. No one could seriously argue now that he was *not* the most powerful human being in Micronesia—an area as large as the United States and its gateway to Asia. Hillblom's promise to give the UMDA shares he'd amassed to the governments of Micronesia had apparently expired at some point during the negotiations with Continental. Instead, he made himself its president.

Air Mike was now King Larry's airline, just as Saipan had become his island and Micronesia was to become his empire via UMDA, which he reimagined as a resort developer, cable television broadcaster, and of course, casino operator. The Continental settlement would provide millions in cash flow and UMDA could buy property outright. But Hillblom needed someone to help him navigate Micronesia's Byzantine political and tribal bureaucracies. Of particular interest were cable systems and resorts. "I'm not investing in anything without land attached," he confided to a friend.

Joe Lifoifoi was the obvious choice, though he was reluctant when Hillblom summoned him to his office shortly after the Continental settlement was signed. Like most islanders, he had worked only for the government and never for private enterprise. Taking a job at UMDA would be a tremendous paradigm shift—from working for the Great Father to the Great Bird.

"I said, 'No. It won't work,'" Lifoifoi recalls. But Hillblom persisted. When Lifoifoi asked him what his job would entail and where his office would be, Hillblom told him not to worry about such things. They would travel as they had during the war with Continental Airlines. It would be another great adventure.

Lifoifoi did not ask about compensation; he just said yes. But when he received his first paycheck a week later, he assumed it was a mistake. Larry was paying him $100,000 a year—more than six times what he had earned as Speaker of the House. Lifoifoi went back to his friend and said that it was too much, but once again, Hillblom brushed him off.

"Don't worry." He grinned. "Your time will come."

Lifoifoi was stunned. He had introduced Hillblom to a few people, drunk a lot of beer, and shared a lot of stories. In San Francisco, he'd done little but sit in a chair and chew betel nut while Larry and his attorneys argued in language that flew over the islander's head. In New York, he'd helped read "Self-Determination Realized" into the record, but that had yielded nothing so far, and most of Lifoifoi's friends were convinced that Larry's views on the Covenant were a little nutty anyway.

"What do you mean," the islander finally grumbled, "my time will come?"

Twenty-Two

Strings

"**L**arry must have been everything to those islanders," Patrick Lupo muses. "He was kind of like their connection to the outside world. He was huge."

Lupo relaxes his tall rancher's frame into a comfortable couch in the solarium that overlooks his generous swimming pool. Decades ago, he might have heard George Harrison or John Lennon jamming at one of their nearby mansions. He tells me how Hillblom visited occasionally in those days, loaded with several DHL pouches packed with vitamins. When Lupo's children opened the refrigerator for their morning cereal, they would instead find dozens of bottles of pills and colorful capsules. They invented a nickname for their father's boss: Larry-the-weird-guy-with-all-the-vitamins.

Unlike Peter Donnici, Lupo never followed Hillblom to Saipan. Instead he was summoned here to run DHL's operations in North and South America. Lupo's immediate boss was a former Lever Brothers executive named Bill Walden, who worked out of a brain trust in Belgium called Management Resources International. Hillblom and his top executives had devised MRI as an outsourced chairman's office—an arrangement that not only saved the company from paying taxes in the United States, but kept the corporation's nationality purposefully ambiguous. His immediate challenge was making DHL competitive in the United States, where it had fallen to a distant third in the express market, behind Federal Express and UPS. While FedEx was already a household name, most Americans still had no idea that DHL even existed.

"It really bothered Larry that DHL still wasn't successful in the U.S.,"

Lupo says, though it certainly was not for lack of trying. After telling Lupo that he had seen the seeds of DHL's demise in the fax machine, Hillblom had insisted that they open fax offices in major cities where customers could send their documents instantly across the country or across the world via satellite machines the size of mainframe computers. The idea was to leapfrog FedEx, but as Japanese companies like Canon and Sharp rolled out cheap, landline-based fax machines, companies simply bought their own and DHL's fax business fizzled. Lupo then hired popular *The Far Side* cartoonist Gary Larson to create an expensive—and offbeat—ad campaign to reintroduce DHL to the United States. The campaign won awards, but no new customers. Hillblom then flew to Memphis to discuss a merger with Federal Express's founder Fred Smith, but Smith, who had served in Vietnam as a marine, had joined the ultra-exclusive Skull and Bones society at Yale, and was on the verge of taking FedEx public on the New York Stock Exchange, did not hide his contempt for his disheveled rival. "Chalk and cheese," Lupo observes. Jim Campbell, who set up the meeting, explains: "They were just very different, strong-minded people. . . . Fred is more polished and civilized, traditional sort. Larry was a Fresno kid who worked his way up through high school and Berkeley and just a different kind of fellow."

In desperation, Hillblom even brought back the dreaded office of the presidency—empty since Curt Carlsmith's ouster—and hired a succession of executives, including Larry Roberts, a brilliant GTE engineer who would later become known as one of the fathers of the Internet. But despite his genius, Roberts proved as short-lived as Carlsmith.

"Hillblom flew to San Francisco," Lupo remembers, "and told Roberts, 'You've just got to improve the publicity. You've got to improve our awareness.' And Roberts says, 'Well, what do you suggest we do?' And Larry says, 'Do *something*! Any news is good news. Any headline is good news!' And Roberts says, 'Like what?' So Hillblom thinks a moment and goes, 'Why don't you jump off the Golden Gate Bridge? 'Chief Executive of DHL Jumps Off of Golden Gate Bridge!'" Lupo gesticulates a newspaper headline and roars. "That was the end of Larry Roberts!"

Hillblom finally offered DHL's presidency to Joe Waechter, a thirty-one-year-old executive who had worked for the company since college. Waechter had run the stations in New York, Houston, and San Francisco. He was known as someone who could motivate employees and solve problems. But as smart and talented as Waechter might have been, the title that Carlsmith had once held remained a dubious one. ("I didn't know what it meant," Steve Kroll says, "except being a front man for Larry.") Yet in many ways, the loyal and grateful Waechter, who had originally been hired by Hillblom's half brother, Grant, proved himself more than up to the task. When Hillblom decided that DHL needed to go toe-to-toe with Federal by flying its own planes, Waechter built a hub in the Midwest and started leasing jets. The airline would turn out to be the most disastrous of the succession of failures in the United States. The domestic company, which had managed to eke out a profit in the early eighties, suddenly began to hemorrhage red ink.

By the time Bill Walden called Patrick Lupo into his office in Belgium and offered him CEO, there was only one solution remaining. "You've got two absolutely first-class, well-capitalized, entrenched companies in Federal Express and UPS," Lupo explains. "And we could get an element of market share from them but other than that, forget it." Since DHL had already tried merging with Federal, they would now have to approach UPS, which obviously meant that Hillblom would have to give up control. Instead of being the puppetmaster of DHL, he would be a major—but still a minority—shareholder in an iconic American corporation. And he would be fabulously wealthy. But Hillblom had other ideas.

The Flying Tiger Line had been awarded its first route authority by the Civil Aeronautics Board two decades before the founding of DHL, making it the first scheduled cargo airline in the United States. Started by ten pilots from the First American Volunteer Group, the quasi-mercenary air force that had defended China from Japan in the first stages of World War II, and known by the AVG's nickname, "Flying Tigers," the company had grown to serve fifty-eight countries on six continents and had surpassed Pan Am as the world's largest cargo operator in 1980. Its impressive fleet of aircraft, including several 747s, was flown by an army of 1,000 pilots, using route authorities accumulated over more than three decades. In addition to its cargo business, Flying Tigers ran passenger flights on a charter basis and had won a number of military contracts over the years, acting as one of the U.S. Army's first private contractors.

Acquiring Flying Tigers, Hillblom figured, would instantly make DHL a major player in packages and freight. Tigers had scale, airplanes, and the permission to fly them all over the world. Lupo loved the idea. "I think this is Larry's genius," he tells me, "as the big picture guy, looking at something completely transformational. . . . His argument was change or die." But Hillblom's audacity was equally obvious. Tigers was a huge, publicly traded corporation. DHL might have had offices in twice as many countries and an impressive client roster, but it still had virtually no assets. At any other time, Hillblom's strategy might have been DOA. Not so in the roaring eighties. In fact, there was an investment bank in New York that was doing such "gnat versus Goliath" deals, as Lupo terms the takeover of Tigers. By 1986, it had become the most profitable investment bank in American history, thanks mainly to a workaholic genius named Michael Milken, who had pioneered the use of so-called junk bonds in order to finance hostile takeovers such as the one that Hillblom and Lupo were now contemplating. The name of the firm was Drexel Burnham Lambert.

Lupo crossed the Atlantic several times to meet with Drexel's hotshot bankers. He had learned by then to use Hillblom strategically. The trick was to bring in his eccentric boss at the last possible moment. When Lupo eventually talked his way into a meeting with Drexel's president, Fred Joseph, he finally summoned Hillblom to the company's offices at 60 Broad Street, a generic steel-and-glass edifice two blocks from the New York Stock Exchange.

Like Fred Smith, Fred Joseph was handsome and Ivy League–educated and had served in Vietnam. He was also fond of suits and was leading by far the hottest company in his industry. "He was a very impressive guy," Lupo recalls, ignoring the ominous. "We said, 'We want to buy Flying Tigers.' And we worked hard on it. But I think, basically, the DHL structure was too fragmented, and our airline was too puny and our capitalization was too thin to really give Drexel the comfort they needed that we could launch any kind of takeover."

So Lupo traveled the short distance to Greenwich, Connecticut, and pitched a novel idea to executives of the only remaining merger possibility: United Parcel Service. Lupo suggested that DHL and UPS merge and then the combined entity would buy Flying Tigers. "That was just a knockout strategy," Lupo says, and beams, "because we had the international market. UPS controlled the domestic market, where we were very weak. Neither of us had an airline of any substance. UPS was just starting theirs. We were just starting ours. Ours was rubbish. Theirs was very good but still old aircraft. Route authorities were difficult, particularly international. And then you'd put the FT airline, freight, on top of that, and then UPS would generate small package traffic. We would have delivered the packages internationally. I'm telling you, it would have been huge. In fact, had that occurred, I would question whether there would be a Federal Express outside the U.S. today. It was really a knockout."

But Lupo could not close the deal. A year later, a UPS vice president suggested a straight buyout of DHL. The courting phase lasted several years. "They just kept putting us through one hoop after another," Lupo groans. "We kept trying to dance and basically got slate. [Now] UPS is basically saying, 'Well, we're going to do our own thing internationally.' So, as these things happen, you get more and more disenchanted with the prospect of doing anything, and so there came a time when I just said, 'We're out of here.'"

With the last of DHL's potential partners out of the picture, and DHL's reputation sullied, Lupo confronted a frustrated Hillblom and his angry partners. Some of the original station owners had waited nineteen years to be rewarded for their hard work and sacrifice. They'd watched the company grow exponentially, but most of them had only unimpressive paycheck stubs to show for it. Thanks to restrictive covenants, they could unload their shares only to another shareholder, and for far less than they were probably worth. One of the shareholders had designed his dream house, anticipating that UPS would buy DHL, and now lived in the garage—the only part of the home he could afford to build. Meanwhile, he and his fellow shareholders had witnessed Hillblom's escape to a tropical island where he now owned an airline and a smattering of smaller businesses. When one of DHL's bankers told Lupo that the company had outgrown its shareholders, he knew the man was right. But there was nothing that anyone could do without bloody Hillblom's approval, and Hillblom had other things on his mind.

Twenty-Three

The Spy

When the young U.S. Navy JAG lawyer Howard Hills found out that Larry Hillblom was coming to New York City in the summer of 1987, he immediately asked his superiors for permission to interview him. Hills, a tall, blond surfer from Laguna Beach, California, said he wanted to discuss Hillblom's relentless opposition to terminating the Trust Territory, but he had a personal fascination with the man who was showing up at Trustee Council and Congressional hearings on a regular basis. They had even chatted a few times in the hallway of the Capitol. "His arguments were very good," the still rather intense Hills tells me, "but his personal presentation cut both ways. He would show up in Congressional meetings or UN receptions wearing sandals, shorts, and a plain white T-shirt that was dirty! Sometimes he would wear jeans and an aloha shirt [where] everyone else was wearing suits. And I envied Larry because I'm a beach guy!"

Permission to interview Micronesia's chief gadfly was granted, mainly because the State Department had no idea how to handle Larry Hillblom. The JAG lawyer was hardly intimidated by his eccentric reputation, however. In every island group, Hills explains, there were a few Americans who had risen to a certain level of political influence. "There were always several people," he remembers, "who found their way out there and looked around and said, 'Wow. This is like the Wild West. This is like being in Dodge City or Keystone, Arizona. This is out here on the frontier.' You always tended to attract Americans who were eccentric but who were very smart people. They tended to be able to give the U.S. government a run for its money."

Larry certainly fit that bill. Not only was he connecting the dots of Micronesia's four nations, befriending politicians and local businessmen alike, but he had run for Congress in the CNMI and had just purchased the Marshallese ambassadorship to Vietnam for $25,000. As an unofficial lobbyist, Hillblom was now helping Palau negotiate more foreign aid from the United States, and he was also arguing against the termination of the UN Trust Territory with respect to the CNMI, which still lacked the required consent of the UN Security Council. Hills wanted to know Hillblom's motives: Was he just trying to protect his tax cut? Keep his tax returns confidential? Was he an egomaniac? Or did he just enjoy fucking with them?

He showed up at Hillblom's hotel in Manhattan on a warm summer night. During the short walk to the Japanese restaurant that Hillblom suggested, the two young men tried to stake out some common ground: the possible fallout of the Iran-Contra affair that had embroiled Ronald Reagan's White House, their favorite beaches in Micronesia, etc. Once they sat down at a small table and ordered sushi and beers, however, the conversation turned to business: Hillblom's opposition to the termination of the Trust Territory.

"I started talking about how I saw the self-determination process and the Trust Territory system," Hills recalls. "I basically told him that I thought that the U.S. had a very dysfunctional territorial policy and law in practice and that I thought free association was probably a better way for the U.S. to go and for the islands to go, and I found that it was interesting that the CNMI had chosen territorial status."

"The decision to go for Commonwealth status was not territorial," Hillblom interrupted.

Hills shook his head. "I think all of the history of the Covenant establishes that it's under the territorial clause of Congress," he shot back. "Any special rights are statutory and therefore under the authority of Congress."

"Under the Covenant," Hillblom said firmly, "the territorial clause does not apply to the CNMI."

"Well," Hills finally said, "let's agree to disagree."

Hillblom nodded. Then he launched into an analysis of the ways in which the territorial clause *might* apply to the CNMI after all. The Covenant, he offered, had created an ambiguous legal situation and that would have to be determined going forward.

Hills tried and ice-breaker: the Territorial Clause issue was irrelevant, anyway. The CNMI, he told Hillblom, was not going to achieve the status that they wanted to achieve in any event. It wasn't just a matter of getting the United States to agree with them, but of the islanders ultimately getting what they wanted. Termination was a good thing, he argued, because it was based on principles. It was not just a ploy by the United States to create a new colony. The Covenant, after all, allowed people to debate whether or not the Territorial Clause applied. Any disagreement would therefore be best fought out in the context of the new status. And the islanders had a lot more leverage to negotiate their rights as U.S. citizens rather than as wards of the UN Trust Territory.

Hillblom fell silent for several moments. "I've never talked to anyone who'd explained this to me as clearly as you've explained it to me," he finally said. "And I can see that there are principles in your policy and that it has a positive agenda. But, I think now more than ever, I realize that I have to do everything I can to prevent termination of the trusteeship."

Hills was shocked. He thought he'd made Hillblom see the light but now the opposite seemed true. "Why?" he blurted.

"Because," Hillblom replied, "I don't think the U.S. is capable of acting in a moral manner toward the Mariana Islands without UN oversight."

"That's interesting," Hills replied, a little flush, "because the UN and the Trusteeship Council had oversight when the U.S. conducted sixty-seven nuclear tests in the Marshall Islands and the Security Council and the Trusteeship Council had the ability to exercise their authority but they acquiesced. So it wasn't just the U.S. who conducted the nuclear tests; it was the UN. And although there were later a lot of questions and concerns, the UN regime that was in place facilitated the nuclear testing program. And if you believe, as I do, that that was, in terms of the impact on the people on the islands, lamentable," he continued, "then it doesn't really sustain the view that the UN makes the U.S. more moral."

Hills tried once more to make Hillblom get it—that keeping the trusteeship in place just allowed Congress to lord it over the islanders and fail to educate them—treat them as subjects instead of citizens. Why not, he implored, bring U.S. law to the Marianas and end what was essentially military rule?

"Because," Hillblom replied calmly, "withholding termination of the

Trust Territory gives the Marianas more leverage in dealing with the U.S. government."

"But the Trust Territory is okay to the U.S. because it gives the U.S. everything it wants! The new structure will introduce limited government. In the end, the U.S. has disproportionate bargaining power. I think you increase their bargaining power by moving to the new status."

"*That* is what's going to happen," Hillblom allowed, "but for now, I think the smart move for the CNMI is to slow it down and keep the UN involved."

The young JAG officer had now exhausted his arguments—legal, political, even moral. Only after returning to his own hotel that night would he realize that that's exactly what Hillblom had wanted all along, to draw all of the government's potential arguments out of him. Hills had hoped to pick Hillblom's brain; instead, it was Hillblom who'd cleaned up.

But Hills had a feeling that, for Hillblom, this wasn't about the Marianas or about the UN or about the Trust Territory. Becoming a linchpin made him a much more important person. And not having the Trust Territory terminate must do something for him business-wise, though what that might be Hills had no idea. How else to explain that his appeals to Hillblom's sense of history and his commitment to democracy and self-government had been so totally ineffective, if not counterproductive?

When Hillblom returned to Saipan, he told his friends that the United States had sent a psychoanalyst posing as a government attorney to size him up over dinner, but that once he had realized what was happening, he'd stormed out.

The former JAG officer enjoys a laugh when I mention Hillblom's version of events. "As I recall," he says, "we parted amicably. It wasn't an official assignment or information-gathering mission. No one had briefed me on him. I just saw him as one more of a long parade of eccentric and interesting people who tended to be the Americans out on the islands."

Polar Bear

In an ambitious bid to become a global air freight carrier, Federal
Express Inc. agreed today to pay $880 million to buy Tiger
International Inc., parent of the Flying Tiger Line, the world's
largest air cargo carrier.

—The New York Times, *December 17, 1988*

The brief *New York Times* article datelined December 17, 1988,
announcing Federal Express's purchase of Flying Tigers might well
have doubled as DHL's eulogy. "It was pretty bleak," Patrick Lupo
admits. Compounding the sense of doom at DHL's headquarters in
Brussels, the U.S. company's latest president, a food service executive
named Charlie Lynch, had recently jumped ship to join a private equity
firm, and Lupo had just fired DHL's European chief for not making his
numbers. Meanwhile, FedEx had begun testing the Japanese market by
flying to Tokyo under a limited route authority—something that both
UPS and DHL had applied for, and lost. "Geez," Lupo said to Larry
during one of their weekly phone calls, "you lose Japan and then what
happens next?"

They both knew the answer. Whether or not Larry was willing to do
what was necessary to save the company, however, was another question. When Lupo had lined up a major new investor not long before,
Hillblom had sabotaged the deal by failing to show up at a key meeting—probably, Lupo had assumed, because Larry was not yet ready
to give up control. DHL *had* outgrown its major shareholder, but
Hillblom wasn't going to relinquish the strings unless he got what he
wanted. And, unbeknownst to anyone besides a few childhood friends

and Carla, what Hillblom wanted more than anything was a deal that would make him a billionaire.

So Lupo focused on the near impossible task of making the hodge-podge of more than one hundred companies that Hillblom had strung together in a tangle of cross-ownership and nominees palatable to Wall Street. Lupo had sold Cocos Island and a number of Larry's other hobbies long ago. He had hired an investment banker from a major New York firm to put the books in order. And DHL itself had already met two crucial goals: expanding the network to more than two hundred countries and stabilizing the technology platforms that would make further growth possible—and none too soon. Documents been had only the crest of a tsunami that DHL had ridden to unimaginable growth. Now there was the inkling of another wave, parcels and cargo, forming behind it. Thanks to the popularity of Japanese electronics like Sony's Walkman and just-in-time inventory practices that required express shipping and logistics, DHL was once again in the right place at exactly the right moment. But Lupo needed long-haul airplanes and transcontinental route authorities—or the money to buy them.

In Asia, Hillblom may have seemed inert, but paranoia was still his most reliable ally. He had always made the big decisions when he sensed that DHL's survival was at stake. On golf courses in Micronesia and Japan, Hillblom now discussed the idea of a strategic alliance with executives of Japan Airlines, one of DHL's major suppliers. Within a couple of months, he'd negotiated a deal to sell one quarter of the company to JAL and an affiliate company called Nissho Iwai. The deal valued the entire DHL network at half a billion dollars—enough to make Hillblom easily one of the wealthiest men in America, if still a ways from making him a billionaire. More important, from Lupo's perspective, is that DHL would leapfrog Federal Express and gain respect. "There was a huge credibility [in having] the biggest airline in Asia," Lupo recalls. "Otherwise, we would have had to acquire the large aircraft. Instead, we used the belly of the JAL planes and concentrated on the hub and spokes." Unlike Federal, which would have to max out Flying Tigers' 747s with small packages in order to be cost-effective, DHL could send packages virtually anywhere in Asia in virtually any quantity at virtually any moment. By flying its own long-haul airplanes, FedEx was guaranteed to create bottlenecks for itself at customs. By using commercial airlines' cargo space, DHL's package flow would be far smoother and less prone to delay.

Hillblom signing the deal that made him one of the world's richest men. Pat Lupo is on his right. Peter Donnici stands behind him.
(Courtesy of L. Patrick Lupo)

But once again, Hillblom swooped in with the grand idea and left it to others to execute. As a small army of attorneys from JAL and Nissho Iwai suddenly invaded DHL's headquarters in Brussels to do their due diligence, the company became overwhelmed. "Two things happened in one day," Lupo sighs. "One is that the manager here rang and said that the lawyers wanted to see each and every lease for every vehicle we had in the UK. And we had over a thousand vehicles. . . . It was just stupid. It was lawyers over-lawyering to generate big fees. Then, in the same day, one of their senior lawyers fronts up and says he wants to basically come into my office and go through all of my files. I said, 'What are you looking for?' And he said, 'Nothing particularly. I just want to go through all of your files.'"

"You gotta be kidding me!" Lupo shot back. "I'm a lawyer; I've done due diligence. That's not how you do diligence."

"That's how we do it," the attorney replied. "We have an approach at our firm and our clients fully subscribe to it. It's called 'open kimono.'"

Lupo lost it. "I don't care what y'all . . ." he growled. "Take that whole team of people and I want them out of the building *now!*"

A minute later, Lupo's phone started ringing. "It was Larry's partners," he remembers. "They rang up and said, 'This is tragic! This is terrible! All this work!'"

Lupo told them to forget it. He was putting his foot down. After seventeen years building DHL and defending Larry Hillblom's company against attack from regulators and competitors, he wasn't about to defend it from its owners. Only one shareholder agreed with him. "Larry supported me a hundred percent," Lupo recalls. "He said, 'Yeah, that's just ridiculous. You don't have to go through that.'"

Two weeks later, Lupo received a full apology from JAL's lead attorney. And once again, DHL's headquarters was swarming with lawyers. This time Lupo bit his tongue—for eight months.

Federal Express had started flying planes into Japan by the time Lupo's secretary announced that Klaus Schlater, chief financial officer of Lufthansa, Germany's largest airline, was on the phone. Like Hillblom, Schlater liked to get to the point.

"I know you've been having these discussions about a cargo airline," he told Lupo in a thick German accent, "and I like to do things a lot bigger, a lot faster. We'd like to buy twenty-five percent of DHL."

"Sorry," Lupo replied, "but we've been going through due diligence for eight months now and this is a really slow process and I'm confident that we will eventually conclude with JAL."

"What if we just take the due diligence that they've done," Schlater offered, "we don't do any of our own, and we will not renegotiate anything? We'll just sign on to the memorandum of understanding that you have with JAL."

Lupo thought about Schlater's proposal for a moment. It was extraordinary—a multibillion-dollar corporation, a flag carrier, offering to sign on the dotted line without peeking behind the curtain or kicking the tires. "That's pretty interesting," he admitted. "We'll go back to JAL and talk about it."

But by the time Lupo arrived in San Francisco to present the deal to Hillblom and DHL's other shareholders, Hillblom had had second thoughts. The deal had gone from a minority stake in DHL to over 50 percent—a quarter each for JAL and Lufthansa, plus another 12.5 percent for Nissho Iwai. Even with the exact ownership of DHL still at issue, Hillblom would obviously no longer be in the position he had enjoyed for three decades, the position that he'd told Carla he wanted—of pulling the strings. Instead, he would be a minority shareholder in a multinational corporation owned by three other, very conservative, multinational corporations. The deal might save DHL but it would also push him out of the picture entirely.

"Larry was not too enthusiastic," Lupo recalls of the shareholder meeting. "But he got the other guys to agree. I think he very much believed in the strategy of the deal. He could see his future evolving in Asia and JAL was a very important force in Japan and in Guam and Saipan and so on. But if the financial mechanics weren't right for him personally, he wasn't going to go along with it."

Eventually, the shareholder issues were resolved by Peter Donnici, who split the company up according to what percentage of DHL's success each of its thirteen shareholders could claim as their own. Hillblom ended up with a clear majority of the domestic company and about half of what would now be known as DHL, International. At signing, Hillblom would receive $120 million for his shares in DHL, International and his stake would be reduced to just above 20 percent. But there was still a possibility of Hillblom's becoming a billionaire. "We're going to TSE this," he said to Lupo one day, referring to an IPO on the Tokyo Stock Exchange, where the price-earnings multiples were such that he could probably consider himself a billionaire already.

The closing was held one year later in the conference room of a New York City law office. "Larry was sitting there," Lupo recalls, "and all the massive documents [occupy] a whole table, and everyone's going around signing their documents. And one lawyer says, 'This transfer was made to this account, blah blah blah.' And then a settlement agent from one of the banks comes in and he says, 'Everything's fine except that we don't have JAL's transfer of so many millions of dollars.' This is after twelve months of due diligence. And Hillblom says to the head guy of JAL, 'You know, before we'd started this process, if you guys had just told us you didn't have the money, it would have saved us all a lot of headache.' And everybody cracked up."

The Japanese christened their takeover of DHL the Polar Bear Deal and passed out white teddy bears after the last rider was initialed. No one remembers the significance of polar bears, except that they are both larger and more ferocious than tigers, perhaps.

Lupo kept two photographs from the occasion. One shows five middle-aged men memorializing the creation of what would soon be the dominant global express company. Four, including Patrick Lupo, are wearing dark suits and ties. The fifth is dressed in a dark sports coat; his shirt is open—no tie—colored glasses. He has not shaved for days and appears to be signing a document, though his hands are blocked by a sloth of teddy bears spread about the conference table. Directly behind him, Peter Donnici looks on, hands folded behind his back, lips locked in a scowl.

Hillblom left Manhattan the next morning with his teddy bear and little else. The year before, a tax specialist in Donnici's firm had arranged the sale of Hillblom's majority stake, held in a Bermuda-based holding corporation, to Po Chung for $226 million. No cash had been exchanged and there was no record of the transaction, other than an unsigned memo in the attorney's files. So the largest share of the DHL payout never even touched American soil, much less stuck to Larry Hillblom—or any corporation with which he was legally affiliated. Yet he was suddenly, officially, a very, very rich man.

When a limousine deposited him at the Continental terminal at Newark Liberty Airport, Hillblom approached the first-class ticket counter. He handed his PS-1 card to the ticket agent, who stared a little curiously at his T-shirt, which was silk-screened to resemble a blazer, oxford, and tie. During the Air Mike negotiations, when Continental's attorneys had finally agreed to give Hillblom his coveted PS-1 pass, they had attached a stipulation that they'd hoped would kill the deal: if Hillblom wanted to travel first-class, he'd have to wear a tie. The ticket agent accepted Hillblom's card, buried her eyes in her computer, and found him a front-row seat to San Francisco, which also happens to be my next destination.

Twenty-Five

Money Problems

"**L**arry was a real character," Jesse Choper, the renowned constitutional law expert, dean of Boalt Hall, and Hillblom's former corporations professor reminisces from behind his desk overlooking campus. Choper is a thin, elegant man who dresses well and wears his silver hair slicked back like Gordon Gekko. For an academic and for an attorney, Choper's attitude is disarmingly candid—as is his smile, which he flashes often when discussing his most infamous student. Several floors below us, in the building's foyer, a huge bronze sign lists Larry Lee Hillblom among the building's major donors, alongside giant law firms like Morrison Foerster. "He was fairly soft-spoken and not terribly articulate," Choper recalls. "I was not initially impressed but eventually he distinguished himself as an original thinker . . . he was pragmatic rather than intellectual."

Throughout the 1970s and 1980s, Hillblom was a regular guest in Choper's Berkeley office. He would show up, usually unannounced, sink into one of the chairs opposite Choper's desk, and pontificate on his two favorite subjects: DHL and Micronesian politics. Choper had followed Hillblom's success from day one. He and his wife, like a few other Boalt Hall professors, had served as DHL couriers several times, and at Choper's request, Hillblom had donated $25,000 to fund a chair in Stefan Riesenfeld's name. Still, the professor-turned-dean remains shocked by how successful his farm boy student became. "It's difficult for me to imagine how he dealt at the higher levels," Choper says. He follows up with a story of when his secretary had once asked if she should call the police when Hillblom showed up asking for the dean; apparently, she assumed he was a deranged student.

That Hillblom could operate at the *highest* levels had, however, turned out to be quite an understatement by the early 1990s. The awkward, soft-spoken boy from the San Joaquin Valley had cultivated a multinational corporation that, according to the *New York Times,* employed 24,000 people and produced revenue approaching $2 billion in 1990. Even more impressive, the philosophy that had caused so much consternation in Choper's lecture room when Hillblom had tried to express it now had a respectable name: "law and economics." And politicians like Margaret Thatcher and George Bush were now preaching that the government should foster economic growth rather than temper it, just as Larry had argued. In law journals, "law and economics" had become the buzz phrase du jour.

So when Choper started a $10 million fund-raising campaign for a new Boalt Hall law school building, he placed Hillblom at the top of his list of possible donors. Japan Airlines and Lufthansa, he'd just read, had acquired a minority stake in DHL. Their investment had not been disclosed but was likely to be in the hundreds of millions, considering the size of Hillblom's company. And Larry was always inviting Choper to come to Saipan. In fact, the dean seemed to remember that Hillblom owned the airline out there. Choper asked his secretary to leave a message at Hillblom's office in Saipan.

Larry, he says, called back almost immediately. "I'm gonna take you up on your offer," Choper informed him, "but I have to warn you that it's a fund-raising visit." Choper's only request was that his new girlfriend be allowed to join him.

Not long after, the dean received two first-class tickets on Continental Micronesia—via DHL, of course. He removed a pledge card from his desk, filled in Hillblom's name and $250,000, then folded it neatly next to the plane tickets. Despite Hillblom's *bonhomie,* something told Choper that getting him to sign on the dotted line was not going to be easy.

The trek to Hillblom's home would only confirm this suspicion. Even in first class, the journey from the States to Saipan is an arduous one: three flights (connecting through Honolulu and Guam) spanning more than twenty hours, fourteen time zones, and two customs clearances. The finish line is the small arrivals hall of Saipan's Polynesian-style airport, where

Hillblom greeted the dean and his date in the summer of 1990, carried their bags to his car, and deposited them at the Hyatt Regency on Micro Beach amid gentle gusts of hot, humid tropical air.

"The next day," Choper recalls, "he drove us around the island in his broken-down Honda with Josephine, whom he'd nicknamed 'Tita.' I think it means 'monkey' in Tagalog. Every time he said it she tried to slap him." Across the island, Hillblom pointed out businesses that he'd either started or bought: a technology company called Saipan Computer Services, a realty firm with an unpronounceable, a pawnshop, condominiums, golf courses, a beachside restaurant, a Honda dealership, a small printing operation that silk-screened T-shirts, the rodeo-brothel complex on the northern tip of the island where he'd erected a giant movie screen and showed first-run films amid a cattle-grazing field and, finally, the island's modest DHL office.

But Hillblom was especially proud of a nondescript building on the southwestern side of the island—a rounded cement bunker supported by several of Micronesia's ubiquitous latte stones. The building housed the CNMI's new Supreme Court, where Hillblom often began his day. The governor had recently appointed Hillblom as a special judge to the court, which had replaced the U.S. district court as the destination for appeals of superior court rulings. Supreme Court rulings could still be appealed to the Ninth Circuit in San Francisco but, under the CNMI Constitution, the Supreme Court would become the island's sole appellate court in fifteen years. At that time, Supreme Court rulings would be appealable only to the U.S. Supreme Court. Hillblom had fought for the establishment of the CNMI Supreme Court for one very simple reason: The U.S. Supreme Court hears a fraction of the cases submitted to it. With the establishment of its own appellate court, the CNMI would at least have judicial sovereignty.

"Larry was very proud of being named an associate justice of the Supreme Court—much more so than of the money he'd made," Choper recalls, slightly misstating Hillblom's position if not its importance. Hillblom was a *special* judge, not an associate judge, meaning that if any of the court's three permanent judges were unable to hear a case, he might be called in. On an island like Saipan, where people frequently travel and where a large part of the population is intimately connected—genetically or otherwise—the odds of a justice's being absent or of having to recuse himself is very high.

Over the next several years, Hillblom sat in on a great many cases and wrote just as many opinions. He took the role very seriously, arriving at the court's modest temporary quarters on Beach Road early in the morning, well before the other justices, and poring over the day's cases next to a steaming pot of Vietnamese coffee. Sometimes he brought fresh wheat bread that he'd baked in a machine in his office. When the justices needed a table for conferencing, Hillblom ordered one custom-built. His opinions were exhaustively researched, though they often meandered to his favorite issue, the Territorial Clause. "I thought they were sound," Choper says of the opinions that Hillblom proudly sent him, like a son seeking approval.

"Larry was a great host," Choper continues. "He took us out for dinner every night and threw a big party for us at that house overlooking the ocean." Hillblom showed off the DeLorean, and walked his old law school professor down the cliff in front of his house, pointing out a surfside cave where he'd lived for a few years—or so he said, at least. But when Choper breached the topic of his pledge, Hillblom became argumentative.

"How much do you need for the job?" Hillblom asked, annoyed. "What are you planning to do?"

"I've told you what we're going to do," Choper replied, more annoyed. "And it's in the literature."

"Are you going to have computers?" Hillblom said.

Choper bristled. He remembered how hard it had been to collect the $25,000 that Hillblom had pledged for Riesenfeld's chair; now he was asking for ten times that amount. What had he been thinking? After a tense back-and-forth, Hillblom put forward a jaw-dropping idea.

"He wanted to manage the construction himself, because, by building it at night, he thought he could nix the union." Choper shakes his head. "Larry insisted that it could be built on the cheap and talked about how he'd built this road in Half Moon Bay at night so there had been no regulation and that's how they should do Boalt Hall and that bit of genius would be his contribution." What Larry didn't tell him was how a local news helicopter had spotted the two huge Caterpillar earthmovers roaming his property and alerted both the public and the local authorities to what he was doing; the reporter he assumed it was a new public road, a bypass to Highway 1, which also happened to be under construction at the time. That fiasco had cost Hillblom a small fortune in legal fees. Even without that knowledge, however, Hillblom's idea inspired more anger than admiration. "I told him that this was a public university," Choper growls, "not a private road on his ranch!"

Hillblom and Ted Mitchell, before the "Clash of the Titans"
(Courtesy of Michael W. Dotts)

Choper waited until the last day to pull out the pledge card. "By then, I knew I'd worn him down," Choper brags. He asked Hillblom to sign it in his presence—something that he had not demanded of any other donor. Such pledges are notoriously difficult to collect, Choper says, even with a signature. But he wanted to impress upon Larry that he owed the money, that it was not something that he could argue his way out of. That night, Choper, his girlfriend, and Hillblom celebrated the visit over dinner at a restaurant near the hotel. Afterward, Larry walked them to Little Ginza, which had been Saipan's bustling downtown during the Japanese occupation. Now it was a mishmash of restaurants, massage parlors, shops, and strip clubs anchored by a cobblestone promenade. Choper and his girlfriend followed Hillblom toward the neon sign of a nightclub. In front of the entrance were several young Asian women in matching leather miniskirts. Hillblom motioned for his reluctant guests to come inside, where he chose a comfortable spot and ordered a round of drinks.

"A few of the girls came over to the table," Choper recalls. "They knew Larry and he them. Clearly, 'Tita' was not the only woman in his life. After the girls walked away, Larry turned to me and my girlfriend. He said he only had sex with virgins, that he'd spent ten million dollars on girls because he was deathly afraid of AIDS and didn't want to have sex with anyone who wasn't a virgin."

An awkward silence followed as the dean and his girlfriend digested what Hillblom had just revealed. Finally, Choper spoke up: "Only virgins, Larry?"

"Yeah," Hillblom replied nonchalantly, as one of the girls delivered their drinks. "You have to be careful."

Choper took a sip of his beer. Maybe, the older man thought, he had not asked for enough.

Jesse Choper was not the only solicitor to descend on Saipan in the wake of the Polar Bear Deal. On May 29, 1991, a Caucasian man in a dark suit presented himself to the receptionist at the CNMI Department of Finance Building near the crest of Saipan's Capital Hill. When prompted, the man announced that he was an auditor from the U.S. Inspector General's office in Washington, D.C.

The Department of Finance holds the tax records of all CNMI residents. Under a unique provision of the Covenant, virtually anyone who makes the request is allowed access to the tax records of all CNMI citizens. But when the Inspector General's auditor demanded to see the records of several residents, including Governor Larry Guerrero and his close friend, Larry Lee Hillblom, the clerk called the governor's office for authorization. A few moments later, she hung up the telephone and apologized. The records, she explained, were not available.

Like Choper, the auditor had traveled thousands of miles on three flights, and he was not about to leave without getting what he'd been sent for. So, once again, the clerk called the governor's office, which in turn called Special Supreme Court Justice Larry Hillblom. "A federal government office doesn't have the authority to demand anything," Hillblom told the governor matter-of-factly. "Allowing the Inspector General access to local tax returns violates not only the CNMI's right to self-government but the privacy rights of its citizens."

Guerrero had good reason to ignore his friend's advice. The feds had provoked an almost identical showdown at the Department of Finance two years before and the governor had quickly given in to the audit.

But Guerrero followed Hillblom's advice anyway and advised the clerk not to allow the Inspector General's auditor access. So the man returned to his hotel, notified his superiors, and found himself leaving Saipan almost as soon as he'd arrived, empty-handed. Hillblom quickly filed a lawsuit on behalf of two locals that demanded an injunction denying the Inspector General access to their tax returns. When the CNMI Superior Court sent the lawsuit to federal court—the proper jurisdiction of any action in which a federal agency is an indispensable party—the litigants appealed to the CNMI Supreme Court. Coincidentally, one of the Court's permanent justices happened to be off-island. His substitute was Larry Hillblom.

Common sense made the conflict of interest obvious: a judge hearing a lawsuit that he himself had filed? But Hillblom did not recuse himself. And on Boxing Day, 1991, the CNMI Supreme Court rendered its decision: the Inspector General was not authorized to audit the tax returns of Commonwealth citizens. As usual, Hillblom crafted an opinion restating his interpretation of the Covenant as well as his opinion that the Territorial Clause did not apply to the CNMI.

United States v. Guerrero was filed in Saipan's federal court two months later. Unfortunately for Hillblom, the Commonwealth's liberal federal judge, Carter appointee Alfred Laureta—the judge who had handed down the default judgments on Continental's executives and allies and ordered the State Department to issue dozens of passports to clients of Hillblom & O'Connor—had recently been replaced by a Reagan appointee named Alex Munson. Munson, a large man with a thick gray mustache who patrolled the island in a giant Lincoln Town Car, did not think much of Hillblom or his legal theories. If Saipan was the Wild West, then Munson was the perfect sheriff sent to tame it—a tough California judge, appointed by a president whose Secret Service code name was Rawhide, in order to restore law and order. He was revered by most of the expats and feared by everyone else. Not surprisingly, Munson quickly and unequivocally sided with the feds. "If it's good enough for Ronald Reagan then it's good enough for me!" the big man declared, as though such logic was self-evident. Munson threatened the governor with huge fines and jail time for every day he refused the Inspector General access to the CNMI's tax records. With no appetite for either, and no way to hide out—as Hillblom had from Judge Roberts's contempt order seven years earlier, and from the CAB's auditors before that—Guerrero folded. But I am told that by the time the auditor returned to Saipan, Hillblom's tax returns had vanished.

That did not prevent Saipan's chief instigator from fighting on. In both of his two major legal victories—*Loomis* and *Continental*—he had started in a defensive position, lost the first round and, several years later, won on appeal. *United States v. Guerrero* was on the same trajectory. More important, it was a near-perfect test of the CNMI's sovereignty—and the legal theories that Hillblom had espoused for ten years. Energized, Hillblom burrowed in his tiny den, among his law books and photocopies of the opinions he had written as a Supreme Court justice; he was cobbling together several core legal theories as a basis to fight for the CNMI's internal sovereignty. He would present an exhaustive appeal of *Guerrero* to the Ninth Circuit in San Francisco, which he himself would argue. Hillblom was determined to remove the Territorial Clause from around the necks of his fellow Micronesians once and for all, to slay the threat of American imperialism. It would, of course, take months to write, to be heard, and, finally, to be adjudicated—maybe longer. In the meantime, he seemed oblivious to the cracks quietly spreading beneath his own feet.

Twenty-Six

Clash of the Titans

A five-minute walk from the Nauru Building, across Beach Road from a narrow park where two young Chamorros are selling fresh yellowtail from a cooler perched on the tailgate of their Nissan pickup truck, lies the newish CNMI courts complex—a two-story white monolith that would look comfortable in just about any small county seat in the States. Under the courthouse's porte cochere, several locals loiter with their cigarettes. One exhales and nods briefly as I approach. A stocky Yapese U.S. Marshal grins a mouthful of submerged red teeth and waves me through the metal detector, which appears to be either broken or unplugged. To the left, behind two glass doors, sits the Larry Lee Hillblom Law Library, announced in metallic Times Roman, but it is the clerk's office that houses Hillblom's legacy, and that is on the opposite side of the tiled two-story lobby.

The irony of Larry Hillblom is that he was an intensely private man whose life is chronicled in millions of pages of very public court filings around the world. Most of those pages reside here, filed under *In the Matter of the Estate of Larry Lee Hillblom,* aka Civil Case #95-626, which seems like as good a place as any to begin an investigation of the second half of Hillblom's life. I have spoken to a few of the workers here by phone already, but none is apparently expecting me or recognizes my name. The very polite young islander in pressed slacks and a perfectly ironed blue polo shirt—Dexter is the unlikely name—seems a bit incredulous that I have flown here from Los Angeles. Certainly I must have more exciting things to do on the mainland, his eyes say. The look is familiar by now; every young islander wishes they were in Los Angeles. Or New York. Or

Cleveland. When I ask "Dex" to have a look at the Hillblom case his eyes widen a little more. "That's a very big case," he says. "It has its own wall in the archives room."

"Well," I reply, "can I just start at the beginning? I'd really like to see the original probate filing and the will at least."

"Hold on," he says, before disappearing into a side office for several minutes. He marches out a little sheepishly.

"My boss wants to know who you are," Dex says.

"I'm a writer," is my reply. "I'm writing a book about Larry Hillblom."

"I see," he says. And then he disappears for another five minutes. "I'm very sorry," Dex tells me as soon as he returns to the counter, "but we're understaffed at the moment. Do you mind coming back later?"

"How much later?"

"We close at four thirty. I'll try to pull the first folder for you before then."

"Done." I smile. "But I'd still love a copy of the original filing—and the will, if you don't mind."

"Copies are twenty-five cents apiece. You pay next door."

"I know." The time difference has made me a little testy. "I read it on the website."

As I stroll back past the Hillblom Law Library and the broken metal detector, it occurs to me that I have absolutely no idea how to fill the rest of the day—no inkling of which friends of Larry's still live here (if any) or what history I could possibly uncover from the documents that will apparently be doled out in small quantities at the whim of an invisible woman in the clerk's office. I spend the next eight hours moving into the Hyatt, walking a long bike path that hugs the western coast, eating Korean barbecue in an empty restaurant, and (finally) exploring the huge DFS mall—several acres of Prada and Hermès and Louis Vuitton, plus a Hard Rock Cafe and a tourist shop that sells "Chamorro Chip" cookies and plush teddy bears with carrot noses called "Saipan-das"—as a polished player piano bangs out Schubert. I visit a tiny museum—the former prison during the Japanese occupation—where photos of skinny Chamorro children wrapped in traditional sumo *mawashi* sit before their glum Japanese teachers/occupiers. Curled up behind the wheel of my impossibly small Toyota, I scour the island for visible evidence of Hillblom's legacy, only to arrive at a disconcerting conclusion: *Maybe I'm too late; maybe he has disappeared.* But later that afternoon, Dex will prove as good as his word; he will hand me copies of the first two dozen pages of CNMI Civil Case #95-626, the closest thing to a biography of the man as has yet been written. A cursory glance of the case's early filings will yield something that I had not known existed: a local nemesis.

Like most enemies, Theodore "Ted" Mitchell began as a friend. "When he arrived on the island," the attorney Mike Dotts tells me over lunch at a beachside café not far from the courthouse, "Mitchell was probably the most prominent attorney on Saipan, and he was Larry's favorite." Dotts is a junior partner in Bob O'Connor's law firm. During the several years before Hillblom's presumed death, he was Larry's personal attorney and a board member of the Bank of Saipan and UMDA, where Mitchell had been general counsel during the Continental Airlines war. "None of us liked him," Dotts continues, "but Larry always stood by him. He'd say, 'If you were accused of murder, who would you want representing you? Some pinstriped lawyer or Ted?'"

Dotts rolls his eyes as he takes a bite of his mahimahi burger. He's a slight man who, like O'Connor, moved here from California seeking a more adventurous life. He had originally interviewed for a position at the CNMI Legislature until being told of an eccentric multimillionaire who needed help suing the federal government. Dotts was game, though initially he was more of a personal assistant—picking up the morning pastries and coffee, overseeing Hillblom's failed rodeo-brothel-turned-drive-in-movie-theater, paying Josephine her monthly stipend, and fending off bill collectors, of whom there were many, since Hillblom cleared both his mail and messages by dumping them into the trash bin, unread. Another attorney who worked for Larry tells me that Hillblom referred to Dotts as "the gerbil," but he was eventually entrusted with Hillblom's personal checkbooks as well as some of his thorniest problems, the thorniest of which was Ted Mitchell.

In July 1991 a victorious Mitchell walked out of the CNMI Supreme Court grasping a momentous ruling. Citing a paragraph of the Commonwealth's Constitution that prohibits nonnatives from owning land, the court on which Larry Hillblom sometimes sat had just invalidated any real estate sales to companies that had been formed by nonnative investors, even if they technically met the 51 percent native ownership requirement. The ruling was a watershed for Mitchell, who had sued Japan Airlines, the owner of Saipan's largest and newest resort, the Nikko, on behalf of the islanders who had originally owned the property underneath the hotel. The islanders technically had sold the property to an entity called Realty Trust Corporation, but Mitchell alleged that RTC was a fraud—a "resultant trust"—that was secretly controlled by nonnatives, i.e., people with less than 25 percent native blood. Under Article XII, the paragraph of the CNMI Constitution that prevented nonnatives from owning real estate, Mitchell argued, resultant trusts like RTC were unconstitutional.

For months, Mitchell had fought virtually alone against a huge Japanese corporation and its large law firm—Carlsmith Ball—and now he had won. And, as everyone knew, the outlawing of "resultant trusts" would transform the island. Virtually all of Saipan's prime beachfront real estate was controlled by foreign or American investors, including Mitchell's old boss, Hillblom. By turning Article XII into an absolute, the Supreme Court had just opened the way for any islanders who had sold or leased their property before Saipan's real estate boom to get their land back— perhaps even with a shiny new hotel and lagoon pool on top. Mitchell gleefully predicted a massive calamity: "The Japanese firms will lose huge chunks of money," he told a reporter from *Guam Business Magazine*. "They will sue Carlsmith and all the lawyers that told them these transactions were legal. It will throw all the lawyers in bankruptcy. It'll be great!"

The one landowner Mitchell refused to take on was Larry Hillblom, even though Hillblom owned several prime properties through his San Roque Beach Development Corporation, including the land underneath his home and a large tract next to the Nikko Hotel. (Most of SRBD's shares were owned by a Chamorro friend, and Hillblom's onetime secretary, Debra Diaz, but neither had invested any money, and Diaz did not even know that she was a shareholder until it was brought to her attention in a deposition.) Dotts tells me that Mitchell was scared of Hillblom's relentless and very personal litigation style. And while it is certainly true that Mitchell knew Hillblom as someone who relished a fight, there was more to Mitchell's avoidance of Hillblom than fear. Both men possessed brilliant legal minds, and they had both supported the establishment of the CNMI Supreme Court and fought the federalization of the islands. The difference, of course, was that Hillblom had made a fortune doing it while Mitchell had not. The disparity was not lost on Mitchell, who had accused Hillblom of being driven by nothing but his own financial and political self-interest. Mitchell, in fact, not so secretly suspected that Hillblom owned a majority of UMDA, which would have been illegal under both its charter, and now, under the "resultant trust" ruling, because of UMDA's large landholdings throughout Micronesia.

Yet they had coexisted, with offices on opposite sides of the same floor in the Nauru Building (now Marianas Business Plaza), for years. After Mitchell had left UMDA, Hillblom had continued to barge into his office for an impromptu legal debate or two. "He always bursts in without warning," Mitchell would complain, "barges into my office and proceeds, depending upon his mood and his subject of the moment, to harangue or pontificate immediately. Sometimes, there is a gem of truth or useful information in the torrent of otherwise confused and confusing rhetoric. Often, he merely repeats his speech of the day or the week before. . . . He talks fast, he moves fast, he jumps from one subject to another in the space of a few minutes." Mitchell ridiculed Hillblom's brains as "scrambled."

But now it was Mitchell's success that inspired his adversary's wrath. Standing in the doorway of Mitchell's modest office, Hillblom shredded the legal reasoning behind the Supreme Court victory, particularly the "resultant trust" idea. "It takes two to tango," Hillblom admonished his former employee, promising that if the opinion was upheld and landowners were forced to give up their holdings, then Mitchell's clients would never see any benefit because they were equally guilty. Echoing a chorus of his friends in the Legislature, he accused Mitchell of trying to enrich himself while destroying the island's economy.

"If I'm greedy," Mitchell shot back, "I'm insane, because the odds are about ten trillion to one that I'm ever going to make a dime off any of this."

Not everyone agreed. As the months wore on, executives at Japan Airlines became concerned enough of Mitchell's possible success that they ordered their engineers to draw up demolition plans for the 400-room Nikko Hotel, which their attorneys at Carlsmith Ball forwarded to every member of the CNMI Legislature. The normally poker-faced Hillblom became increasingly nervous; he knew that Mitchell was smarter than all of the attorneys at Carlsmith combined and that if they lost the Nikko, the other hotel-resorts along Saipan's west coast would crumble like dominoes. Then his own house. Then UMDA. But there was nothing that he could do. Without Mitchell's suing him personally, Hillblom had no way to advance his own legal arguments about Article XII in court. He was reduced to sitting back and watching Carlsmith milk JAL and fuck up everything.

"Larry was dying to get a dog in the fight," Dotts recalls. And he did, eventually, using a familiar tactic: he filed bankruptcy on San Roque. Of course, neither he nor his real estate company was really broke, but it had worked for People of Micronesia, hadn't it? Hillblom once again argued that the mere threat of litigation—and the Carlsmith firm's assumedly incompetent response to it—would inevitably bankrupt his real estate development company. Whether the new federal judge on Saipan would agree was questionable, so Hillblom went a step further. He threatened Carlsmith with a massive malpractice suit. If Saipan's largest law firm did not do his bidding, Hillblom would ruin them himself.

Dotts smiles. "That ruse worked."

Twenty-Seven

SMART

The year 1992–93 was one that most [Saipan] residents would
probably like to forget. There were setbacks for the government,
a serious blow to private enterprise, and social problems such
as illegal drugs began to have a very serious impact on society.
Little that could be considered positive occurred.

—The Contemporary Pacific

"You're looking at the luckiest guy in the world!" Hillblom shouted
from the center of his resort-style swimming pool, where he was
relaxing at his swim-up bar under the shade of a terra-cotta gazebo. He had
just turned fifty years old—a milestone, he told his friend Bob O'Connor,
that guaranteed he would live much longer. After twenty-four years of
struggle and constant worrying, 1993 was to be a new beginning. Hillblom had accomplished nearly everything in life that he had set out to. He
had both shrunk the world and expanded his empire. The hard work now
was protecting it. The previous summer, Hillblom had entered a congressional hearing room for the first time in fifteen years to deliver a confident defense of his island, which the World Health Organization and two
U.S. senators had called out as a hotbed of corruption, human trafficking,
and prostitution. (Hillblom argued convincingly that the CNMI's human
rights record was far superior to that of its former occupier.) Meanwhile,
DHL soaring on the wings of its new owners; Lufthansa and JAL's jumbo
jets were literally propelling Hillblom's brainchild to record sales and profits. Budweiser in hand, and with Josephine at his side in a microscopic
bikini, the second chapter of his life spread out before him as infinite as
the view from the edge of his swimming pool.

Larry Hillblom *should* have been the luckiest guy in the world that day, but the photocopies that Dex has just handed me suggest that his luck had begun to run out by then, that even the barstool upon which he sat was under siege.

Hillblom was served in his office on April 7. Mitchell's complaint, which I have the guilty pleasure of reading fifteen years later, might have been written by Hillblom himself for its hyperbole and the almost frantic tone of its accusations. First, Mitchell calls out Hillblom's real estate development company as a "mere sham" and demands that he return his mansion to its rightful owner, who happens to be Mitchell's client. Hillblom, the complaint asserts, had always known that buying real estate on Saipan violated the CNMI Constitution, but rather than bow to local law, Hillblom had chosen to embark on a conspiratorial end run around it, going so far as to fund the lawsuits of several taxpayers demanding that any land recovered should not go to Mitchell's clients but to the CNMI government. Once Hillblom's scheme is exposed, Mitchell promises to have him impeached of his special judge status. But that's just the beginning. The main assault is not on Hillblom's constitutional theories or legislative escapades; it is on the Hillblom mythos. DHL's success, Mitchell argues, is almost all due to Peter Donnici, not Larry Hillblom. In fact, he says, DHL has succeeded despite Hillblom's "erratic, unpredictable and unprofitable" behavior. Its founder is, in fact, one of the worst businessmen that Mitchell has met in his entire life!

Hillblom's response was immediate, if predictable. He stormed across the Nauru Building's third-floor mezzanine to Mitchell's office, where he once again excoriated Mitchell's arguments and his tactics. The Battle of the Titans had begun.

Within weeks, an alliance of influential individuals and business leaders materialized from thin air. They called themselves SMART, an acronym for Saipanese Mobilized on Article Twelve. (Article Twelve is the paragraph in the CNMI Constitution that forbids nonnative ownership of land.) Mitchell seethed at the ploy, but Hillblom's name was nowhere to be found—although one of SMART's leaders was none other than Mike Dotts, now Larry Hillblom's personal attorney, and the movement was suspiciously similar to Hillblom's earlier campaigns against both the CAB and the postal monopolies. And the arguments proffered by SMART, broadcast in a series of television ads, were identical to those that Mitchell had heard Hillblom pontificate countless times from his office doorway. By late summer, those arguments had been neatly wrapped into a bill that, among other things, eliminated contingency fees for lawyers in Article XII cases and invalidated Mitchell's "resultant trust" theory by name. Mike Dotts and Joe Lifoifoi were soon lobbying the Legislature to pass the bill quickly. So was Carlsmith Ball's managing partner, a mild-mannered Pacific Northwesterner named David Nevitt.

Mitchell, his beard turned thick and white, his once-taut frame now spilling over his waist, drove up to Capital Hill and delivered his response to the Speaker of the House in person. He accused Hillblom of writing the legislation, ridiculed Hillblom's minions as the "not so-SMART lobbyists," and accused Mike Dotts of having a "hidden relationship" with his boss. But he read desperate. Everyone knew that Hillblom had penned legislation in the past; and no one, particularly an attorney as savvy as Mitchell, could profess shock that any wealthy businessman would cue up his personal attorney to do his bidding. Mitchell could have hoped that the many politicians who had sold land before Saipan's property boom would vote their self-interest, but Hillblom had largely convinced them that clawing back their property would have the opposite effect: it would render their property worthless, because no one would dare touch it from that point forward. Those lucky enough to prove native status would be left to trade land among themselves.

One senses, in the documents that Mitchell has left behind (he died several years ago of cancer), an almost insatiable anger, an obsession with Larry Hillblom that bordered on the pathological; by the summer of 1993, the pages of his briefs had become little more than rants against "King Larry." Mitchell subpoenaed the corporate minutes of DHL meetings; he unearthed several letters Hillblom had sent the president of Palau offering UMDA stock in exchange for air routes to Japan—proof of corruption, Mitchell noted; he reminded the court that Hillblom had yet to return his 25,000 UMDA shares to local governments as promised but had illegally kept them for himself; in a burst of ego, he proclaimed that Hillblom "has known from the beginning that I would not be his sycophant and that he could not win my uncritical allegiance with financial favors."

The obsessed Mitchell got only one shot at his nemesis—a deposition in Mike Dotts's office at the Nauru Building. No transcript remains, and Dotts admits that he ended the deposition prematurely, no doubt fearing an inquisition of DHL, Vietnam, and Hillblom's personal tax situation. In any case, on July 14, 1993, Hillblom countersued in federal court, alleging that Mitchell was engaged in a comprehensive scheme to financially injure and damage him through unlawful acts, including violations of the Racketeer Influenced and Corrupt Organizations Act—the same statute he used to bring down Frank Lorenzo almost a decade earlier. Mitchell seemed to draw energy from being attacked. King Larry had not ignored him. "Hillblom is scared!" he told a reporter, promising that his nemesis would soon be exposed for masterminding both SMART and the lawsuits demanding that lands be returned to the government rather than the islanders. "We are on the verge of finding out who is really behind these actions and he is cutting and running," Mitchell continued. "He got scared because we are narrowing it down to him. Who else could it be?"

Mitchell did have one ace in the hole. Several years earlier, when he was the general counsel of UMDA, Peter Donnici had told him that the disclosure of Hillblom's tax returns would have dire consequences both for him personally and for DHL. If Mitchell remembered correctly, the exact word that Donnici used was *disastrous*.

Twenty-Eight

Taxes

On Friday, August 6, 1993, Hillblom drove his trusty Honda Civic up the winding road to Capital Hill. Midway to the top, he turned left, into the Saipan offices of Deloitte and Touche Tohmatsu. His accountant had scheduled a meeting with two auditors from the CNMI Department of Finance—Revenue & Taxation regarding an audit they had just completed of Hillblom's personal income taxes dating back to 1988.

No taxpayer looks forward to a meeting with the tax man, but Larry Hillblom had placed himself in a uniquely, almost unbelievably, precarious position. First, he had not reported any income from the sale of his DHL shares to JAL and Lufthansa; second, that money, funneled through Po Chung in Hong Kong, was already being spent; finally, his unreported income had flowed into a country where it was illegal for him to do business.

As Hillblom shifted in his chair, exhibiting his many tics, one of the auditors produced a statement showing the department's calculations of his income versus what he had claimed on his returns. In each of the four years they'd analyzed, Hillblom had reported income of roughly $200,000, but the department's figures were considerably higher.

In 1988, for example, Hillblom had failed to report over $100,000 in interest from ARW, a partnership he'd founded along with a few other DHLers to invest in real estate and cellular licenses.* The situation in 1990

---

* Hillblom had been interested in communications since the days that he'd envisioned a satellite fax network sending DHL's clients' documents instantly around the world, and DHL had even entered

was similar. In 1991, the discrepancy was far greater. That year, Hillblom had deposited nearly $800,000 into his checking account at the Bank of Saipan that had not been reported on his returns. But 1989 was the killer. In addition to the $201,000 Hillblom had reported on his return, the auditors had discovered another $20,000 in deposits to his local bank account—plus a capital gain of *more than $226 million.* The total difference, including interest—but not penalties—amounted to just under $29 million.

Hillblom challenged the auditors' chart. The $226 million, he explained, was for the sale of his interest in a company that he co-owned with DHL's Asia head and his longtime nominee, Po Chung. He'd never received any cash for it, he said, and the gain was closer to $30 million.

The auditors asked for a cost basis that would justify the lower amount, but neither Hillblom nor his accountant could provide one. Monterrey, the company co-owned by Hillblom and Po Chung, contained only one asset: their shares in DHL, International, which he had started back in 1969 with $3,000 and Adrian Dalsey's credit cards.

So Hillblom argued that Monterrey should be treated as a "fresh start" transaction, meaning that the auditors should have calculated the capital gains based on the investment's value when Hillblom had moved to Saipan. But once again, the auditors demurred. The "fresh start" provision of the CNMI tax code applied only to investments sold before 1984, they reminded him. Because Hillblom had never sold shares in Monterrey, taxes would be calculated based on the full amount. Unless he could establish a cost basis, Hillblom was now staring at a tax bill of more than $97 million, including full penalties and interest.

If Hillblom was suddenly contemplating financial ruin, he refused to let it show. Nine days after leaving that meeting, he gingerly invited a lawyer

---

into a joint venture with the fax manufacturer Canon for a short time, but cellular telephony was an even more exciting prospect to Hillblom for a simple reason. "In the early days of U.S. cellular," Lupo explains, "you could file as part of a lottery, and as long as you had engineering drawings, you'd file and then you'd negotiate with the other people who had filed, and then you might come up with an application and then you might get the license. So Larry ended up with three or four interests in different cellular companies."

he'd recently hired named Bruce Jorgensen on a joyride. Jorgensen lived in Hillblom's pool house. He had been tasked with writing the SMART legislation and lobbying the CNMI Legislature for its passage. And just in case that did not happen—or in case the law was subsequently ruled unconstitutional—Jorgensen had also worked on the lawsuits that would return recovered property to the Public Land Trust rather than to the previous owners—a personal attack that had enraged Mitchell every bit as much as Hillblom's legislative activities.

Jorgensen's boss wanted to show off the new engine on a small plane he'd bought to indulge his on-again, off-again passion for flying. Jorgensen agreed to go, perhaps unaware that Hillblom's student pilot license had expired—and that the offer had been extended to him because most of Hillblom's friends knew better than to fly with him.

Twenty-Nine

Disaster

The Cessna 182, also known as the Skylane, is a two-door, three-wheel, four-seat airplane powered by a single propeller. Popular with flight instructors and weekenders, the 182 weighs less than a small BMW sedan, and its engine produces fewer horses than a modern sportscar. The ubiquitous 182 has been manufactured since the early 1950s and remains one of the most common aircraft in the world; its design, featuring a wing that rests above the cockpit attached by two aluminum alloy rods to the small body, is one of the most familiar in aviation. Hillblom's 182 was built in 1960 and had been repainted cherry red. The plane had been bought used by Hillblom and Jim Sirok, a local collections attorney and amateur pilot who had been coplaintiff in one of Larry's antigovernment lawsuits. It had been flown across the Pacific Ocean to Saipan from Spokane, Washington—a near-miracle made possible by a number of island stops and the addition of auxiliary fuel tanks in the cabin. Its maximum speed of roughly 140 knots and the fact that its cabin was not pressurized had no doubt made for a long, rough, and very cold two weeks.

When Jorgensen and Hillblom arrived at the Pacific Aviation hangar near the end of the Saipan International Airport's extraordinarily long runway, Adonis Gotas, a young Filipino whom Hillblom had hired as his mechanic, was checking on the more powerful engine that he had recently installed. Jorgensen noticed that Hillblom had no time for the standard checklist that pilots are taught to perform before flying, much less inspecting the new engine. Gotas was quickly directed to the rear seat of the airplane and Jorgensen climbed into the tiny front seat, cramping his lanky frame. Hillblom jumped in next to him, secured his door, and started up the engine. Then he pulled a headset over his ears as Jorgensen and Gotas did the same, but when the propeller began spinning, creating a loud drone, it became apparent that Gotas's microphone did not work.

Hillblom glanced at the instrument panel as he contacted the control tower for permission to take off. Warned that a Continental Micronesia 737 was incoming, he immediately opened the throttle and turned toward the end of the runway. Once aligned with the large white stripes and pointed toward a seemingly infinite strip of concrete, Hillblom let it go. Within seconds, they were airborne. Hillblom banked crosswind to avoid the incoming jet.

The sky was perfect, as usual, a gleaming turquoise. But, as Jorgensen would later recall, his boss was having difficulty trimming the throttle and reducing the engine's speed. So Hillblom banked again, bringing the tiny plane parallel with the runway, a trajectory that pointed them toward the narrow channel separating Saipan and Tinian. As Saipan disappeared from beneath them, however, the plane was suddenly cloaked in a foamy white cloud. Jorgensen was now very concerned. There was no way now that they would be able to see the incoming 737.

Hillblom glared at the instruments for a moment longer, then turned back to Gotas and shouted at him to examine the throttle cable housing. But Gotas quickly gave the thumbs-up. Jorgensen stole a glance at the plane's tachometer. The needle had not moved. Hillblom looked frustrated. The RPMs, he suddenly shouted, were still way too high. He asked Jorgensen if he should attempt a landing on Tinian.

But the young lawyer shook his head. They should return to Saipan, he said. And Hillblom should broadcast a radio distress message. Saipan had a longer runway than Tinian; and if they did crash, Saipan also had a real hospital.

Instead of making the U-turn, however, Hillblom continued toward Tinian. He made no attempt to broadcast a distress signal as he frantically decreased the engine's power by turning off the fuel mixture, obviously hoping to slow the plane down enough to land by starving the engine.

There was no more time to argue. Jorgensen turned back to Gotas and jerked on his seat belt, which had seemed too loose before. Unlike Larry, they were both preparing for the worst. By then they were midway over Tinian's runway, but Hillblom had not lowered the flaps and he had clearly lost control. Suddenly, he remembered the flaps, but as soon as they engaged the plane flared. Realizing his mistake, Hillblom immediately pulled up to abort the landing.

As Hillblom desperately tried to gain altitude, he seemed unaware that the flaps were still engaged. He jerked the steering yoke repeatedly in a panic, causing the plane to sway violently up and down in a porpoising motion. The stall siren began to shriek as the violent swings induced a series of aerodynamic stalls. Jorgensen looked down to see the end of the runway. Then silence. The engine had failed.

Hillblom yanked the steering yoke hard, inducing another stall as the siren wailed. Jorgensen yelled at him to drop the nose down and straighten out, but once again he was ignored. Jungle was approaching fast through the windshield. They were going down.

Jorgensen braced himself as the landing gear hit something—a treetop, he assumed—beneath his feet. The wingtip impacted next. And then he was upside-down. *Silence.* Behind him, Gotas was unconscious. Inches to his left, Hillblom was gushing crimson blood; the impact had forced the steering yoke directly into his face. Through the cracked windshield, thick black smoke poured over the wreckage and into the sky.

Jorgensen forced open his door with his right shoulder, exited the plane, and ripped his shirt off. His first instinct was to smother the engine and suffocate the smoke. That accomplished, he walked over to the other side of the plane and tried to open Larry's door, but the impact had jammed it shut. He returned to the open door on his side of the plane. In the backseat, Gotas's small frame was crumpled upside-down and his eyeballs appeared to be completely rolled back in his head. Larry was still bleeding profusely and his neck was hugging the dashboard at an unnatural angle.

Amid a rush of adrenaline, Jorgensen pulled Gotas out of the plane and laid his body on the inverted wing. He was too scared of breaking Hillblom's neck to touch him. Instead, he grabbed his shirt off the engine and started waving it frantically at a small plane that was just taking off. Unsure whether or not he'd been seen, he rushed toward the tiny airport, finding a fire truck close to the perimeter. Thankfully, it was occupied. Jorgensen ran up to the driver's side and told a stunned islander that Hillblom and Gotas were badly injured and to radio medical personnel and a medevac. They'd need to fly them to the hospital on Saipan immediately.

Satisfied that help was on the way, Jorgensen now ran back to the wreckage, the plane gleaming amid the dense jungle like a ruby. Crouching down next to the open passenger door, he could see that Hillblom had regained consciousness. Larry begged him to pull him out, but Jorgensen refused. So Hillblom slid a bloody hand down to his lap belt, unclipped the buckle, and immediately collapsed headfirst into the cabin ceiling, moaning in excruciating pain.

Jorgensen managed to wrench his seat aside and pull Hillblom from the open doorway. Then he laid him on the wing next to Gotas. The right side of Larry's face was gone. Blood was streaming out of a huge gash beneath his eye, where the steering yoke had lanced the face. Jorgensen grabbed his shirt, bundled it up, and pressed it into Hillblom's wound, trying to stem the flow of blood. But Larry refused to sit still. He was clearly in shock. He was rambling something about not having a pilot's license or insurance. Suddenly he shot off a bunch of nonsensical questions, rapid-fire: "What happened to my face? Where are we? What happened?" And, pointing to Gotas, "Who is that?"

Jorgensen maneuvered behind Hillblom's body, sat down behind him, and wrapped his arms around his torso in an attempt to immobilize his boss. But Larry kept trying to get up to see what he'd done. Finally, an emergency vehicle arrived and a couple of locals relieved Jorgensen of his duty. They slid Larry onto a backboard and secured him with rope so he couldn't move. Jorgensen turned around to see Gotas stirring; he was alive. They traveled to Tinian's small hospital in the ambulance together. Once there, Jorgensen grabbed a hospital telephone and dialed the only man presently capable of saving Hillblom's life: Joe Lifoifoi.

Recovery

"**H**as anyone mentioned suicide?" the tall, sixty-ish man in the white lab coat inquires offhandedly.

"No," I stammer. "Why? Do you think—"

"Oh no." The doctor grins. "I was just wondering." He is Douglas Ousterhout, MD, the preeminent craniofacial surgeon in the United States, author of *Aesthetic Contouring of the Craniofacial Skeleton,* protégé of the great French surgeon Paul Tessier. He has just shown me a PowerPoint presentation of grotesquely deformed skulls, mostly belonging to children. "There are many more out there. Cleft palates, cloverleaf skulls, and so forth. We just don't *see* them because they do not show themselves. Jackie Kennedy is a good example of a public figure with a craniofacial abnormality. She's bug-eyed. If you look, the eyes are too far apart."

Larry Hillblom's route to Ousterhout's office at the Davies Medical Center* here in San Francisco was a circuitous one. From Tinian, he had been airlifted back across the channel to Saipan's Commonwealth Health Center—by far the largest and best-equipped hospital in Micronesia— where he was rushed into the emergency room on a backboard, his neck cradled in a white brace and the shattered right side of his face buried, mummy-like, beneath bandages. Joe Lifoifoi, Mike Dotts, and Joseph Waechter were waiting for him there.

Jorgensen had contacted Lifoifoi, who had arranged for the medevac,

---

* CPMC Davies Campus.

but it was Waechter who had taken over from there. On the far side of his thirties, with prematurely white hair and the overfed and underslept body of a road warrior, Waechter had lived in Micronesia for four years. Hillblom had recruited him to run his disparate businesses in Asia, including UMDA a few years earlier. Waechter diverted an Air Mike DC-10 bound for Manila to Saipan. It had then been emptied of its passengers and flown to Honolulu carrying Hillblom and a small medical team.

The young doctor who examined Hillblom on Saipan had not seen the purpose of flying a fatally wounded man 4,000 miles in a jumbo jet, but Waechter had insisted that the hospital free up a couple of nurses and an MD for the trip. Michael Dotts, terrified that he would be in the airplane when his boss expired, had refused to make the trip. So Waechter and Lifoifoi had gone instead.

Onboard, time had passed slowly with nothing to do but watch Hillblom fight for his life. They had managed to keep him alive until they'd arrived in Honolulu, where a plastic surgeon named Jim Penoff had rewrapped his wounds and made an incision in his chest where he inserted a drainage tube to release pressure, then stabilized Hillblom for the flight on to San Francisco, where Penoff had referred Waechter to the best craniofacial surgeon he knew: Douglas K. Ousterhout.

"I was quite surprised that Hillblom survived the plane rides," Ousterhout says and smiles, "because I'd heard he had a pneumothorax [collapsed lung]—what's called a tension pneumothorax, to be exact, where the pneumothorax is so bad on one side it moves all the contents over to the left side and you have no lung space and you die of suffocation.

"Most of Hillblom's fractures were on the right side of his face," Ousterhout continues, reaching behind his chair for a human skull that he likes to use as a prop. "He didn't have any neurological damage, but there was a great deal of shattering of the nose and face. The first surgery was performed right away, as soon as swelling ceased, which would have been six or seven days after the crash."

The first operation had lasted well over ten hours, as Ousterhout reattached and grafted dozens of bone fragments to Hillblom's skull. One of the nurses remarked that she had never seen so many screws in one human being, but Hillblom's face had eventually resurfaced. Three days later, the bandages came off, revealing a good start but also that Hillblom's right eye

had died. "A great disappointment to me," Ousterhout sighs, "but even more so to him, I'm sure."

Initially, Hillblom recovered in a private room at the hospital. He received several visitors, among them his half brother, Grant, who had long since quit DHL and was now tending the peach farm on Zedicker, as well as his brother, Terry, now a lawyer. They'd brought him a huge basket filled with fruit from the San Joaquin Valley. Even Helen had stopped by for a visit. Mother and son had not seen each other for fifteen years or so, and the reunion was smoothed over by the fact that Hillblom could not speak. (An emotional Helen told her golden boy that she loved him and then left.) Finally, after a friend of Hillblom's helped her secure a visa, Josephine showed up, and moved him to the Embassy Suites Hotel near the San Francisco Airport, where they checked in under an assumed name. Eventually, they were driven to the ranch in Half Moon Bay, which would be home for several months as Larry endured several follow-up surgeries under Ousterhout's knife. Josephine and Larry were taken care of by a hearty Englishman named John Spice, who had worked for DHL in London, UMDA in Palau, and now oversaw Hillblom's pet projects at the ranch.

"When the operations were done," Ousterhout remembers, "Larry told me that he didn't want to return to Saipan or to Vietnam until he looked better. So he came back here for a face-lift in 1994." A few days after that procedure, Spice drove Hillblom back to Davies for his last follow-up. He was feeling elated, as only a man who has dodged a bullet can, and he was delighted with his new face, which made him look years younger even as the tightening of the skin made his face oddly translucent. After checking his patient's chart and completing a pleased appraisal of his work, Ousterhout decided to drop the bomb. "I just sensed that it was the time to ask him for a donation!" the surgeon trills. "He was very, very interested in the surgery and the work I do. So I asked him for three million dollars for the Larry Hillblom Chair at Davies and he said yes immediately. I think it took five minutes! He said that he wanted to take care of kids."

So, that Thanksgiving, Ousterhout and his wife traveled to Guam and Saipan as Hillblom's guests. He had told the surgeon that he wanted him to perform cleft-lip operations on Saipan. Hillblom envisioned the trip as a reconnaissance mission; other doctors would join them for a junket to

Vietnam. While Jesse Choper and his girlfriend had been relegated to a hotel, however, Hillblom loaned Ousterhout and his wife his bedroom at the house in Dandan. "I had to peek in the closet because of the way he dressed." The surgeon laughs. "All he ever wore were jeans and T-shirts. And sure enough, all I saw in his closets were jeans and T-shirts!"

After a few days, they boarded an Air Mike 737 to Guam, spent a couple of days trolling the medical centers there, and picked up the other doctors. The expanded group then flew another Air Mike jet across the Philippine Sea to Manila, where they would have to visit the Vietnamese embassy for visas. Although the decades-old embargo with Vietnam had been lifted in February of that year, there was still no embassy anywhere in the United States. That night, Larry decided to give Ousterhout and his wife a taste of his life outside of Saipan. He met them at their hotel in a red Mitsubishi van driven by a taxi driver named Guido who often served as his personal driver, took them to dinner and then to a street lined with nightclubs flanked by young girls in bikinis and tall boots. Inside were more girls. Hillblom, it soon became obvious, was a regular. In fact, Hillblom bragged that the owner of the club had been the one who secured Josephine's visa, because he had so many clients at the U.S. Embassy. As he had with Choper and his wife, Larry sat Ousterhout and his girlfriend at a small table and ordered a round of drinks. Directly in front of them was a small stage where dozens of very young girls in bikinis shimmied their adolescent chests to pop music.

Ousterhout clutched his wife's hand. He was horrified. Each girl had a piece of paper attached to her bikini top: a number. Every few minutes, a girl would be summoned from the stage and a new girl would step forward to take her place.

Nursing a Bud Light a few inches to his right, Hillblom was staring intently ahead. Finally, he nudged Ousterhout with his left elbow. "Don't you want a girl?" He grinned. "What about her? Number Twenty-three . . . ? Don't you think she's pretty?"

Ousterhout clutched his wife's hand a little harder. "Oh, Larry!" was all the normally verbose surgeon could muster.

Later, Hillblom would tell Ousterhout what he had told Choper—that he slept only with virgins because he was terrified of HIV. And he would show Ousterhout the diplomatic passport proclaiming him the Marshallese ambassador to Vietnam. "Three percent flat income tax," Hillblom explained. "I'm gonna make you a citizen." For once, Ousterhout was impressed. Maybe he could become the Marshallese ambassador to somewhere, he told himself, before laughing off the thought.

As soon as the visas were processed, they returned to the Manila airport, where a jet flew them the 1,100 miles across the South China Sea to Hanoi, Vietnam's capital city. The trip was a typical Hillblom whirlwind. First they toured the stoic communist buildings of Hanoi, then flew south, to Ho Chi Minh City, and finally, to Dalat, where they golfed on a course that Hillblom said he owned. It was not yet complete, and Ousterhout was shocked to see women in traditional hats planting grass seeds one by one. But he was more disturbed by another vision. "In Dalat," he recalls, "there's a flatcar and engine—a relic from the old days—that Hillblom bought. He put a picnic table on the flatcar and drove it five miles through the fields, and I hate to tell this story, but one of the farmers kind of gave us the finger as we passed."

They also visited hospitals, but none of the doctors, including Ousterhout, did any actual medical work. The surgeon would depart Vietnam after only a few days, secure in two beliefs: that Hillblom cared about helping children and that whoever was building his golf course was screwing him—but he kept that last observation to himself. After all, Larry Hillblom was both a shrewd businessman and his benefactor. So, despite their common interests in medicine and the easy rapport the two had developed, he knew that Hillblom was not quite his friend.

"Do you think he's still alive?" Ousterhout asks me suddenly.

"I assume he's not—" I reply.

"You know, I flew with him once," the surgeon says out of the blue. "My sons and I met him at an airport north of Nevado. He took us on a short flight and we landed at a lake near Napa in his seaplane. I wasn't nervous at all!"

Ousterhout relishes the shock value for a moment. Then he releases the skull still clutched in his thin, expert fingers and spins his chair around to conjure up a PowerPoint presentation on the computer behind him. This, he says, is his current work: male-to-female face reconstruction. The results are remarkable, I gush. Ousterhout's patients are unrecognizable as their former selves or even as men. They have disappeared. "Larry would have been fascinated by what I'm doing," he says proudly, and I am not prone to disagree. How better to vanish than to completely change your appearance? What better alias than an entirely new face?

Hillblom, Ousterhout continues, was actually one of the last purely reconstructive surgeries he performed; those stopped when he received $270 from an insurance company for a fifteen-hour operation. Changing someone's identity, on the other hand, is mostly cash and very remunerative. Plus, the clientele tends to be far more exotic. A major Hollywood director is among his current patients.

On my way out, the doctor remembers one more thing that might be of interest to me. Standing up, he begins perusing his modest bookshelf, stacked with medical tomes—including his own—a black-and-white photograph of his mentor, Tessier, and more than a few random mementos. Amid these is a small plastic container, not much larger than a prescription bottle, filled with a sliver of what appears to be human tissue. It is, he reveals, what remains of Larry Hillblom—a thin slice taken during Hillblom's face-lift. "This has sat on my bookshelf since 1993." Ousterhout smiles. "I still can't understand why no one asked me for it. I guess I should really just throw it away."

Thirty-One

The Playground

Why would I spend $500 on dinner? I'd rather spend it on pussy.

—Hillblom to a friend in 1993

"**L**ast year, in August, of 1993," the attorney Bob O'Connor wrote in response to a letter from the Internal Revenue Service, "Mr. Hillblom was in a very serious airplane crash when a private plane he was in took off from Saipan, developed engine problems, and was forced into a crash landing on the nearby island of Tinian in the Commonwealth of the Northern Mariana Islands ('CNMI'). Mr. Hillblom was near death suffering from massive injuries to his face and head and cervical spine fracture. He has undergone numerous operations (one which lasted 14½ hours). He is currently still recuperating from his most recent surgery and the overall trauma of the accident. Mr. Hillblom has no plans to be in the United States in the foreseeable future."

If not an outright lie, the letter was certainly a stretch. Hillblom *had* spent months recovering from the plane crash. But by the time O'Connor typed his letter to the IRS, Hillblom was hardly immobile. He'd spent weeks crisscrossing Asia in a Learjet, fretting over the golf course in Vietnam that was spiraling overbudget, and exploring a raft of new opportunities, including purchasing Philippine Airlines and starting a new airline in the north of Vietnam, where the trade embargo had finally lifted in February. While "recuperating," Hillblom had also met with the billionaire financier David Bonderman at a Moroccan restaurant in Washington, D.C., and agreed to invest millions of dollars in Air Partners, a buyout fund that had just purchased Continental Airlines out of bankruptcy. And he had been spotted at the United Nations building in New York City once again, this time imploring the Security Council to explain, as he put it, "how the Administering Authority can take a position on democratic ideals concerning Nicaragua, Eastern Europe, the Soviet Union and China, while taking a totally contrary position when dealing with the Northern Marianas."

Hillblom's appearances on Saipan had become less frequent but more memorable. With his newly taut face looking at least a decade younger, he gave a glib interview to a reporter from his own TV station, in which he appeared to brush off the seriousness of the accident and incorrectly claimed that the FAA had said he'd done everything right; in fact, they had forbidden him from flying and revoked his already expired license. In another instance, police were called to his house at 3:00 a.m. when a crazed woman from Palau started banging on his windows, demanding child support for her son. On yet another occasion, police dragged a drunk, cursing Hillblom out of the CNMI Legislature during a late-night tax-writing session and arrested him when he claimed to have a bomb. More in character, he was spotted a few days later bounding down the stairs of the Nauru Building, waving a photocopy of his middle finger that he had just faxed the State Department, in response to an inquiry about his activities in Vietnam. Finally, Ted Mitchell had encountered him stocking up on sale-priced frozen broccoli at Costco; according to Mitchell's law partner, the two nemeses had somehow managed a civil conversation.

But from the date of O'Connor's letter forward, Larry Hillblom was noticeably absent from the island where he had once seemed intent on building his empire. Where he had disappeared to was known by fewer than a handful of men, only one of whom is willing to talk to me about those days.

"Larry never worried about anything," says my lunch guest, an expat businessman who was Hillblom's frequent companion during the last twelve months of his life. I will call him Jim because there are things that happened back then that he does not want his children to know. I can reveal our location, the crown of the Nauru Building, which has miraculously begun to rotate again, just one week before my departure from the island, and is now home to a tourist restaurant called 360. "Larry's feeling"— Jim grins—"was that there would always be another deal and there would always be another girl."

When he'd first started making the four-hour flight to Manila in the early eighties, Hillblom would stay at the Admiral Hotel, a stately if spartan white edifice on Roxas Boulevard across from Manila Bay. Like a lot of sex tourists, Hillblom loved the Admiral because whatever rate they charged you the first time was your rate for life. Several years later, he bought two small condos in the Chateau de Baie, a twenty-four-story condo building overlooking Manila Bay in Malate, not far from the strip clubs on Del Pilar Street. He also bought a studio in Makati, Manila's upscale financial district.

Hillblom's sex life had always been an open secret—with one exception. He would lie to Josephine, telling her that he was going to Guam, where she was not allowed to travel on her limited work visa, and instead used it as a stopover on his way to the Philippines. Hillblom traveled under an alias and, if he had one, he would force his companion to do so as well. One of his favorites was Fred Flintstone—his companion being Barney Rubble for the evening—though he sometimes picked the name of his favorite rock star at the time. Most of the locals would have no idea that he was making fun. (There are, in fact, a number of stories of such jokes being lost in translation—some with serious endings. Case in point: an Elvis impersonator who met his wife because she didn't know that Elvis was dead; apparently, she thought she had hooked Elvis.)

But Hillblom went a step further than most. He kept two passports, in addition to his diplomatic ID, as a ruse so that Josephine wouldn't see the Manila stamp when he returned. When she found a pair of panties in his luggage, Hillblom snatched them away and ordered Mike Dotts to find a Barbie doll wearing a dress in the same color, so that he could pretend that the panties she'd seen were something much more innocent— though Dotts is at a loss to explain how Hillblom rationalized carrying a Barbie dress in his bag. Regardless of what was said, Josephine became proactive and started writing her name on Hillblom's underwear in permanent marker.

These deceptions did not seem to bother my lunch companion. "When

Larry recovered from his surgeries," Jim remembers, "we met up at the Chateau, and after that we traveled to Manila frequently. He gave me a key, but you needed two, so it was kind of useless. One of the first things Larry told me was that he'd slept with 132 virgins, which was kind of a harbinger of things to come."

The billionaire who was more comfortable in a
rickshaw than a limousine
(Courtesy of Michael W. Dotts)

Their days in Manila revolved around Hillblom's twin pursuits: empire-building and pleasure. Though he purposefully avoided routines for security reasons, mornings usually started with a series of phone calls to the United States, followed by a quick visit to the driving range or a longer outing to Tagaytay—a village in the highlands thirty-five miles south of the city popular with local celebrities, where Hillblom liked to play golf. Jim, as with most of Hillblom's friends, had a skill that was extremely valuable—a willingness to drive in Manila. "I'd drive his Mitsubishi L300 van," Jim recalls, "which he was very proud of, by the way, to the golf course while Hillblom slept in the back. At night, we'd go out to the strip clubs. I guess you know how they work." In the morning, he tells me a little sheepishly, there were usually girls around.

Neither age nor the plane crash had tempered Hillblom's neuroses or his virility. He was still carting around huge bottles of vitamins and obsessing over certain kinds of foods, usually fruit. "At one point he was obsessed with papaya until he read in a magazine that it reduced your sex drive." Jim laughs. "I ran into him in the airport lounge after that and he came running up to me: 'Don't eat the papaya!'" But Hillblom also loved fried chicken. The KFC on Roxas was one of his favorite restaurants. He drank gallons of strong Vietnamese coffee. And Hillblom was borderline obsessed with tuna fish sandwiches made with canned tuna drowned in heavy mayonnaise.

"One morning," Jim remembers, "I woke up late. Hillblom was on the phone but when he saw that I was up he offered me a plate of greasy tuna fish sandwiches. Anyway, I took a sandwich and then he poured me some coffee, but he wouldn't get off of the phone. When he finally hung up, he turned to me and said, 'Bonderman and I just bought America West Airlines.'"

Jim was impressed. Like most of Hillblom's friends, he knew that Larry was rich, but not *that* rich. David Bonderman was one of the most successful investors in the world. His buyout of Continental Airlines had made it the top-performing stock on the New York Stock Exchange that year. If Larry was on a first-name basis with someone like that, investing together and giving advice, Jim thought, they must be on the same level: billionaire.

So when, a few days later, Hillblom turned to him, smiled, and said, "You wanna see something really different?" Jim's response was automatic.

"Hell, yes," he replied. How often, he told himself, do you get that kind of offer from a *billionaire*?

Jim followed Hillblom down the elevator to the lobby, then stepped out onto Roxas Boulevard and into an small, beat-up taxi that Hillblom had evidently rented for the occasion. Instead of heading to Makati or Del Pilar Street, as usual, the taxi ferried them to the outskirts of Manila, down a dirt road and up to a small building that had a single San Miguel beer sign outside. Jim's excitement evaporated. Maybe, he thought, this was another one of Hillblom's practical jokes, taking him to a dive bar that no haole in his right mind would enter.

Sure enough, the first thing Jim noticed when they walked inside was that he and Hillblom were the only Americans. Worse, perhaps, there were only two drink options: a Coke for sixty cents and a beer for eighty cents. Then the girls paraded out from a back door onto a pathetic stage. "I thought that they looked eleven years old, tops," Jim says. But the girls immediately ran over to Larry, eyes lit up, all smiles. "We missed you!" a few of them purred in pubescent voices. "We wrote you letters but didn't have your address!'"

A mama-san, maybe one of the girls' mothers, materialized, but Hillblom already knew the price: twenty bucks per girl. A bargain by Manila standards, which explained Hillblom's excitement. Jim watched as his friend chose four or five. His turn was up next and the mama-san focused a familiar dragon smile on his face. He chose the oldest-looking one—maybe fourteen or fifteen, he guessed. Then he followed Hillblom and his entourage into the back. Each chose a small private room furnished with a single couch, as they always were.

Jim finished with his girl first and returned to the bar for another drink. An hour or so later, Hillblom emerged from the backroom and Jim followed him outside to the waiting taxi. On the way home, neither man said a word.

Jim shakes his head. He knows how it sounds. "People in the States don't understand what goes on out here," he protests to an invisible judge. "There's a very different attitude about sex. What happens is that the parents borrow money and then the daughters have to pay off the debt by working. I know that Larry'd bought several girls out of slavery, but after the plane crash, these girls were repossessed immediately by their mothers and ended up back at work. Who knows what's happened to them all since?"

It is, of course, a rhetorical question. Jim knows that I have no intention of trolling Manila in search of a lone San Miguel sign long since faded by multiple typhoons—if it exists at this point. Any trace of Larry or his girls has long been washed away. There is, however, one place where Hillblom's trail remains fresh, a country where Hillblom had once hoped to build a third empire, a country steeped in guilt and mystery.

Thirty-Two

Vietnam

*T*raveling to Vietnam is not difficult but it is not effortless, either. First, you must send your passport to the Vietnamese Embassy in Washington in order to secure a visa, which is good for only thirty days, and trust that the U.S. Postal Service will deliver it back by the day of your flight. Vietnam Airlines flights may not be booked over the Internet but only through a handful of government-sanctioned travel agencies. Since these do not accept credit cards, you must deposit the cost of your ticket into the travel agency's bank account or send them certified funds and hope that they send you a paper plane ticket in return, which you are forbidden to lose. If you jump through these hoops, however, upon arrival at the Ho Chi Minh City Airport, a tiny old man in a blue uniform will wave you through customs with barely a nod, into an oppressive, smoggy heat. And you will be slightly amazed that your iPhone works perfectly—an unexpected windfall of information that, in my case, includes a flurry of texts that I am in the wrong place. My interview is one more flight away, in Dalat.

A few hours later, I am sharing a taxi with a U.S. Army veteran who is probably close to Hillblom's age, had he lived. The man tells me how he came to realize, ten years ago, that he preferred Vietnam to America. He's on his way home to his Vietnamese wife and children, having spent several days viewing what he says are amazing Buddha statues in neighboring Cambodia. When I drop Larry Hillblom's name, the man nods knowingly, then asks what happened to the girl in *the* photograph. Of course I know who he's talking about, and I tell him that I hope to find out. He jokes that he'll buy me a drink at Larry's Bar if I do. Then he recites his phone number, which I dutifully punch into my iPhone.

At first glance, Dalat is an endless honeycomb of tiny hotels constructed around a small lake where newlyweds take paddleboat rides as their elders, mostly women, stroll a walking path dotted with a few tourist restaurants. (It is the third place where Hillblom lived that is known as a "honeymoon capital." I've been counting.) A two-lane road cuts past the small lake and through the city; a half mile up a modest hill, the taxi turns off at a cobblestone driveway, passes a vintage Citroën limousine, and finally stops in front of the Palace Hotel, a colonial-era hunting lodge with a sprawling lawn that slopes back down to the lake. After checking in, I'm escorted to a large room decorated with antiques and Persian carpets. The bathroom boasts an enormous claw-foot tub. Before heading to the restaurant on the first floor, I spelunk the sprawling basement christened Larry's Bar, where clusters of expatriates are eating pizza and drinking beer beneath portraits of Hillblom and Nick Faldo, the famous golfer. When a young woman offers me a drink, I find it difficult to look away from Larry's face in order to politely decline. I have a meeting scheduled with her new boss in a moment, upstairs. . . .

"He told me that he came to Vietnam because of the girls, but I thought I saw Larry's anti-Americanism at work," attorney Barry Israel tells me a few minutes later, motioning toward a rather ornate seat in the Palace Hotel's empty formal dining room. "On a plane once, Larry showed me a picture of a gorgeous girl—his Vietnamese teacher—that he was madly in love with. He hadn't slept with her yet. I know he's fucked a few girls here at the hotel."

Israel is the kind of man you encounter in airport business-class lounges: wire-rimmed glasses, wrinkled oxford shirt and business-casual slacks, doughy hands. Only a few months ago, Israel negotiated the sale of all of Hillblom's Vietnam properties, including the Palace Hotel, to a Chinese investor group called Red Dragon. He has lived in Asia for a decade now—by choice or maybe by necessity, having developed an appetite for Asian women that he credits with ending his first marriage. But Israel seems almost fated to be connected to Hillblom forever. Despite the settlement of *People of Micronesia v. Continental Airlines* more than a quarter century ago, a $70 million default judgment from the federal district court on Saipan remains on Israel's credit report. That stubborn bit of Hillblom's legal handiwork was, Israel tells me with a laugh, discovered by his banker the last time he refinanced his mortgage.

"When I first started coming here," Israel tells me, "they knew where I was and when I was coming. The police once knocked on my door and demanded to know if I had a girl in my apartment. I did, and she was arrested. Dalat is very racist. It's the Deep South and we're the blacks. Larry had to be brought to Dalat in the trunk of a car the first time because it was still sealed. The government thought that he was CIA. But Larry eventually hooked himself to a pretty powerful guy here who died three years ago."

By all accounts, Hillblom was the first private American investor in Vietnam, though doing business in a communist country would have been adventurous enough without violating your country's Trading with the Enemy Act. Most banks would not finance projects in a place where private enterprise is considered public property, or where the law is, by definition, agnostic. ("How do you swear in a witness in a country that does not believe in the Bible?" an attorney will ask me later.) Vietnam was especially challenging. Shut off from trade with the world's economic engine, the government lacked capital. The deal offered foreign investors was therefore that the government provided the land and sometimes the buildings, but the investor had to put up all of the cash for only a percentage of the business. The terms of Hillblom's Dalat deal, for example, were 50/50; Hillblom put in $20 million in cash and the government contributed land and buildings valued at another $20 million. Each got a 50 percent stake in the properties, though Larry was solely liable for any cost overruns. The split for the Riverside Apartments he built on the Saigon River was much better, at 80/20. Phan Thiet, the last property he purchased—an unfinished hotel sitting on a huge plot of land roughly 120 miles north of Saigon that he hoped to turn into a golf resort—was divided 70/30. In his excitement to snap up three prime properties, Hillblom signed deals that he knew were less than optimal. According to Israel, he must have assumed that he could fix them later.

"He bought Dalat for corporate retreats," Israel says of Hillblom's master plan. "Riverside Apartments for housing staff, and Phan Thiet for tourists. He saw Vietnam as virgin territory and Ho Chi Minh as a central hub.

He was twenty years ahead of its time. He got properties no one will ever get again in Vietnam. The property in Phan Thiet is one half of the city. The Riverside complex is the most valuable property in Ho Chi Minh City and is next to the international school, which turned out to be very lucky because he built a lot of one-bedroom apartments. The properties here are the center of the city."

Over four years, Hillblom would spend $120 million of his own money in Vietnam and see only two of his projects—the hotel in Dalat and its golf course—through to completion. He would fly out the entire board of directors of Continental Airlines, including David Bonderman, to try to convince them to fly their jumbo jets into the country—something that has yet to happen. Finally, he would summon Patrick Lupo, hoping to convince DHL's chairman to build a massive Asian hub at the Ho Chi Minh City Airport.

"I'm sure at this time," Lupo explains, "DHL must have just been a complete nuisance to him, because there was some issue I had and he rang up one day and said, 'How are things going?' And I said, 'Terrible.' I ran through this litany of woes. 'You think you've got problems?' Larry goes, referring to the golf course in Vietnam. 'I've got fungus on my greens!'

"In other words," Lupo continues, "'I couldn't give a shit about DHL's problems.' DHL really became just a marquee, a cardholder for him."

But fungus was the least of Hillblom's problems in Vietnam. Ten thousand ponderosa pine trees that he imported from California for the golf course in Dalat simply refused to grow. Theft was rampant. Staircases had to be rebuilt multiple times because the local carpenters did not understand how to build them. Hillblom became so frustrated at times that he would order the construction workers out of their earthmovers and bulldozers and do the job himself. But the Vietnamese were becoming just as disgusted with him. At one point, a fistfight broke out at a meeting with angry provincial leaders as delays ate into their promised profits. It was as though Hillblom had finally found a place impervious to his charisma, his wealth, or his carefully choreographed dog and pony shows. Trotting out Ousterhout and the other doctors, then the Continental Airlines board, then DHL's chairman did little to sway the provincial governments in his favor if his lease payments were late. Nor did the economic arguments that had won over the legislatures of Hong Kong, the CNMI, and even the United States work here. Even Joe Waechter, brought in to oversee all of the Vietnam projects in February 1994—the month it became legal for him to enter the country—could not fix Hillblom's most expensive and most intractable mess.

Dinner with Israel is off the record. The conversation first orbits around Washington, D.C., because he is still a political junkie, a pedigree that dates back to his days working for Clark Clifford, then shifts to Israel's wife, Tam, whom he introduces as the most beautiful woman in Dalat. Tam is also very ambitious; they are developing property together, largely because as an American, Israel, like all foreigners, is forbidden from personally owning property here. The next morning, a chauffeured Ford Escape with tiny television sets mounted in the front headrests rolls up the driveway, and I join Israel in the backseat. The SUV maneuvers in and out of morning traffic, then climbs slightly until the clusters of tiny hotels are replaced by forest dotted with provincial villas. Then the forest breaks and lush valleys appear below us on either side. When I tell Israel that, of all the places Hillblom lived, this feels by far the most like Larry, and that Larry's Bar actually gave me chills the day before, Israel nods appreciatively.

"Dalat is the San Joaquin Valley of Vietnam," he explains. "There's a huge amount of produce grown here and flowers are the biggest export. The soil is incredibly fertile. The Vietnamese, ironically, are the most entrepreneurial people on earth. It's all small businesses."

A moment later, our driver turns down a long driveway with a massive iron gate, where a young Vietnamese woman in a flowing, brilliant white wedding gown is being photographed on the front lawn. Beyond that, maybe a hundred yards, sits a four-story colonial-style château that you might expect in the leafy suburbs outside of Paris. As a guard waves us through, Israel cautions against wandering the grounds; the forest surrounding the villa is peppered with land mines from the war, he says. My eyes are drawn to a couple of rusted artillery stations on the driveway's edge, still pointed outward.

"This was one of Bao Dai's summer palaces," Israel says as we circle the building's exterior. Bao, a puppet of the French government, has become

a symbol of the evils of colonialism and the people's determination to govern themselves. His old villa appears neglected, despite the millions of Hillblom's fortune that have been heaped upon it. The plaster is peeling in places and the green shutters seem ready to fall off at any moment. At one point, Hillblom envisioned this villa becoming a gleaming Las Vegas–style casino, but the government refused to invest any cash and by then he had run out. So instead, Hillblom made Villa Number One his frat house. "You know," Israel says suddenly, returning to the reason that Hillblom gave for coming here in the first place, and inadvertently referencing *the* photo, "Be Lory was conceived here."

I nod my head. I had no idea.

Thirty-Three

The Photo

Outside, only a few feet from the storefront, dozens of Japanese and German luxury sedans are emulsified amid one of the relentless rivers of Honda scooters that propel this city while the three of us—two Vietnamese whom I have met only this morning and myself—sit comfortably around a Formica desk inside a small travel office. All eyes are fixated on a small Sony Trinitron television as a VHS tape flickers to life, revealing the rolling lawn of the Palace Hotel Dalat, familiar from my visit there several months earlier. Except that this time, the lawn is full of people, mostly grim-faced communists in dress shirts and dark slacks but also children and a few familiar faces: Joe Lifoifoi, Joe Waechter, Po Chung, and Carl Gutierrez, then the governor of Guam and a close Hillblom friend.

He appears roughly a minute in, dressed in a dark blue suit with a pressed white shirt and no tie. (Suits always hung too loosely on Larry Hillblom, as though he had not grown into them yet.) He mingles with a few guests, then strides to a podium planted in the grass, in front of the grand veranda where I enjoyed breakfast the morning Israel showed me the villa. The cameraman pans jerkily across the lawn, where the guests are settling into wooden folding chairs. Hillblom is awkward but clearly happy, almost serene. His leg is not shaking; he no longer parts his hair with his pinkie or beats his forehead with a fist. He apologizes for his soft voice—on account of the plane accident, he explains, which occurred only six months before. He draws the microphone a bit closer as the camera zooms out to a two-shot, revealing a beautiful young Vietnamese woman dressed in the traditional two-piece satin dress known as *ao dai*. The woman is a translator. She dutifully repeats his apology, then turns to him and bows her head slightly.

188

Larry acknowledges her with a subtly lascivious grin, then unfolds his script, a single white sheet of paper. He thanks Po Chung, Lifoifoi, Waechter, and his government partners in Danao International Holdings, as well as his partners in Dalat Resort Incorporated, the local joint venture, to muted applause. Next, he claims that he has been an investor in Vietnam only since the embargo was lifted—just a few weeks earlier. It's an obvious and gratuitous lie that generates chuckles around me; it can only be meant for the State Department spies in the audience, if there are any, or in case the videotape ends up in their hands someday. With that caveat out of the way, Hillblom observes that this is an extraordinary day—the first fruits of the first partnership between an American and the communist Vietnamese since the war. A pause to acknowledge history in the making but more so, perhaps, to acknowledge how stupid those decades of embargo were to begin with. There is more polite applause as the translator converts his remarks to the native tongue.

Finished—and mercifully brief—Hillblom grins as the translator completes her work. He bows slightly to more applause and then steps into the audience, the camera following from a respectable distance. Amid his mercenaries, a cadre of pasty expats with thinning hair, Hillblom seems out of place. He is rail thin, gangly, neither young nor old, while they have grown up and out, and are attached to women and even children. Larry is still Larry-with-the-scraggly-beard—though there is something far more measured, far more mature, and far less awkward about him than in the past. When he mingles with a group of Vietnamese, he becomes suddenly tall and white, though there is an unmistakable Asian-ness to his features—especially the perpetually squinting eyes that have always appeared too narrow for a Caucasian.

Cut to the golf course across the lake, a little later. Surrounded by smiling young girls in *ao dai*, Hillblom slices a red ribbon with a pair of scissors, revealing a quaint clubhouse. The girls giggle and Hillblom hams it up a little for the cameras. He seems utterly relaxed now, as though this may be one of the happiest days of his life. The video then cuts to the first hole of the golf course, where he ditches his blazer and wanders in circles for several moments until someone hands him a driver and a ball. He sinks a tee into the earth, hits a drive out of frame, and beams. Enthusiastic applause as he walks out of frame. Then the television fizzles into snow.

"How much does Mr. Toan want for the videotape?" I ask the interpreter sitting next to me—a young man wearing the round, metallic-rimmed glasses that I sported in high school.

"One moment, please." He consults the man next to him—a middle-aged Vietnamese with an eager face—before returning a sales pitch: "Mr. Toan has hundreds of photographs of Mr. Larry, too, including the famous one of his lady friend holding Mr. Larry's baby. He gave that photo to Mr. Larry himself but he didn't want it."

"How much for everything, then?"

"Mr. Toan is aware that Disney recently paid a million dollars for some film footage that they used in a movie."

"You want a million dollars?" I say incredulously.

Mr. Toan frowns. "You can make an offer," the interpreter says.

"I need to talk to my publisher first," is my lame reply—lame because I know that my publisher, *any* publisher, would laugh at the notion of paying anything for a short videotape and a bunch of photos of a man that most Americans have never heard of. Why I cannot bring myself to tell Mr. Toan this right now, I have no idea. Maybe because I am a terrible negotiator, or maybe because I do not want him to know that his great bird was something far less in his own country: a prophet without honor, a disgraced man, brief fodder for tabloid news shows and glossy magazines.

Over the next several weeks, I will exchange a few e-mails with Mr. Toan via his interpreter; we will not agree on terms for the video or the photographs, my starting offer being in the very low four figures. The morning spent at his office will be tossed into the vast memory pile of hundreds of encounters that seemed promising at one time but ultimately proved useless, except as evidence that Larry Hillblom was eluding me as he had eluded everyone else in his life.

"Larry was wherever he was at the time," one of Hillblom's friends explains over the phone one day, as though my effort to create a unified portrait of the man was doomed from the start. There is no collage, only fragments, which all lead up to May 21, 1995—the day that Hillblom would hop into the front seat of his seaplane and escape forever. A friend, poring over my first attempt at a manuscript, suggests that I should title my book *The ADD Billionaire*. Fair enough, but the feeling that I have missed something nags constantly.

Not long after, hunched over my desk in Los Angeles, I open a letter postmarked Ho Chi Minh City. The sender is a Mr. Toan. His English is broken but the portrait he paints of Hillblom's last year is not. Toan reveals that Hillblom came to Vietnam in early 1990 and one year later founded Danao* International Holdings, Ltd., with Po Chung in order to circumvent the embargo. Toan explains how they hired a Chinese-Canadian businessman named Wong to oversee the development, and how Wong discovered the parcel of land beside the Saigon river, which had been former president Vo Van Kiet's "pleasure house" before the evacuation in 1975—the site where Riverside Apartments was ultimately built. Toan describes how the "pleasure house" soon became known as "Larry's house," as he lived and worked there, rising at five thirty in the morning to a breakfast of coffee, bread, egg whites, canned fish seasoned with red pepper sauce, and carrot juice. Toan relates Hillblom's optimism after the plane crash and how the surgery had not diminished his taste for girls, then describes how he kept the names and numbers of the girls that Larry liked—often waitresses he met while dining alone—in a black book, so that when Hillblom wanted one, he could simply point and Toan would arrange for that girl to come over for the night. When Hillblom traveled to Dalat, Toan explains, there were usually some "girls" following him—girls with whom he would have sex after work.

Finally, Toan reveals how Hillblom met Nguyen Thi Be, the woman in the famous photograph. In May 1995, he tells me, the month that the Palace Hotel opened, a Ms. Tuyet mistakenly drove six girls from Phan Thiet and Phan Rang to Dalat after receiving Toan's order of four girls for four guests. So after Hillblom and his guests had paired up, there were two girls left over. Ms. Be, Toan writes, was among the two leftovers, which created an awkward several minutes until Hillblom called out from his bedroom: "I'll take her!" Toan says that they had never met before and that by the time Hillblom's death was announced a few days later, Thi Be was long gone.

---

* There is debate over the origin of the name. I will assume that it is a nickname for "Mindanao," which was one of Hillblom's favorite beaches in the Philippines.

It is Thi Be's photo and her story that have captivated the Vietnamese press for years now, but the final paragraph of Toan's letter is what will resonate in my head for months to come as I wrestle with the implications of Hillblom's life and, even more so, his death:

> *Mr. Larry's life was very strange. His life was very active, but simple and kind-hearted. He loved to be with poor people. I admire Mr. Larry so much and I will remember him forever. The period of time I spent beside Mr. Larry has become a precious time in my life.*
>
>

Sincerely,

Mr. Toan

Part III

Probate

It is my intention to give the residue of my estate to a charitable trust which will entitle my estate to a charitable deduction under Internal Revenue Code Section 2055 and my Executor is directed to take whatever steps are necessary to ensure this result and to carry out the charitable intention set forth within.

It is my request that substantially all of the funds applied shall be for Medical Research and that the Board of Managers show particular attention to and benefit the research programs conducted by the University of California.
—*From the Last Will and Testament of Larry Lee Hillblom, d. 1982*

Thirty-Four

His Majesty

On a moist, sun-drenched morning in December 1871, the only survivor of the shipwrecked merchant ship *Belvidere* was discovered unconscious atop the reef of Nif Island by a Yapese medicine man.

He was David Dean O'Keefe, age forty, an American of Irish descent. O'Keefe's biographer would describe him as a man's man, the hero of a child's adventure book made real: "six feet four inches tall, with carrot-red hair that protruded in thick curls from beneath his gold-braided captain's cap and grew down his cheeks in heavy burnsides." He was a captain, though not of the doomed ship that had brought him to Micronesia. O'Keefe had boarded *Belvidere* to escape murder charges in his hometown of Savannah, Georgia. In his haste, O'Keefe had unwittingly traded a wife, a young daughter, a career, and a charming seaside home for exile on one of Micronesia's most primitive islands. He arrived badly injured and destitute.

The Yap Islands, which are 650 miles north-northeast of Saipan and comprise the third largest state within the Federated States of Micronesia, were then administered by a single, perpetually frustrated German, who ultimately allowed O'Keefe to stay. But as a white man and an American, O'Keefe was an interloper twice over in Micronesia. His presence inspired suspicion among the islanders and disdain from the European colonists who considered the islands theirs, even if they had no idea what to do with them. Yet O'Keefe soon married a beautiful islander, then started both a family and a successful business. And, within a decade, O'Keefe would accomplish a feat that no other colonist had: coronation. He would become His Majesty O'Keefe, king of Yap, with every island and every tribe in the archipelago swearing its loyalty to him in exchange for protection. O'Keefe negotiated the first pact of free association in Micronesia, an arrangement that left the islands to the natives while leaving the seas to the colonists. (So indifferent were the Micronesians to foreign affairs that one chief kept a stack of flags in his hut; whenever a warship sailed into the bay, he would raise the matching flag.) The islanders' respect for O'Keefe's negotiating skills was such that he became their de facto appellate judge, resolving their disputes based upon a quasi-American legal code of his own invention.

O'Keefe made a fortune trading the islands' bounteous sea slugs and copra—a fortune that was kept by his nominee and business partner, a Hong Kong dentist met by chance who had provided his first ship in exchange for a percentage of future profits. But it was the role of banker that solidified O'Keefe's power. With the help of modern tools unavailable to the islanders, he mined huge rounded stones called *pil* that served as their currency in greater quantities than the islanders thought possible and brought them home in the massive hull of his ship. (The stones had previously been transported, one at a time, in canoes that often sank.) Instead of giving them away, O'Keefe kept the *pil* at his mansion, allowing the removal of a stone only after his subjects had filled the belly of one of his ships—Micronesia's first pawnshop.

The German administrator tried to emulate O'Keefe's success, but he could never figure out how O'Keefe cajoled the islanders to work so hard for so little. The man soon lost patience and returned to Bavaria. Another, more ambitious, administrator sailed in, with the same result. The Europeans simply could not grasp that the *pil* was less important than O'Keefe himself, that his willingness to think and live like the islanders rather than patronize them—or subjugate them, for that matter—had ultimately given him carte blanche to manipulate them. Rather than concede defeat and lower his monarch's flag, however, the new administrator lobbied his superiors to make O'Keefe an outlaw. How else to explain his success?

O'Keefe disappeared ten years after he had arrived, presumably lost at sea after sailing into a storm in order to escape arrest by the German navy—though neither the wreckage of his ship nor his body was ever found. He was then the wealthiest man in Micronesia and, according to a bevy of women scattered around the Western Pacific who soon came forward claiming to have borne O'Keefe's heirs, one of the most prolific. Although he had left behind a will that left most of his fortune to his island wife, American lawyers representing his original family descended on Yap to claim his estate for themselves and begin the daunting task of cataloging his far-flung assets—a task made far more difficult when O'Keefe's enigmatic Hong Kong business partner declined to cooperate with the family or the probate court. With no independent means of establishing O'Keefe's interests, the court was forced to accept what the Hong Kong dentist told them and negotiate a compromise among O'Keefe's legal wife and the island women and children.

In bars from Majuro to Hong Kong, O'Keefe's friends recalled how the king had first cheated death when *Belvidere* crashed on Nif's reef. They spread the (true) rumor that the German navy had dispatched a ship to arrest O'Keefe for tax evasion shortly before his disappearance. After a few whiskeys, most would insist that the king had not perished in the open sea after all; he was enjoying retirement nestled beneath a coconut palm on one of Micronesia's two thousand islands, indulged by topless native girls and safely beyond reach of the German navy.

In the 1950s, the decade that Larry Hillblom became a teenager, Warner Bros adapted Lawrence Klingman's biography of O'Keefe into a film starring Burt Lancaster as the sailor-turned-monarch and Joan Rice as his islander wife, Dalabo. The quickly forgotten film was never shown in Kingsburg and no one can tell me whether or not Larry saw the film elsewhere. But, in the following decades, Hillblom's life would emulate that of David Dean O'Keefe to a remarkable degree. So would his death.

Thirty-Five

Panic

*T*he morning of Monday, May 22, 1995, Saipan awoke from an uneasy
sleep to confront the unthinkable: Larry was gone. Not off-island or
unreachable, but *gone*. The day before, at around 6:30, he had called Josephine from his seaplane and told her to drive to the airport to pick him up. He
was over Anatahan, a small island roughly eighty miles northeast of Saipan.
Josephine had driven the sporty Toyota MR2 that Larry had given her to the
Pacific Aviation hangar but he hadn't shown. Several hours later she called
Mike Dotts. He contacted the islands' Emergency Management Office, as
well as Joseph Waechter and Peter Donnici, both of whom were in San Francisco. But at that hour, the Western North Pacific Ocean would have been
as foreboding and as opaque as a black hole. If the ocean had swallowed up
Hillblom's little airplane, they would have to wait until morning to find out.

The CNMI's two search and rescue boats left at dawn, followed by a
succession of fishing and pleasure boats, including the governor's, until a
small armada was headed toward Anatahan. A helicopter was dispatched
to the search area, as was a coast guard cutter from Guam. The Emergency
Management Office rented a private plane, which traced Hillblom's flight
path to Pagan and back, and chartered six private boats that afternoon.
A command post was set up at the Smiley Cove Marina just north of the
Hyatt Regency Hotel. Technically, the operation was under the command
of EMO director Robert Guerrero, a stocky, no-nonsense Gulf War veteran, but the governor kept a close watch over him. And Hillblom's friends
set up their own command center at Peter Donnici's office in downtown
San Francisco; they requested assistance from the navy and the air force,
both of which had major bases on Guam.

At Coffee Care, the Little Ginza café where many of the island's attorneys and politicians began their day, news of Hillblom's disappearance dominated the early-morning rush. "It was a difficult time for pretty much the whole island," Mike Dotts remembers. "Everybody was trying to find where the plane was. It was panic." By 9:00 a.m., gas station attendants were briefing those who had somehow managed to avoid both their televisions and cell phones that morning. It was the beginning of the workweek, but for anyone who knew Larry—which was nearly everyone on the island—it felt like an ending.

Updates were painfully slow to arrive. Even with the help of drift patterns that pinpointed where the wreckage—if it existed—would have traveled given the ocean currents, Hillblom's search party would have to comb an area of hundreds of square miles for something not much bigger than a large dolphin. That no SOS had been broadcast meant that they could not be quite sure where the airplane had gone down. Given the area's huge swells, and its numerous sharks, the chances of Hillblom's surviving had evaporated overnight. So difficult was it thought to survive in the Western North Pacific that the EMO's operating procedures called for searches to be called off after just three days. But if anyone could have survived, Hillblom's friends told themselves, it would be Larry.

The next day, the crew of a fishing boat pulled two bodies from the ocean—one islander and one Caucasian. A local news camera videotaped the bodies as they arrived at the marina. After they were transported to the hospital morgue, rumors swirled that Hillblom's body had been positively identified. But when Josephine arrived the following morning, she told the doctors that she knew it wasn't Larry. The body was too large, for one thing. And there was a "Bob" tattoo on one of the shoulders. The man they'd recovered was Robert Long, Larry's pilot.

At four that afternoon, the helicopter spotted something bobbing in the swells not far from where Long had been found floating. A cameraman in the passenger seat recorded the object on a video camera. From above, it resembled a white piece of flotsam, but the shape was hard to discern. The only hint that this might be a human body was the mob of large fish that encircled it. The pilot radioed the command center, which declined to send a boat to the location. Darkness was falling too quickly, the pilot was told; apparently, out of the dozen or so boats trolling the area, none was close enough to reach the object by dusk.

In the coming months and years, whether or not the object was actually Hillblom would be the subject of much debate, because when the helicopter returned to the area the following morning, it was gone. "By that time," Dotts theorizes, "the body had sunk again, and that's why the body was not recovered." But then he pauses. "Another reason Larry's body was not found," he continues, "is that Larry was very thin and hence not a lot of fat on his body, so that's one more reason why his body sunk as opposed to the other bodies that came to the surface."

The search continued for eleven more days, yielding nothing. Larry Lee Hillblom was declared lost at sea. The videotape was tucked away, to be used as evidence in securing a proper death certificate. In the meantime, three separate memorials were held: one for family and friends at the Concordia Lutheran Church in Kingsburg; one for business associates at the ranch in Half Moon Bay; and one for the islanders at Joe Lifoifoi's church on Saipan, where the bishop presided. Hillblom was universally extolled as being unique, curious, and, above all, adventurous. At the family service in Kingsburg, a DHL courier spoke of Hillblom's humility, bringing more than a few members of the audience to tears. At the ceremony in Half Moon Bay, Patrick Lupo recalled talking to Hillblom the day before the accident. "He told me that he was preparing a joint venture for a new satellite with a group of cable companies and that they would have an audience of 1.5 billion," Lupo reminisced. "I rolled my eyes but in thinking about it, this was an example of Larry's vision. If he was ever stymied in his quest to achieve it, it was because of our inability to manage his incredible vision."

But there was business to attend to as well. After the Kingsburg service, Dotts met with one of Peter Donnici's law partners in San Francisco. Although Dotts had not been invited to the reading of the will—a snub that both he and his boss, Bob O'Connor, resent to this day—Dotts was ordered to make an inventory of his Hillblom files so that arrangements could be made to transfer everything to San Francisco. No record of Larry Hillblom's business or personal affairs was to remain on Saipan. "Very quickly after Larry died," Dotts says, "they [Donnici and Waechter] were sort of closing ranks and gathering information and cutting off other people to sources of information."

According to the thousands of photocopied pages of *In the Matter of the Estate of Larry Lee Hillblom* that have since made their way from the bowels of the Saipan Superior Court Building to a cluster of plastic containers in my spare bedroom, Joseph Waechter became vice president of the Bank of Saipan's trust department on June 24, 1995—the same date that the bank, which still operated a single branch in a small strip mall next to a Subway Sandwiches franchise, founded its trust department to service the trust called for in Hillblom's will. Three weeks later, Waechter strode into a tiny building not far from Oleai Beach, a cement structure supported by latte stones and cooled by the trade winds that drifted in and out of its open-air windows. He was accompanied by an attorney from the Carlsmith firm, a bearded lumberjack of a man named John Osborn. Awaiting Waechter was a young Filipino carrying a steno pad and pen, a well-liked reporter for the *Marianas Variety* newspaper named Ferdie de la Torre, but Osborn motioned his client past the gallery to a small wooden chair at one of the tables in the front of the courtroom. Already seated at the opposing counsel's desk were two African-American attorneys.

Waechter had been in San Francisco at the time of Hillblom's disappearance, looking for a loan to complete the Vietnam projects, which were spiraling overbudget. The prematurely white-haired Waechter was exactly six months from resigning from Danao, Hillblom's Vietnam holding company. He was looking forward to moving back to Saipan to be with his Filipina wife, Annie, and their young daughter, who had refused to live in the communist country. Waechter had worked there for a year and a half, in very trying conditions, and he had spent five years attempting to fix UMDA, now a typical Hillblom clusterfuck featuring everything from Air Mike to a giant ecoresort Hillblom had planned in a remote village on Palau to a laser-based television network on Guam. Waechter was ready to get out. But then Peter Donnici had sat the terminally loyal Waechter down at his office and pulled out the trump card: Waechter *owed* it to Larry to protect his last will and testament, he'd said. After all, with the exception of two unhappy years at a buttoned-down venture capital firm, Waechter had worked for Larry Hillblom his entire professional life. But that was a double-edged sword. Waechter's days as DHL president had ended badly when he was fired by Patrick Lupo.

Waechter had attended the Kingsburg service the next day, then he'd flown back to Saipan, where he'd delivered a self-deprecating eulogy at the last Hillblom memorial and driven up Capital Hill to meet with the estate's law firm.

That Peter Donnici had engaged the very firm that he and Larry had vanquished in the Continental case might have been irony enough, but the Carlsmith firm's managing partner at the time turned out to be someone with an even more personal connection to Hillblom: David Nevitt, the FSM's former attorney general and a named defendant in *People of Micronesia v. Continental Airlines*. Apparently, that kind of personal history did not matter on a place as small as Saipan, where Carlsmith was the only law firm of any real size and depth.

Waechter had shifted uneasily in his seat as Nevitt briefed him on what was to be his number one priority: taking control of the Bank of Saipan, which Hillblom had named as the executor in his will. "How can someone like me," Waechter had asked, "avoid conflicts of interest? I'm on the boards of several companies owned by Larry's estate, including the third most valuable: UMDA." Nevitt had brushed him off with the folksiness he'd honed as a country lawyer in rural Washington State. Carlsmith, he'd assured Waechter, would bring in the big guns from Los Angeles if necessary, and the whole enchilada would be wrapped up within six months.

Of course, Waechter hadn't believed him. No one who knew Larry would have. When Joe Lifoifoi found out that he had agreed to be the executor of Hillblom's estate, the islander had proffered a warning. "Watch out for the Palauan boy," Lifoifoi had growled between gentle sloshes of betel nut juice. "He's going to come after you."

And so he was. The two African-American lawyers sitting a few feet away from Waechter now were proof of that. Their client was a thirteen-year-old Palauan boy named Junior Larry Hillbroom, né Junior Larry Barusch. Junior's mother, Kaelani Kinney, had had a brief relationship with Hillblom in the early 1980s, but Hillblom had cut it off after she'd gotten pregnant.

Kinney had suddenly reappeared; she was suing for paternity on

behalf of her son. As her lawyers conferenced one last time before entering her claim, Judge Alex C. Castro entered the courtroom, his burly frame hidden beneath the traditional black robe. A former police officer and attorney general distinguished by a thin mustache, Castro often came across as foreboding but, among his acquaintances, he was known for a robust sense of humor. One such acquaintance had been his fellow judge Larry Hillblom.

Joe Hill, the shorter of Kinney's two lawyers, stood first and motioned for an injunction to delay probate until his client had a chance to prove paternity. Castro interrupted him almost immediately to correct Hill's spelling: "Hillblom, not Hillbroom," Castro admonished.

Hill replied that the spelling was correct. Junior's mother, he explained, was half Japanese. Because Japanese often pronounce the English "l" as an "r," that's how it had been officially recorded. (It was actually more convoluted than that. Kinney originally had put down the name Larry Barusch on the birth certificate, believing that Hillblom was Barusch, a Guam attorney who had never even been to Palau. "Larry could have been using the name," Dotts admits. "Later, she kind of figured out that it was Hillblom. So she changed it.")

Waechter sat respectfully as the lawyer continued. Hill was a well-known figure on-island. He had come to Saipan from Alaska seeking adventure and found it fighting on behalf of the island's thousands of guest workers, particularly the Chinese who toiled in third-world conditions at the island's two dozen garment factories. But Hill was more thoughtful than fearsome. Castro immediately denied his motion to delay probate until Junior Larry Hillbroom's paternity could be proven.

As Hill returned to his seat, Waechter rose for the executor oath, which was quickly administered by Castro's clerk: "I. Joe Waechter. Do solemnly swear. That I will faithfully. Impartially. And to the best of my ability. Discharge all of the duties. Of my trust. According to law. As executor. Of the last will. And testament. Of Larry Lee Hillblom."

Castro nodded. "Thank you. You can be seated."

Waechter stepped forward and sat down in the witness chair, gripping a copy of his first "Petition for Letters and Instructions"—essentially a to-do list forwarded for the court's approval that Carlsmith had prepared. His attorney eased into a light volley of questions establishing the long-standing friendship and business relationship that had existed between Waechter and Hillblom. Then it was time to get down to business. Larry had died with only about $200,000 in the bank versus millions in short-term debts. The estate was already experiencing its first cash crunch.

"Your Honor," Waechter explained, "we need to borrow twelve million dollars from DHL, International, and three million from DHL Corporation. And these obligations will be secured by the estate's stock holdings in those companies. The funds will be used to complete development in Vietnam as well as buy the estate's holding company in order to solidify the estate's position in the bank."

"Is there some urgency with regard to this particular request?" Castro asked.

"This is a loan that would have taken place if Mr. Hillblom had lived," Waechter said, not mentioning his unsuccessful attempts to get the loan elsewhere. "Mr. Hillblom has—the largest portion of the proceeds will go to continue developments in Vietnam investments there. Today, Mr. Hillblom has invested $63,413,000 in Vietnam. And in coming to close of development and construction there, and without this continued funding, the construction stops. Those projects never get into operation. There is never a return on the investment. So it's urgent that this loan take place and that those monies be sent to Vietnam immediately."

"All right," Castro said. "Subsection C, please?"

"Yeah," Waechter replied, thumbing through his copy of the petition until he reached it. "This is to loan," Waechter started before stumbling. "Again," he said, "part of that fifteen million dollars is to loan $3.7 million to the Commonwealth Holding Corporation for acquisition of the Bank of Saipan . . . to ensure control of the executor and provide for an orderly and efficient administration of the estate and its assets."

Once again, Castro nodded his approval. The judge had no objection—not even a single question, although Castro might have misunderstood what, exactly, Commonwealth Holding Corporation, aka CHC, was. Waechter had obfuscated by calling CHC the "estate's holding company," a statement that was factually incorrect. CHC was not owned by the estate. It had been crafted by David Nevitt and his associates as a nominee for Larry Hillblom's former business associates; the company's owners were none other than himself, Joe Lifoifoi, and Peter Donnici. In other words, Hillblom's best friends were borrowing from his estate in order to gain control of it, while what Waechter had just described to Castro sounded more like the estate fortifying itself.

Waechter sailed on. "The rest are pretty much cleaning house, including paying off one loan at thirteen percent and investing to finish an apartment complex on Saipan." Two recent typhoons had done $350,000 in damage to an apartment complex that Larry owned on Mount Tapochau. Those bills were now coming due, and the estate was already delinquent on lease payments for a parcel of land that Hillblom had purchased near the old navy base. Finally, Waechter had thrown in expenses for the mansion in Dandan, still occupied by Josephine and her brother Jaime.

"Is there anything unusual that's in the, any of those household expenses?" Castro inquired.

"No," Waechter replied. "Nothing unusual there. It's the telephone, utilities, cable television bill, employees, the maintenance guy's salary, pool maintenance."

Castro thumbed his copy of the petition. "Based on your prior relationship with Mr. Hillblom and your knowledge of his business affairs," the judge finally asked, "are these the types of actions that Mr. Hillblom would take himself were he to be alive?"

Waechter nodded, taking time to choose his words carefully. "I believe all of these actions would of—or are things that happen in the normal course of Mr. Hillblom's business affairs would have taken place had he been alive." That was an important point, he thought. Hillblom's will expressly authorized its executor to do what he would have done.

The judge made an appropriately grim face and paused. "Petitioner," Castro announced, "is hereby authorized to do all acts requested in this petition within the four corners of his fiduciary duty to this court."

Copies of his final order would be stuffed into the attorneys' pigeonholes at the clerk's office a few hours later. Castro's only concession to Joe Hill was that Waechter submit monthly reports detailing the estate's activity and that copies of those reports be sent to all interested parties.

Of course, "interested parties" was a relative term. Few people were *not* interested in Larry Hillblom's estate—or more to the point, in who would win it.

Thirty-Six

Secrets

*U*nder oath, Joe Waechter would later admit that he had been aware of "the Palauan boy" for some time. The eleven-year-old had been conceived on one of Hillblom's junkets as a legal adviser to the CNMI in the early 1980s. He and Donnici had traveled to a pan-Asian political conference held in the neighboring archipelago of Palau, known as one of the most beautiful places on earth and home to some of the best diving waters in the world. The purpose of the conference had been to promote tourism in Micronesia, although the downing of a Korean Airways jumbo jet by Soviet fighters that year had cast such a pall over the conference that its delegates would end up talking more about fighting communist aggression than luring honeymooners. During the day sessions, Larry had been atypically passive, sitting against the wall in an aloha shirt loaned to him by a Palauan senator to cover up his dirty tee—an abomination in the eyes of the Japanese and Taiwanese delegates—but on the second night, Hillblom had cut loose in the bars, which is where he'd met a kind of tough, foulmouthed sixteen-year-old named Kaelani Kinney. Later that evening, he had taken her back to his room at the Nikko Hotel.

Eight years later, Waechter had been in Koror, Palau's capital, working on a couple of UMDA projects when Joe Lifoifoi had found him in his hotel and told him a story: Earlier that day, as Lifoifoi and Larry and their entourage of local politicians were returning from the Rock Islands in Larry's boat, a deranged woman had appeared on the dock and attacked Larry from behind. She was demanding money and yelling that Hillblom was the father of her child. Lifoifoi had told Waechter that Larry's friends had had the woman, whom Waechter described as "crazed," arrested.

Lifoifoi had urged Waechter to prevent future embarrassments. UMDA was then building the island's cable television system and negotiating to lease several large plots of land in order to develop resorts and an eighteen-hole golf course. Lifoifoi, UMDA's de facto ambassador, had said the locals were bothered by Larry's behavior. So Waechter had brought the issue up with Larry the next day: "Why would this woman attack you?" he had asked him. "Is this your child or what? It must be . . ."

Larry had squinted over Waechter's shoulder: "Absolutely not. Not my kid. Can't be. Not mine. Absolutely not. She's out of her mind. Crazy."

Larry had left Palau the next day, before the "crazy woman" was released from jail, leaving Waechter to deal with it. He'd put it out of his mind until a short time later, after he'd returned to Saipan to hear that the crazy woman had appeared at Larry's mansion in Dandan at two o'clock that morning, climbed the fence, and started screaming, once again demanding money. She'd woken Larry and Josephine. Larry had called the police and had her arrested, but later that morning, at the house, Waechter could see that Josephine was still upset. So he'd prodded: "What's going on here, Larry? Is it dangerous? Is this woman going to have you knocked off? Is this your kid?"

"Absolutely not."

"Are you sure this is not your kid?" Waechter had persisted. "Because you ought to do something to take care of it if this woman keeps coming back."

"This is not my kid," Larry had replied, kind of agitated. "She just wants my money."

Waechter had broached the subject a third time, after a Palauan businessman named Polycarp Basilius offered to take Waechter to see the boy. By then, UMDA's investments there had begun to sour. The leases they'd signed were being challenged in court by local tribal chiefs after they'd already sunk millions on deposits and built a road out to a remote village where they'd planned a huge resort. Waechter had politely declined Basilius's offer, unsure how Larry would react or whether it was really his job or not to settle Hillblom's family issues, but the next day at breakfast, several of their Palauan partners started chiming in about Larry's kid. Lifoifoi was growling louder that something had to be done, that it didn't look good, that Larry needed to do the right thing. So when Waechter had returned to Saipan, he'd given Larry the "come to Jesus" speech.

"Larry," he'd said, "if this is your kid you've got to do something about it, recognize it or support him or whatever. Are you sure this is not your child?"

"Absolutely," Larry had repeated.

"Then you need to take affirmative action to prove that it's not. It's jeopardizing our business, hurting our business relationships down there. It's a small island."

But Larry had become indignant, defensive even. "I don't have to prove anything," he snapped. "If these people think he's my kid, let them prove it. I'll do a blood test." Later, the woman had shown up at Mike Dotts's office on Saipan looking for Hillblom. Bob O'Connor had been instructed to give her some cash and a plane ticket back to Palau rather than call the police.

By August 1995, Waechter must have been well aware of at least the possibility of more children in the Philippines and Vietnam. He had, after all, personally witnessed the constant flow of women in and out of the villa in Dalat and had been introduced to two of Larry's Filipina girlfriends often enough to remember their unlikely names: Angelica and Mercedes—or, as Larry had giddily called her, "the Benz."

However, when a reporter for the *Guam Business Magazine* called Waechter's office at UMDA later that month for a cover story/eulogy of Micronesia's most successful businessman, Waechter tried to avoid the subject by waxing sentimental. "We all like to think we'll make our mark while on this earth and shine bright," he told the reporter, "but Larry's star shone much brighter than the rest of us ordinary men." "Larry was the happiest guy I ever knew," Waechter continued. "He had two interests in life: business and the law. I got to talk to him a lot about business, but not about the law, over the twenty-three years that I worked for him. It developed into more than a business relationship. Larry became one of my best friends. I thought about that last month when I was in Vietnam. It hit me hard in Vietnam. I was doing that job for Larry. I've lost a tremendous friend. To me it's like losing a brother. He's someone who's been there for over twenty-three years through good and bad times. He's changed my life completely."

When the interview turned to Hillblom's personal life, Waechter equivocated. "I don't know what you've been told," he said, "but it's a myth that Larry was with ten girls a day in the Philippines. In reality, Larry had one girlfriend here: Josephine Nocasa, and he was very faithful and loyal when they were together." Then, addressing rumors of pedophilia, he contradicted himself: "They weren't twelve or thirteen years old," Waechter said. "Larry preferred them to be eighteen to twenty. At any time he had three or four girlfriends." Finally, the reporter brought up rumors of a girlfriend in Vietnam, where Waechter and Hillblom had shared a villa for the last fifteen months. "He had a female friend for several years," Waechter acknowledged, "but they were never intimate. She was teaching him Vietnamese. He kept thinking that sooner or later, she'd cave in, but . . . he enjoyed the chase more than the conquest."

"Shortly after Larry died," Mike Dotts explains toward the end of our second lunch, "Ted Mitchell tried to get Josephine as a client." Soliciting his enemy's girlfriend was such an audacious move that no one, including Dotts, had seen it coming. Nor would anyone have predicted Josephine's response. She did not say no, though she did not say yes, either. Instead, she told her good friend Annie Waechter, Joe's wife.

Dotts received a call from Waechter a short time after that. "Joe asked me if I would talk to Josephine and persuade her not to hire Ted," he recalls.

"Well, who is she going to hire?" Dotts replied. As everyone knew, most of the attorneys on Saipan were looking for kids. Hillblom's probate was already being called a feeding frenzy.

"No one," was the reply.

"Let her hire me then," Dotts said, though he knew that was easier said than done. First, Bob O'Connor, his boss, had forbidden him to become involved; he didn't want the pain of Larry's death lingering around the office. Second, Dotts was a director of the Bank of Saipan, which was legally the executor. The estate would have to waive the obvious conflict of a bank director filing a multimillion-dollar claim against the bank.

Waechter seemed reluctant to allow anyone to represent Josephine, but he agreed to call Peter Donnici and see if they could work something out. Dotts was convinced that Hillblom would have wanted Josephine to be provided for. He considered her a widow, even if the law might not. Saipan's marriage statute was a holdover from the Trust Territory days, when the U.S. Navy Administrator had eliminated common-law marriages because several young sailors had attended local ceremonies with their island sweethearts and found themselves unwittingly married. So, even though Josephine and Larry had lived together and traveled together for ten years, Dotts would either have to invalidate the old statute or offer some proof that a marriage ceremony had occurred. This already daunting task was made thornier by the fact that Dotts himself had drawn up the employment contract that defined Josephine as Hillblom's maid—the contract that had allowed Larry not to marry her.

At least, Dotts told himself, he would not face opposition from the estate. Both me Donnici and Waechter knew Josephine and they knew Larry's feelings for her. Dotts told himself that they would do the right thing. As he hopped into his Jeep and navigated the southern tip of the island toward Dandan, Dotts thought his biggest problem would be keeping his new client a secret from his boss.

Curled up in one of the couches of Larry's favorite room twenty minutes later, Josephine told Dotts how she had become a recluse, hiding from the press and news of Junior. But he was not her first visitor that week, she said. Joe Waechter had also come by to remove all of Larry's files and his computer. In total, Josephine estimated that Waechter had made off with thirteen or fourteen boxes, although the computer was broken anyway.

But later that day, Josephine continued, she had received a call from Waechter. He had decided that removing the files was not enough. He wanted to make sure that she cleaned the house and especially, that she vacuumed the carpet thoroughly. And, he told her, get rid of Larry's nail cutter and his combs. When she asked why, he explained that Junior's lawyer was going to come to look for evidence. As she would testify under oath later: "He told me that Junior was going to try and take away Larry's money. And that it would be wrong for that to happen, because he said that Larry didn't have a son." Finally, he asked her to get rid of Larry's clothes and his personal things. Specifically, Josephine would recall, "He told me to burn them."

Their maid had flown home to the Philippines to visit family so Josephine, her brother, and Hillblom's pool man had teamed up to expunge the last evidence of Larry Hillblom from his home. While she'd gathered his modest wardrobe in large trash bags, the two men had cleaned the yard and the swimming pool. But instead of burning Hillblom's clothes, Josephine had decided to bury them in the backyard. She'd called up the only equipment rental shop on the island and rented a backhoe for a hundred bucks. She'd directed the driver to come all the way down the driveway to the garage and dig a large hole next to the tennis court. Josephine had chosen a spot that would be overgrown with tangan-tangan within a few days. Since then, she'd fretted over the hundred dollars; that equated to roughly half her monthly salary and, with Larry gone, she had no idea how she would feed herself, her brother, or even her cat.

A few days later, when Waechter had called back and asked her if she was done cleaning the house, Josephine had simply said yes. And he hadn't followed up to make certain that the clothes had been burned, so she'd let him believe that she had done as she was told.

But Waechter had not been the only one on the estate side to contact Josephine in recent days. David Nevitt, the estate's lead attorney, had taken her to lunch at a resort hotel where he told her that he would do everything he could to make sure that Junior didn't get a penny of Hillblom's money. Then he had made her an offer. "He said," Josephine would remember, "that if I didn't hire a lawyer, that I'd have a house to live in for the rest of my life." In addition to the house, Nevitt also promised her $1 million, paid by the Bank of Saipan, on the condition that she not file a claim. Which, he added, was really in her best interests because if she did not hire a lawyer, then she would have all of the money for herself! Of course, the poor girl from the provinces was supposed to be impressed by the white man in the tie and his big number but she wasn't. Larry had promised her more than that, she told Dotts. He'd told her that she would inherit the house as well as her Toyota MR2 and his stock in UMDA. She had pressed Larry to write down these promises, but he'd refused, joking that she would want him dead if he did. Instead, he'd bought her some land in Manila, an SUV for herself, and a Jeepney for one of her brothers.

Dotts froze. He was now staring at a very long, complicated path to settlement. In the inventory of the estate's assets that he'd filed with the court, Waechter had estimated Hillblom's UMDA shares at $50 million. If Nevitt had offered her only a million dollars, Josephine and the estate would start their negotiations tens of millions of dollars apart. To further complicate matters, Josephine had just admitted to destroying evidence. If Junior's attorneys found out about that, the chances that they would allow a settlement with Josephine were next to nil. They might even go after Dotts for contempt. Or disbarment.

"The trick"—Dotts smiles—"was not revealing Josephine's complicity in hiding Hillblom's personal effects until after a settlement. I had to get lucky and I had to just keep delaying."

Thirty-Seven

Sparring

By the time a copy of *Guam Business* landed on Joe Waechter's desk several weeks later, the cover a watercolor portrait of Hillblom in which he seemed to be either drowning or suspended in an aquamarine haze, Waechter had received more than two dozen claims against the estate. While most would be easy to deal with—a claim for work done on one of Hillblom's apartment buildings on Saipan, for example—there were a few curveballs, none more perplexing than a malicious prosecution lawsuit demanding $1.5 million from the estate. The lawsuit had been filed by Ted Mitchell, who happened to be quoted at length in the *Guam Business* article.

Mitchell's lawsuit became much more menacing when Waechter received a call from Guy Coombs, the longtime head of DHL's Philippines subsidiary. Coombs told him about a strange call he'd just received from a man posing as an estate attorney. The man, Coombs said, had asked a lot of questions about Larry—where he'd gotten the cash for his Manila junkets, for example, and what had happened to the condos that he'd purchased there, as well as any personal effects that remained. The caller had seemed especially interested in whether or not Hillblom had owned any property in the Philippines through nominees, as he had on Saipan. When Coombs had become suspicious, the line had suddenly gone dead.

Waechter thanked Coombs for the information and hung up the phone. If he had not yet appreciated the precariousness of his position, the reality now settled in the pit of his stomach. He was no longer Larry's fixer. As executor, he *was* Larry. And so he had just been pulled into the final, and most personal, phase of the Clash of the Titans.

Monday, September 8, 1995, started hot and stayed that way. In the early afternoon, Mike Dotts rode the escalator down to the first floor of the Nauru Building, traversed the parking lot, and walked the well-worn dirt path to Castro's courtroom for an emergency hearing inspired by Hillblom's old nemesis, Ted Mitchell. The last time the two men had sparred, Dotts had enraged the bombastic litigator by yanking Larry out of his deposition. He suspected (based on purely circumstantial evidence, it should be noted) that Mitchell had gotten his revenge by sabotaging Larry's Cessna shortly thereafter—nearly killing him. Now it appeared that Mitchell had flown to Manila to dig up dirt, which he had neatly sifted and categorized in an emergency pleading to Judge Castro—the emergency being Mitchell's suspicion that Joseph Waechter was secretly disposing of estate assets in the Philippines. But given the relatively minuscule value of Hillblom's property there, Mitchell's emergency seemed like a pretense, one that conveniently allowed him to crucify Larry as a tax evader, a real estate fraudster, and a pedophile.

Among other things, Mitchell alleged:

- Hillblom had often "borrowed" cash from the DHL office in Manila for his sex junkets. The revolving loans had been repaid by Donnici's office in San Francisco. At the time of his death, about $25,000 worth of these loans were outstanding.
- Hillblom's studio apartment in Makati, Manila, was inhabited by a "little girl" whom he was sending to school.
- Waechter had given power of attorney to a DHL lawyer named Domingo Jhocson to dispose of Larry's assets in the Philippines without court approval. The implications of this were twofold: Waechter was trying to cover Larry's tracks by immediately clearing out his residences; and Larry had illegally purchased property in the Philippines, where, as on Saipan, foreigners are not allowed to own real estate.

Dotts took a seat in the courtroom as Waechter and John Osborn crossed the bar. Several feet away, Ted Mitchell, Joe Hill, and a stocky islander dressed in a deafeningly loud aloha shirt took their seats at the opposing table.

Castro entered in his long black robe and asked for appearances. The only witness that day would be Joseph Waechter, who dutifully slouched to the witness chair and promised to tell the truth. But before Mitchell got his shot at him, the executor was given the opportunity to explain how he had gone about marshaling Hillblom's assets in the Philippines. Waechter said he had executed the power of attorney with Jhocson—a close associate—only to explore the sale of Hillblom's Manila condos and certainly not to destroy evidence, as Mitchell's affidavit had suggested. Of course, Waechter said, he had always planned to come back to the court and obtain its approval if they received any offers, but they hadn't. In fact, nothing of Hillblom's had been sold yet.

Mitchell shifted in his seat, taking notes, or pretending to, as the islander attorney suddenly asked Castro permission to approach the witness. The judge acquiesced with a warm smile.

The islander attorney's name was David Lujan, pronounced with a soft "j," accent on the second syllable (loo-HAN). Physically, he was compact and thick—a bulldog with a mocha complexion—and he moved like a fighter. He was obviously Chamorro. Dotts watched closely as Lujan stood and thanked Castro for allowing him the opportunity to question the witness. But as he turned to face Waechter, Lujan's smile morphed into a smirk. Then the islander attorney began to pace, waving a thin double-spaced document with his right hand: the power of attorney.

Lujan rattled off a number of establishing questions: Did Waechter really understand his duties as executor? Did he understand what the power of attorney he'd signed actually meant? Did he get that this was not a limited power of attorney, as he had intimated, but actually a very broad authorization that gave Jhocson not only the power to sell assets himself but also to anoint another attorney with the power to operate as the executor within the Philippines? What exactly was Waechter's relationship with Jhocson?

"Sir," the islander asked Waechter, "are you aware that Mr. Hillblom sometimes buys properties and puts it in other people's names?"

"I'm not aware of that," Waechter replied.

"The Rooster," attorney David Lujan. The photo is from an article in *GQ* magazine on the Hillblom probate. (Courtesy of Robbie McClaran)

"You're not aware of it?" Lujan asked, raising an eyebrow.

"No."

The attorney turned back to Castro and asked the judge to consider the whopper that had just escaped the lips of one of Hillblom's closest business associates. Then he swapped the power of attorney for a copy of Mitchell's affidavit and called Waechter's attention to Mitchell's assertion that Guy Coombs, DHL's manager in the Philippines, had told him that Hillblom owned a house north of Manila that was held in Coombs's wife's name.

"I see that," Waechter admitted.

"Are you aware of that?" the attorney asked.

"I'm not aware of that, no."

"You're not aware of it?"

They sparred awhile longer before Waechter questioned why they were spending so much time arguing over less than a million dollars. If they went through this exercise for every asset in Hillblom's estate, he admonished the islander, they would be in court for three years.

Lujan smirked. Was Waechter blaming him for being suspicious of his actions? he asked.

John Osborn immediately objected. Overruled.

Lujan repeated his question, a little more emphatically: "Do you blame me for being suspicious?"

"Well," Waechter stammered, "I don't know what—the word, *blame*. I don't know what you mean by 'blame.'"

The attorney ignored him. He asked Castro's permission to delve into something potentially more substantive than the Philippine assets—something that predated his entry into the case but seemed very suspicious: a brand-new entity called Commonwealth Holdings Corporation that now owned the majority of the Bank of Saipan, the estate's executor. But Castro refused, promising that it could be discussed at a future hearing. Disappointed, Lujan sat down and ceded the floor.

Attorneys like Dotts are used to the repetitive nature of cross-examinations, but Waechter, an executive used to short meetings and quick decisions, was already flustered. Now Ted Mitchell finally stood up to have his turn. And for several minutes, Mitchell repeated many of the questions that Lujan had already asked, eliciting the same responses in an increasingly agitated tone. When Mitchell inquired as to why Waechter had not consulted with the eminent auction house Sotheby's before disposing of Hillblom's television and VCR, Waechter finally lost it.

"I checked with Sotheby's about a VCR?" Waechter said, incredulous.

"Isn't it," Mitchell replied, "*conceivable* that something with Larry Hillblom's name on it, or a golf bag that has his name on it, or that it belonged to him . . . You laugh? They're having auctions at Sotheby's every few days of Elvis Presley's effects, aren't they? And other similar celebrity's effects?"

"No," Waechter answered firmly. "It's *not* conceivable."

"You don't think that Larry Hillblom's effects would have any special value?" Mitchell demanded.

"*I* think," Waechter replied, "you're living in a dream world. That's not—I don't believe it's conceivable."

"It is not legal," Mitchell continued, then paused a moment to rephrase. "Is it your understanding that Mr. Hillblom could legally buy real estate in the Philippines in his own name? What is your understanding?"

Osborn objected again. Overruled.

"I don't know whether you can or not," Waechter mused. "I've never bought property in the Philippines. I don't know. I mean, I don't know what their law is about buying property. Mr. Hillblom owns two condominiums there, owns two golf course memberships there. I don't know what their law is, if that's the question."

"You don't know," Mitchell thundered, "*anything* about the Philippine law with respect to alien ownership of real property in the Philippines?"

"I've never bought property there."

"That's not my question, Mr. Waechter."

"Well," Waechter admitted, "I don't know anything about it. I don't know anything about their law."

Mitchell started to ask the question again, but he had exasperated the judge every bit as much as the witness. "Asked and answered," Castro interjected. "Next question."

Thirty-Eight

The Rooster

"**Y**ou know how they did it in the old days?" David Lujan asks rhetorically, raising his hand above an empty coffee mug and making a forward motion with his index finger. "They brought you before the judge for a good look. Side by side with your father. That's how the judge made his decision."

Lujan, ensconced in a less than comfortable chair in the atrium restaurant of a Guam hotel, has already spoken for more than two hours, filling my head with useless factoids and opinions: Hong Kong is his favorite city; he gets more work done on the Air Mike flight between Honolulu, where he owns a second home, and Guam than any time else; his father, a judge, would disappear every weekend but Lujan and his mother knew that the old man was at the cockfights; he considers the Northern Mariana Islands to be American colonies; Patrick Lupo and Peter Donnici are worse than rapists and murderers.

The rapid-fire delivery has allowed him to steer the conversation, though every now and then, his cell phone interrupts and he leans back, barks a few sentences in Chamorro—a language that splits the difference between the indigenous tongue and Spanish—and then picks up wherever he left off.

At the moment, Lujan, who wears a military haircut and lots of gold jewelry, is explaining how he decided to take Junior Larry Hillbroom's case. First came the call, from a small family law firm called the Family and Immigration Law Clinic. The FILC consisted of four American attorneys, one of whom had been the attorney general on Guam. They represented the mother of Junior Larry Hillbroom, the only known child of Larry

Hillblom. But to take on Hillblom's friends, the FILC needed a fighter and they needed someone with cash, because they had none. Lujan was Guam's most successful criminal attorney. He'd built a thriving practice representing local drug dealers, murderers, and rapists.

The prospect of representing Larry Hillblom's son intrigued Lujan immediately. But before committing any of his own time or money, he had remembered his father the judge, and he'd had the boy brought before him for a good look. Junior was a handsome, barely adolescent young man with the skin of an islander but the smooth features of a Caucasian: big ears and a button nose. Lujan thought that the boy looked like Hillblom; in order to be certain, he had called the clerks at CNMI Superior Court, where Junior had made an appearance a couple of weeks earlier. The clerks all said the same thing: Junior looked just like Larry. Spitting image, in fact. So Lujan had agreed to spend a quarter of a million dollars of his own money to establish Junior Larry Hillbroom's heirship. In exchange, he would receive 8 percent of Junior's inheritance—nearly half the contingency fee that FILC had negotiated with Junior's mother, Kaelani Kinney.

On his native Guam, Lujan is still known as the lawyer you call when you can't win. He has litigated hundreds of cases, mostly small-time criminal matters, and one of the first things he tells me is that he has never lost, though one of his clients had been forced to pay a $1.5 million settlement just before Hillblom's disappearance. Defeats, however rare, are taken personally and hard-fought. Lujan is famous for his exhaustive cross-examinations. Opposing witnesses, even if victims of serious crimes like rape, are interrogated ruthlessly, sometimes tearfully.

Lujan tells me that he learned how to fight in the underground gambling dens on Guam. As a small kid, he dealt cards for poker matches that often turned violent. Sometimes the cops beat him up, but he was tough. He did time in juvie, which he considered the best education a young man could have, then he became a bill collector, which he considers the second-best education. In his thirties and married, he decided to change his life and put himself through Notre Dame Law School by playing professional chess. Lujan claims he never studied, and still feigns near ignorance of the technicalities of the law. What he knows is how to win and how criminals think. His first client, Lujan tells me, was his cellmate from juvie, who had been indicted for the murder of his other cellmate.

From his father, the judge, he has inherited a gambler's intensity. His mother taught him about money. One of them blessed him with a photographic memory. Lujan favors suits in very bright tropical hues, apparently because islanders like bright colors. (Today, he sports a pastel aloha shirt and white slacks.) Like Hillblom, the man is intensely competitive and unpretentious. He has likened himself to Guam's ubiquitous boonie dogs, of which he has adopted many. In a rare interview with the men's lifestyle magazine *GQ*, Lujan accused his stateside opponents of dismissing him as a "brown nigger." The assistant U.S. attorney on Guam likes to call Lujan the Rooster but, having spent the past couple of hours with him, I think that Shark might be more apt.

Weeks before the SeaBee crash, Lujan tells me, he and his wife had accepted an invitation from Larry to stay at his new hotel in Vietnam. The two men had become friendly several years earlier when the assistant U.S. attorney, a former marine named George Proctor, had indicted Jesus P. Mafnas, former speaker of the CNMI House of Representatives, for corruption. *United States v. Mafnas* was the first case that the U.S. attorney's office tried on Saipan, which had established such a dangerous reputation that FBI agents refused to stay overnight. Money laundering was rampant; a police informant had been murdered on the beach shortly before a trial; Chinese triad gangs and the Japanese Yakuza were expanding highly profitable trades in forced prostitution and drugs; and politicians were selling everything from jobs to choice apartments and accepting everything, including sex, for payment. Convicting Mafnas of bribery was meant to send a clear signal about who was in charge and what would no longer be tolerated.

During high school, Mafnas had lived at the Lujans' home in order to attend school on Guam, and he had become Lujan's brother's best friend, so Lujan did not hesitate to defend him against the feds. During the trial, Lujan would become a frequent visitor at Mafnas's house on Saipan, where, he tells me, a cartel of the island's political elite gathered every morning before dawn to talk over the issues of the day: the soaring real estate market, Willie Tan's garment factories, the proliferation of video poker dens. The only haole was a well-known businessman named Larry

Hillblom, who would sneak into the kitchen before Mafnas's wife and children were out of bed and make coffee for himself while he waited for someone else to show. During those early-morning sessions, Hillblom had been frequently chided by his friends for being the father of "that boy on Palau." Sometimes he would deny it. Sometimes he would just smile and take another sip of his coffee.

Lujan tells me that Hillblom agreed to be his local counsel on Saipan—an assertion that is not verified by my research but is also not as outlandish as it might seem. At the time, Hillblom was ingratiating himself with the CNMI Legislature, but his interest in Mafnas's case would have been even more personal. They shared an enemy. Guam's FBI agents had told the U.S. attorney that if they did not "get" Larry Hillblom at some point, they would consider their presence on Saipan to be a failure, while Hillblom publicly characterized the FBI's presence as an illegal invasion. When Lujan delivered his final argument in front of a jury of eleven islanders and one American housewife, he says that Hillblom had a front-row seat. (The prosecutor, who is now a federal immigration judge, does not remember Hillblom ever attending.)

Lujan won Mafnas's acquittal on an eleven-to-one vote. He says that Hillblom had been so impressed, he'd asked to hire him as counsel for a lawsuit that was percolating on Guam. Lujan agreed but the lawsuit never materialized. So in the coming years, the two attorneys would exchange greetings when fate brought them together on airplanes or at the occasional barbecue. Then, on May 22, 1995, Lujan received word that Hillblom had been lost at sea near the northern island of Anatahan, along with his pilot and one other passenger—Lujan's good friend and former client Jess Mafnas. Shortly thereafter, Lujan got the call from the FILC.

After meeting Junior, Lujan imagined the case would be easy. A single $10,000 DNA test would establish the young man's heirship; a trust would be formed until he came of age, allowing him to enjoy the remainder of his youth raising his fighting cock and spear-fishing, or being sent to the best schools as Hillblom himself had once promised. Thanks to the O. J. Simpson case, everyone seemed to know just how simple establishing a "genetic fingerprint" could be. All you needed was a sweat-stained T-shirt, a comb, a toothbrush, a drop of congealed blood. Lujan worried more about finding words. He agonized over every sentence of every pleading, never sure if what he'd written was quite done. A friend had cowritten his first motion.

Not that Lujan was scared. His opponents—he smiles—underestimated his tenacity. They'd never expected someone to gamble everything again and again, as he would.

Thirty-Nine

Evidence

Executor, its agents, employees, servants, representatives, attorneys, occupants and/or custodians . . . are hereby restrained from cleaning, disturbing, destroying, altering or removing any contents . . . or ordering any other actions which may have the foreseeable result of destroying or disposing of items which may contain body tissues, blood, hair or fingernail clippings of the decedent.

—*Order from Judge Alex C. Castro, September 13, 1995*

"I took the Junior case on trust for David," Barry Israel says via cell phone from Ho Chi Minh City. "I crashed in David's office. I would work on the law while he worked on the facts, but whereas I would study all night, David could look at the documents once and go to sleep."

Three months after Hillblom's disappearance, Israel was named cocounsel of Junior Larry Hillbroom's growing legal team. Lujan had met him years earlier while serving on Guam's Political Status Commission and invited him in as an equal partner. Israel signed on after a long talk with his daughters in Santa Barbara, the wealthy coastal enclave they called home; he'd had to warn them that things were going to be different. The Hillblom case wasn't going to be like billing a government or a corporation. There was going to be risk involved. He was going to have to invest money, maybe get a second mortgage on the house. Their comfortable lifestyle might suffer. Of course, if things went the way that he hoped, Israel would be far wealthier than most attorneys could dream of.

Yet Israel must have wondered what, exactly, he had gotten himself into when he arrived on Guam a short time later. Legally, Junior was still a client of the Family and Immigration Law Clinic, the four-partner firm that had signed his mother to a contingency agreement. Theoretically, the FILC called the shots while Lujan and Israel were expected to do the heavy lifting. They were also expected to contribute all of the capital, assumedly because the FILC was broke. But that, Israel soon discovered, was actually the least of FILC's problems.

Of their four partners, one was not only sleeping with Junior's mother but getting drunk with her in public. Two of the others simply seemed lazy or ineffective, perhaps due to illnesses. The fourth, a guy by the name of Roland Fairfield, was handling the DNA portion of the case. It was Fairfield's job to get biological evidence so that Lujan could negotiate the settlement with the estate. Now Israel learned that Fairfield had already panicked and offered Hillblom's brothers 40 percent of the estate in exchange for DNA proving Junior's paternity. The offer had been promptly rejected by the Hillbloms' California attorney, but not before seriously undermining Lujan's trust in his partners, and Israel's confidence.

While Israel moved into Lujan's spare bedroom on Guam, Lujan flew to Saipan to discuss a more promising settlement offer that the Carlsmith firm was supposedly preparing. When David Nevitt kept Lujan stewing on-island for several days with no offer, the criminal lawyer became suspicious and decided to visit Larry Hillblom's house with his local counsel, Joe Hill.

Hill collected Lujan at his hotel in Garapan and drove south along Beach Road toward the airport as a small storm emerged overhead. By the time they reached Dandan, the rain was falling hard, and by the time Hill found the aluminum fence delineating Hillblom's property, the sky was unleashing torrents of water. Up ahead, past the fence, the driveway that led down to the garage and the poolhouse was barely visible. To the right, equally obscured by the rain-soaked windshield, was the upper floor of the house and, in front of that, a red Honda.

Lujan stepped out of Hill's car, planted a polished shoe in the muddy grass, and walked up to the fence, but it was locked. He could see that the Honda's doors were wide open—odd, considering the storm. Even stranger, two figures were crouched in the front seats from either side while their legs and feet dangled in the rain. The howl of a vacuum cleaner could be heard above the rainstorm and the incessant barking of the neighbor's dogs.

Lujan began to shake the fence until the figures froze. He yelled at them to stop. Hill jumped out of the car and joined him until a man and a woman, both tiny and dark-skinned, emerged from either side of the car. Lujan warned them that what they were doing was illegal. He was an attorney, he yelled, an officer of the court, and they were potentially destroying evidence. The two islanders slammed the car's doors shut, grabbed the vacuum cleaner, and ran into the house. Lujan and Hill raced back to Hill's office near the courthouse to prepare an emergency motion demanding that the estate not destroy any potential DNA evidence.

Judge Castro issued a restraining order the following day. Then, as if to level the playing field after one team has made a questionable play, Castro designated Junior Larry Hillbroom an "interested party" in the proceedings. As such, Hillbroom's attorneys were entitled to review all of the estate's records, including legal bills.

The Saipan office of the law firm of Carlsmith Ball is the westernmost of twin two-story stone buildings set into a hillside scattered with sugarcane as thin and precarious as errant whiskers. Oversize tinted windows peer over a two-lane cement road that winds its way from the government buildings at the top of the hill down to the island's western flats and dead-ends into a massive lagoon where honeymooners from Japan and Korea frolic on Jet Skis, locals fish for mahimahi in knee-deep water, and a half dozen forward positioning warships anchor, each holding enough weapons in its belly to invade a small country. I have driven past the building countless times on my way to a restaurant just beyond that serves the only decent burger on the island, though I have never been welcomed inside, as David Lujan was one morning in mid-September 1995.

Joe Hill drove him there, and both men were politely ushered to a conference room with a large table that had been buried in unmarked boxes containing all manner of files—a document dump. Document dumps are meant to overwhelm, but Lujan, armed with several yellow legal pads and a pen, approached each box methodically. He had no intention of leaving until he had reviewed every piece of correspondence, every invoice, and every receipt.

He stayed for hours, glued to a chair as a handful of Carlsmith staffers curiously popped their heads in from time to time. Before long, Lujan was convinced that the conference room was a crime scene and that the papers splayed out before him evidenced a vast conspiracy in which Joe Lifoifoi, Joe Waechter, and Peter Donnici had illegally hijacked the estate of Larry Lee Hillblom from under Judge Castro's nose.

As outlined by Lujan, the conspiracy he imagined had been set in motion less than one week after Larry Hillblom's death, well before Lujan's entry into the case. That's when Donnici had gathered Waechter, Joe Lifoifoi, Ed "Champ" Calvo (a well-known Guam attorney and a Bank of Saipan director and shareholder), and a few other of Hillblom's old associates in his office in San Francisco the morning after his memorial service. He had told them how Hillblom's will called for the bank to be the executor of the estate, but also how, at the time the will had been written, Hillblom had owned over 90 percent of the shares. Now his estate owned only a third. Therefore, in order to keep control of the estate, they would have to buy at least 20 percent of the bank's outstanding stock.

But it soon became clear that one of the bank's major shareholders, Chinese-American billionaire Willie Tan, wanted a huge premium for his stock. After a little research, the estate's lawyers discovered the solution: a large amount of unissued shares they could buy instead. But that turned out to reveal a second problem: no one had the $3.5 million that those shares were probably worth. So Donnici, Lifoifoi, and Waechter had formed a shell entity called Commonwealth Holdings Corporation whose sole purpose would be to buy the unissued shares. To get the money, Waechter had then run to Castro's court claiming that a financial crisis in Vietnam—along with their need for $3.7 million to buy shares in the Bank of Saipan—necessitated two emergency loans from DHL Corporation and DHL, International in the total amount of $15 million, of which $3.7 million would go to CHC.

Castro had approved the two DHL loans, which had (conveniently) already been negotiated by Peter Donnici, even though Donnici was a shareholder in both DHL companies—and despite the fact that he and other DHL shareholders had claims against the estate for DHL stock that they said Hillblom had promised them.

The net was this: Donnici and Co. had borrowed from the estate to take control of it. And of the $3.7 million that CHC received from the estate, only $3.5 million was paid to the Bank of Saipan for the unissued shares. Waechter had told Castro that most of the loans were needed for Vietnam, but Lujan could find no record of the estate buying stock in Hillblom's Vietnam holding company or loaning it a penny.*

Lujan wondered if Castro knew any of this. The judge certainly did not know who CHC's shareholders were, because Waechter had never told anyone. To the contrary, in open court, Waechter had implied that CHC was owned by the estate, which Lujan now knew was not true.

As Lujan made his way through more papers, he discovered more evidence of insider dealings that troubled him. There was, for example, a "right of first refusal" agreement that gave DHL's existing shareholders a short window of time in which to purchase Hillblom's shares in the event of his death at fair market value—but that window began only after notice of Hillblom's death was served on DHL, whose executives claimed that notice had not yet been given. Considering that Hillblom had been declared dead for nearly six months now, and that DHL itself had hosted one of his memorial services, it was hard to imagine why not—unless that too was part of the conspiracy. DHL was apparently being given plenty of time to raise cash to buy the shares.

Also, several hundred shares of DHL stock were missing from Waechter's inventory of the estate's assets. Waechter had simply deducted shares that Donnici, Pat Lupo, and others claimed Hillblom had promised them in exchange for work dating back to the Continental Airlines/UMDA litigation without telling Castro. But the transfer of those shares required approval by the court. Instead of standing in line with the other claimants, Hillblom's friends appeared to have simply taken what they thought

---

*It would later emerge that $11 million had been paid, but the paperwork did not surface in time to give Lujan a different view of the events.

was theirs. (Ultimately, their receipt of the shares was approved by the court.)

Finally, Po Chung, the head of DHL's Asia operations, claimed that he owned 10 percent of Danao, Hillblom's Vietnamese holding company. But there was no written evidence that Chung had contributed anything to Danao. Hillblom, meanwhile, had invested close to $70 million and received no stock certificate. At best, Chung seemed to be hiding the fact that Larry had been operating in Vietnam illegally since at least 1991— three years before the U.S. embargo was lifted—a clear violation of the Trading with the Enemy Act.

As Lujan pushed his chair from the polished table and stood up, grabbing the yellow legal pads that he'd filled with notes, he wondered what else Hillblom's friends were hiding. Almost as an afterthought, he grabbed a stray piece of paper and stuffed it into his shirt pocket. This scrap had nearly been lost amid the volumes of more important correspondence. It was a cash receipt for several containers of muriatic acid, paid for by Hillblom's estate and approved as a household expense by Judge Castro.

Forty

The Pilot

As Lujan prepared an emergency pleading late that night, the bustling expat bars and strip clubs hummed with answers to a singular question: Why had the SeaBee crashed to begin with? FAA inspectors had come and gone, expressing doubt that the cause would ever be known for certain, but the question lingered. For some it was a night's entertainment; others had a more personal connection. Hillblom had invited at least four friends to ride with him that day; only one had gone. The rest considered themselves wise or lucky. One had averted death because he did not have Hillblom's cell phone number; another had received Hillblom's voice-mail invitation too late. Others, like the widows of the two men aboard the airplane, had financial motives. So too did DHL's insurance company, which still refused to pay out Hillblom's life insurance policy, for months citing uncertainty as to whether Hillblom was, in fact, deceased.

Speculation as to what had transpired aboard the plane increased as a few small parts of the SeaBee began to wash up on the shores of Anatahan. Most people assumed that some type of mechanical failure had crippled the plane, but alternative theories abounded. Sam MacPhetres thought that Hillblom might have detonated an explosive shortly after parachuting out of the plane to be rescued by an awaiting submarine. A member of the search team doubted that Hillblom had been on the plane to begin with. Lujan theorized that Larry had been illegally flying the plane, citing as evidence the fact that only the pilot's seat had a seat belt and only Hillblom's body was never found. Therefore, Hillblom's seat must have sunk with him in it. According to Lujan's reasoning, the estate had Bob Long's and Jess Mafnas's blood on its hands.

The flaw of (most of) these theories is not their implausibility but that they are all based entirely on circumstantial evidence. As of today, the largest piece of Hillblom's plane to be recovered is a tiny pontoon that washed ashore and is now displayed on the wall of a Guam steakhouse. The only eyewitness was World War II hero Guy Gabaldon, now deceased, and Gabaldon only saw the SeaBee take off. His affidavit expresses little more than his opinion that Hillblom's plane was an antique and might have had trouble gaining altitude.

In fact, the only evidence are two cell phone calls from that afternoon, both of which occurred shortly before the SeaBee was to return. Jess Mafnas had phoned his wife to tell her that they had been unable to land on Pagan, as planned, due to a storm and that they were headed back to the Saipan airport; Mafnas had added that he was presently staring down at Anatahan's crater. Not long afterward, Josephine had received a call from Larry himself. Neither Hillblom nor Mafnas had mentioned anything out of the ordinary.

But to Bob Christian, a straight-talking former marine and Vietnam veteran who runs Saipan's only FAA-certified shop, even eyewitness accounts and phone calls are beside the point. What matters, he tells me during a long-distance conversation, is the location of the crash, the condition of the plane, and the mentality of those on board—one in particular. "Larry had a tendency to read the two first pages in a book and think he knew the rest," Christian sighs. "He kind of marched to the beat of a different drum. He didn't do it if he didn't think it was necessary." And by "it" Christian means that Larry didn't maintain his aircraft.

Christian was never interviewed during the NTSB investigation, nor was he deposed in either Bob Long's or Jess Mafnas's wrongful death case—odd because he is uniquely qualified to comment on the crash. He is one of the few men besides Hillblom and Long who actually flew the SeaBee. He'd even piloted the plane on one of the test runs to Pagan—the same route that Hillblom had been flying when he disappeared. Christian had done some mechanical work on the plane, too, including installing a much larger oil cooler to prevent the propellers from feathering. He says he repeatedly warned Hillblom that there was a fine line between an antique and a piece of junk. "Things were constantly falling on and off the airplane!" he groans. When Christian refused to fly the plane any longer and Hillblom became too cheap to use his shop, Christian had looked the other way as Hillblom's pilot would "borrow" equipment from Christian's hangar to do Band-Aid repairs. One area that got a lot of attention was the SeaBee's tail, which Hillblom eventually replaced with another that was just as old.

Christian, however, tells me that the tail was not the problem per se. The SeaBee's fatal flaw, he says, was that the transfer line to the auxiliary fuel tank in the tail didn't work. In a plane like the SeaBee, the auxiliary fuel tank is extraordinarily important. To land on water, the tank needs to be full in order to balance the plane; otherwise, the nose will collapse into the water—catastrophic at 120 miles per hour. On the other hand, if you're flying from Saipan to Pagan and back, you'd need to transfer the fuel into the main tank at some point in order to make it all the way home.

When he'd heard that Hillblom's plane had gone missing, Christian says that he had immediately thought of the auxiliary fuel tank. But, he continues, two equally serious problems had also come to mind: Bob Long and Larry Hillblom.

Long, he says, had come out to Saipan from the western United States with an inspector authorization for airframes and power plants, meaning that he could sign off on the annual inspections of aircraft. Christian had hired him, but let him go in 1990 when it became clear that Long did not possess the attention to detail required of a certified shop mechanic. Christian thought Long might have more luck as a pilot, so he had hired an FAA observer to do a check ride that would certify his fellow Vietnam veteran to fly commercially.

The check ride, Christian recalls, should have been a formality considering the numerous combat missions Long claimed to have flown over Southeast Asia. But once he was up in the air with the FAA observer calling out procedures, Long froze. He couldn't even follow instructions. When they returned to the hangar, both Christian and the FAA observer agreed that Bob Long wasn't cut out to be a pilot. So to make ends meet, Long started freelancing as a mechanic. One of his first clients was Larry Hillblom.

By then, Christian was familiar enough with Saipan's wealthiest citizen to think he was full of shit—the type, Christian recalls, who wants people to think he's a pilot, but Hillblom sure as hell didn't know about flying.

Hillblom claimed, for example, that he'd soloed in Hawaii, though he didn't have the records. And it only took one flight for Christian to realize there was no way in hell that Hillblom possessed the skill level he claimed. He figured that Hillblom would keep his distance from someone who knew his little secret, but an arm's-length friendship developed based on Hillblom's need for Christian's skills.

Since then, Christian had flown with Hillblom in several planes to various islands in the Northern Marianas. He'd offered his help and advice on all but one occasion: a month before the SeaBee crash, Long had asked him if he would do some touch-and-gos—quick landings and immediate take-offs—in the lagoon. Christian had refused for two reasons: first off, the lagoon was too rocky; second, in order to land the plane on the water, you needed to take off from the water to know the proper *attitude*.[*] Unlike a land plane, where the pilot normally turns off the power before the wheels hit and catch the nose, a seaplane needs to land with the same power and the same configuration with which it took off. Then the pilot starts to ease back, as with a boat, to bring the plane to a stop.

Long didn't seem to understand the principle of *attitude*, nor did he have any experience with water landings. Worse, Hillblom had more than once pontificated his bullshit theory of water landing: if anything went wrong, you just land it on the water. "That's true, Larry," Christian says he deadpanned, "but it doesn't mean you'll live to tell about it. You'll hit the ocean at 120 miles per hour and the plane will disintegrate."

"Did he listen?" Christian asks rhetorically. "Probably not. Did Bob Long have the personal fortitude to stand up to someone like Hillblom when he told one of his whoppers? Definitely not. Long was hiding his own ignorance." So, in the fall of 1995, when Long's widow, a pretty Filipina, showed up in Christian's office at the Saipan airport to gather evidence for her wrongful death claim, Christian says he sympathized with her but not enough to ignore the obvious. Given the amount of fuel in the main tanks, the SeaBee would have had enough gas to get to Pagan, make a U-turn, and reach Anatahan before dropping out of the sky. Even if the plane's notoriously faulty instruments had alerted Long to trouble,

---

[*] Attitude (not altitude) is a combination of factors unique to every airplane and water situation.

Christian doubted that Hillblom would have interpreted the lack of fuel as dire. Instead, he speculates that Hillblom would have instructed his pilot to glide down and land her on the ocean, even if their only chance was attempting a power-off landing on land. The easily intimidated Long, he reasons, would have complied with the know-it-all billionaire's fatal orders.

Christian tells me that he declined to reveal any of this to Long's widow because he was unwilling to help her squeeze money out of Hillblom's estate. It was Long's job to know his airplane and its capabilities. If the maintenance log was a series of blank pages—and Christian says that it was—then Long had no business flying the plane to begin with. But he *had,* of course, killing himself and two other people with him. When Long's widow asked him what he thought might have happened, Christian bit his tongue.

"I wasn't on the airplane," he told her. "I just don't know."

Forty-One

Emergency

Hearing their version versus the reality is like reading *Bambi* versus a novel by Stephen King, John le Carré, and John Grisham.

—*Barry Israel*

Within a week of David Lujan filing his emergency motion alleging "the grand puppeteer" Peter Donnici's conspiracy to loot Hillblom's estate, the judge ordered up a comprehensive set of hearings to investigate further. These would be officiated not by Castro himself but by a "Special Master"—an officer of the court appointed to investigate a particular issue. Castro wanted to know which of the supposed misdeeds that Lujan had uncovered constituted conflicts of interest or insider dealings. The special master would be given sweeping powers to investigate, not the least of which was the ability to subpoena witnesses. Like a jury, he (or she) would also render judgment on the testimony of those witnesses. And while Castro reserved the ultimate power to issue findings and order remedies, the judge made it clear that he did not plan to second-guess or meddle.

Castro's decision marked a dramatic turnaround from the first hearing, when he had asked Joe Waechter if he was doing what Hillblom might have done, then rubberstamped the executor's to-do list—including the estate's $3.7 million loan to CHC. Peter Donnici's reaction to the appointment of the special master was swift and critical. Neither he nor Waechter, he asserted in a response to Lujan's emergency motion, had done anything wrong. If there were conflicts of interest within the estate, that was Larry Hillblom's fault, not theirs. The special master hearings,

Donnici warned, would turn into nothing more than a fishing expedition for Junior's attorneys.

For the first time, David Lujan happily agreed with him.

Before choosing a special master from the CNMI Bar Association's abnormally thick directory—"Litigation is our biggest industry," Mike Dotts cheerfully informs me—Castro ordered up another fishing expedition. On October 4, the judge subpoenaed Hillblom's medical records from Davies Medical Center, the Straub Medical Center, and Douglas Ousterhout's office. Then he ordered Junior's attorneys and the estate to sign a stipulation providing for the search of Hillblom's residences in Saipan and California, as well as of his Cessna 182 Skylane, which was apparently still impaled upside-down in the Tinian jungle, barely touched since Bruce Jorgensen had reluctantly dragged him from it two years earlier. Each side was to hire biologists for a DNA-gathering junket that would last several weeks and be overseen by a clerk of the court; that way, neither party could dispute the DNA samples' authenticity. For several weeks, Roland Fairfield, the FILC attorney who was handling the DNA portion of Junior's case, skirmished with Carlsmith's big guns in Los Angeles over the extent of the search, as well as the schedule. The estate's attorneys did not want Hillblom's medical records inspected, nor did they want the junket to begin in early October, as ordered by the court. But at eight o'clock on the morning of October 11, on court orders, a team from Carlsmith arrived at Hillblom's front door in Dandan to begin the quest for a piece of Larry Hillblom. They were greeted by David Lujan, Roland Fairfield, and two DNA experts, including a young Canadian molecular biologist named Bradley Popovich. Popovich was paid large sums of money as an expert witness in criminal cases, most famously the double-murder trial of football star O. J. Simpson. Popovich had vouched for the integrity of the DNA samples gathered by police at Simpson's home, but the famed running back had just been acquitted by a jury in California anyway.

As Junior's team moved about Hillblom's empty home (at Mike Dotts's behest, Josephine had moved back to the Philippines for a few weeks) they were followed closely by the estate's attorneys. Popovich's companion, a quirky lab technician from California named Peter Barnett, immedi-

ately noticed something odd. "It was pretty apparent that the house was either not in a condition that somebody would have lived in or the person that lived there was a very strange person," he says. "There weren't a lot of clothing and toiletries and the stuff you'd normally expect to see in a house." In fact, there wasn't anything of Hillblom's at all. When Barnett examined the drains in the master bathroom, they were spotless. Finally, he opened the cabinet beneath the sink, knelt down, and unscrewed the U-shaped trap, which was sure to have gathered some hair, skin flecks, or, at minimum, saliva.

Nothing. The trap was as clean as the day it had been purchased, as though someone had flushed it with acid.

"You know when you stay in a luxury hotel and go in the bathroom?" Barnett remarked to a grim Lujan, standing over him. "Well, this bathroom is probably cleaner than that."

A moment later, they walked out the open front door, empty-handed, and hiked down the long driveway to Hillblom's garage. But the invalid DeLorean and the Civic and even Josephine's MR2 were clean, too, and despite the basketball court and the swimming pool and the tennis court and scattered hand weights, there was no trace of a sweaty gym sock or used towel anywhere on the grounds. For the scientists, who had been flown six thousand miles and were being paid a generous stipend, the search must have been almost as frustrating as it was for David Lujan. But these were not amateurs. They still had their backstop, their *sure* sure thing; the day before, Popovich had sent a pilot to Tinian to confirm the existence of dried blood on the Cessna's instrument panel. Neither of the two passengers in the crash had bled. So by default, the dried blood had to be Hillblom's.

Each of the teams boarded a chartered prop plane at the Saipan airport an hour or so later, lifting off from the same runway that Larry Hillblom, Robert Long, and Jess Mafnas had used four months before. Ten minutes later, they landed at Tinian's tiny airport and migrated toward a macabre crimson sculpture embedded in the jungle just west of the runway.

If not for a tree stump, the Cessna's cockpit might have remained intact, the instrument panel in place, rather than flung forward into the pilot's headrest. Abandoned, quarantined from civilization and cradled by dense knots of vine, the wreckage was an impressive piece of evidence by

anyone's standards. A couple of typhoons had blown through in the past year, but the interior of the plane, including the instrument panel that had crushed the right side of Hillblom's face, had remained sheltered from the elements. As Lujan watched expectantly, Popovich crouched down to peer into the sunlit cockpit where Larry Hillblom had nearly lost his life.

Years later, according to a colleague, Popovich would recall this moment—the moment he realized that the cabin had recently been wiped clean of Hillblom's blood. Nursing a glass of red wine, the molecular biologist would tell his friend how he'd let his imagination get the better of him as he realized that whoever was capable of tampering with evidence despite a court order was probably capable of murder as well. (And what, after all, were the chances of Larry Hillblom's being in two plane crashes within eighteen months?) Popovich had then taken aside one of the dozen attorneys and demanded that at least two members of the estate's team travel back to Saipan on his airplane or else he would make arrangements for himself on the ferry.

Joe Waechter declined to participate in the DNA junket, probably because there were at least a dozen crises for the estate's chief administrator to attend to that month—most recently a letter from the CNMI Department of Finance demanding the immediate payment of more than $11 million in unpaid income taxes and a fax from the Thai contractor building Hillblom's sprawling golf course in Phan Thiet threatening a work stoppage due to nonpayment. However, Waechter was certainly aware of what was going on in Tinian and he knew that Lujan and Co. would soon board an Air Mike flight to Honolulu, in order to inspect Hillblom's medical records at the Straub Clinic. From there they would trek to UCSF–Davies, the site of Hillblom's numerous surgeries, and finally to the ranch at Half Moon Bay, where Hillblom had spent the last few weeks of his recovery in bed with Josephine.

As Lujan, Popovich, and the others boarded the Air Mike flight to Honolulu, Waechter received a call from David Nevitt. At first, Waechter declined to take the call. But his secretary sounded insistent. She said that the estate's lead attorney had some "interesting news" to report.

When he picked up the phone, Nevitt sounded excited. He'd explained

how a lawyer friend had located Junior's *real* father on Palau. Nevitt's friend had refused to give a name though he'd promised that his client would submit to a DNA test as long as the estate agreed to pay him $1 million, $50,000 up front. If the man flunked the test, they would part ways and everything would be kept confidential.

"You're out of your fucking mind, Dave," Waechter barked. The estate wasn't going to pay anything up front. And the notion that anything could be kept confidential on Saipan, particularly anything involving Larry Hillblom's probate, was nuts.

But Nevitt persisted. "Even if it's one in a million, Joe," he implored, "why not do it?"

Waechter let out a deep sigh and promised to talk to Donnici later that night, which was early morning in San Francisco. To his surprise, Donnici agreed with Nevitt: even at one-in-a-million odds, it was worth doing the test. To maintain confidentiality, they would fly Junior's "father" to California. Of course, they would also need Junior's blood to test against, but Waechter suspected this would be the easiest part. One of David Lujan's cocounsels, a guy named Roland Fairfield, had been contacting him since day one. He was desperate to settle. Fairfield, Waechter knew, would get them the blood. It would just have to be their little secret.

Forty-Two

Fishing Expeditions

Larry L. Hillblom's wealth, his unique behavior and his prolific love life make people want to peep, poke and prod into his extraordinary life. The poor are interested in the rich, and the rich are curious about each other, making his life great fodder for any pulp novel.

—Guam Business Magazine

*T*o ensure that no secrets escaped the special master hearings, David Lujan submitted subpoena requests for Peter Donnici, Po Chung, Bill Robinson, Dennis Kerwin, Patrick Donnici, David Jones, Pat Lupo, Steven Schwartz (Hillblom's tax attorney), and every one of the more than two dozen estate claimants, including the Saudi prince who had sent Hillblom the DeLorean. Lujan also filed a request for estate documents listing forty-eight sections, plus subsections. Finally, he demanded Hillblom's medical records and "any and all specimens of tissue, blood, hair and/or fingernail clippings" of Hillblom's family members. Lujan demanded that these be produced within ten days, in time for the hearings, along with the judge's order that approved the estate's loaning money to the Vietnam entities—probably because Lujan knew that no such order existed.

The estate submitted its request to call seventeen witnesses a few days later, but Judge Castro was only too happy to refer both motions to the intense young California native he had just recruited to oversee the interrogations for a fee of $195 an hour, in a vacant federal courtroom a mile up Beach Road.

Rexford "Rex" Kosack was an athlete-trim, handsome former CNMI attorney general. He could have passed for Bob O'Connor's older brother;

in fact, Kosack had taught O'Connor how to surf when they'd both worked in the Ventura County DA's office, and it was Kosack who had recruited O'Connor to Saipan. But where O'Connor seemed laid-back, Kosack had earned a reputation as a meticulous taskmaster who gravitated toward the strictest interpretation of the law. The Carlsmith firm's primary defense would be that Waechter, Donnici, and Lifoifoi had simply acted as Hillblom would have—however unconventional such behavior might appear from the outside. Yet by choosing Kosack to investigate the CHC deal and the two loans that DHL had made to the estate, Castro had sent a clear message: The "What Would Larry Do?" defense would no longer hold.

They used it anyway, with the inevitable result. Waechter's first deposition was such a fiasco that the minute he left the stand he told his attorneys that the estate had lost. "Nonsense," David Nevitt assured him in his folksy twang. "As long as you acted in good faith, you have nothing to worry about."

Peter Donnici only made matters worse. Dragged before Kosack, Lujan, and Israel a few weeks later, Hillblom's former consigliere contradicted Waechter's version of Hillblom's investing in Vietnam, which now seemed clearly illegal, and denied that he had any knowledge of Hillblom doing anything in Vietnam before 1994. (This from the man who had assured the court that he knew more about Larry's business than any living person.) Under a blistering cross-examination, he admitted that the CHC deal—"original sin," as it was now known among some Bank of Saipan directors—had not passed the smell test. "I can see how," Donnici said, "Mr. Lujan could look at this and say, wait a minute, these guys went out and used estate money to buy shares in their name. That stinks! And, maybe, if I had to do it all over again, now, you know being able to be a Monday-morning quarterback and looking back and say, well, maybe I wouldn't have done that."

Things went no better in Brussels, where Pat Lupo was deposed in his office at DHL headquarters, along with the company's chief financial officer, Geoffrey Cruikshanks. Cruikshanks admitted that Junior's inheritance of Hillblom's DHL stock was their "nightmare scenario" while Lupo struggled to convince Kosack and Lujan that Peter Donnici was doing the best he could under very trying circumstances: "Pete was just really trying to do what he knew Larry would have done and he was just absolutely hammered as a consequence of that." Lupo uses a single word to describe his deposition: *disastrous.*

By the time Kosack wrapped up his hearings after Thanksgiving, Po Chung was probably the only one of Hillblom's former associates who emerged unscathed, largely because he did what Larry might have done: he never showed up.

If only that had been the only disaster that winter, or the special master hearings the only fishing expedition. But in late November, with the special master hearings winding down, a Saipan attorney named Randy Fennell walked into the Superior Court Building and filed a lawsuit on behalf of one Baby Jane Doe—the infant daughter of a young bar girl who alleged that Hillblom had met her at a dance club in Manila, taken her back to his condo at the Chateau de Baie, and raped her on an air mattress. When Hillblom subsequently learned that she was pregnant, the mother claimed, he had given her a few hundred dollars and ordered her to get an abortion. Instead, she had fled to a relative's house in the provinces and had the child.

Fennell was a well-respected attorney and dealmaker. He had known Hillblom personally, though he had never been part of his inner circle. Like Hillblom, he had tried to bring casino gambling to Micronesia, had dabbled in banking and real estate, and had been the target of one of Ted Mitchell's Article XII lawsuits. But when Fennell had heard of Hillblom's disappearance and his outdated will, Fennell had sensed an even more lucrative opportunity. He'd flown to Manila, hired a private investigator and an attorney, and posted signs around the local strip clubs Larry had frequented with a photo of Hillblom's face and a local telephone number to call. Fennell's flyers were not unlike the "Wanted" posters that one sees in the post office, except what was wanted in this case were girls who had slept with Larry Hillblom—and who had then either given birth or were now pregnant.

Alongside Baby Jane Doe's paternity claim, Fennell asked the court to order the estate to release anything related to the Philippines in general and Hillblom's Chateau de Baie condominium in particular. Finally, in a pointed reference to allegations that Hillblom's associates had hidden or tampered with evidence, Fennell demanded that the estate produce anything that might establish Hillblom's whereabouts from January 1994 until his death, as well as evidence of the cleaning or removal of bodily DNA evidence from his residences. A few days later, Fennell served deposition notices on Joe Lifoifoi, Waechter, and Josephine. Then he called on his competitor.

"What's alleged," Dotts tells me, "is that Randy tells David: 'What we need to do is settle our current cases for cheap, so that we can get a war chest. Just settle the Palauan boy and this other Filipina for cheap now, because I've got another child that nobody knows about in the Philippines. Once we have the financial means, then we can go full tilt for the entire fortune, for this third child.'"

But Lujan rejected Fennell's overtures. He'd convinced himself that Junior was the only heir; anyone who might take from his share of the pie was therefore the enemy. Yet, within a week of entering the case, Fennell proved that he could be an ally. A stateside attorney he'd hired made a game-changing discovery while examining Hillblom's medical records: a tissue sample that had been cut from Hillblom's face during one of his surgeries in 1993. The "mole," as it quickly became known, was currently stored at the Davies Medical Center lab in downtown San Francisco. Lujan quickly drafted an agreement that would make them Junior and Fennell's client partners—at least until Hillblom's DNA was successfully tested. He attached three conditions. The first was that Fennell would have to immediately disclose the identity of his client and her mother. The second was that they would split the costs 50/50. Finally, Lujan wanted to be reimbursed for half of the money he'd spent on the unsuccessful DNA junket. Only a few months in, the $250,000 that Lujan had committed for the entire case was nearly gone.

The Hillblom probate was becoming a war of attrition, and that clearly favored the estate—a fact that was not lost on its lead attorney, David Nevitt. Not only did Carlsmith have access to the estate's assets, but Pat Lupo had promised Peter Donnici that DHL would loan the Hillblom Charitable Trust millions of dollars to tag-team David Lujan and

Randy Fennell. On December 1, a confident Nevitt asserted the special master hearings had proved Lujan's claims to be "wholly without merit." Alongside that audacious rewriting of recent history, moreover, was an uncomfortable reality: Junior's blood had not matched the Palauan man who claimed to be his father. Further, a well-connected private investigator—the former police chief of the FSM—whom Nevitt had hired to find other potential fathers had failed to do so. And an exhaustive search for Hillblom's vasectomy records, inspired by interviews with Grant Anderson and Carla Bostom, had turned up nothing.

By December 3, as Nevitt looked out his office window and onto the shimmering Saipan Lagoon below, he was caving in to the inevitable—a settlement offer. He knew that Donnici thought reaching out to Lujan was a mistake; he believed that by offering Junior anything, they were simply setting the bar for a protracted negotiation with David Lujan and Randy Fennell while inviting other "heirs" to come forward. Deep in thought, Nevitt barely heard the knock as his secretary walked in and deposited a fax on his desk. Her eyes told him it was urgent.

Randy Fennell was the sender. In uncharacteristically clipped sentences, Fennell excoriated Joe Waechter's refusal thus far to negotiate a settlement with Junior and Baby Jane Doe, and then accused the executor of engineering the vanishing, and potentially the murder, of a second potential Hillblom heiress—referred to simply as "Baby M." Fennell also alleged that Waechter had ordered him and Jane Doe roughed up by airport security on their way out of the Philippines a few days before. Of course, Nevitt would plead ignorance, but Fennell had given him an ultimatum: if the estate did not come clean on its involvement in or knowledge of "M"'s disappearance by 9:30 a.m.—the following day—Fennell would go to the press.

Nevitt called Baby Jane Doe's attorney to buy some time. Fennell stewed for several days but then proved as good as his word. On December 8, under the headline "For Immediate Dissemination," Fennell launched an incendiary fax—addressed not to Nevitt but to the press. First, he wrote, his office had been "led to believe" that Joe Waechter had contacted "M," Baby M's mother, a serious breach of legal ethics. "M," Fennell continued, was only fifteen years old, and was only fourteen when she had been "sexually accosted and impregnated by Larry

Lee Hillblom." Waechter, Fennell alleged, may have co-opted a poor, uneducated, and vulnerable young girl and was probably steering her to use the estate's handpicked attorneys. Why? "They know," Fennell wrote, "the mother can testify to Hillblom's sexual relations with minors and to Hillblom's employees' and business associates' knowledge of these relations." Not only that, Fennell wrote, but Hillblom's employees had broken U.S., Philippine, and CNMI law by procuring minors for sex with him. Waechter and his goons, Fennell predicted, would soon launch a PR campaign to divert attention from Larry Hillblom's criminal pedophilia.

A few days later, Fennell folded the press release's major points into an affidavit that added a startling new accusation: a DHL employee in Manila had recently asked Waechter if he wanted M and her daughter killed. Though the affidavit acknowledged that Waechter had declined the offer, Fennell laid out the possibility of a conspiracy between the estate and M's mother to silence Fennell's unborn client:

> On Monday, November 27, 1995, I received a telephone call from one of the Philippines attorneys who frantically informed me that M and her family was [sic] missing. The attorney told me that M and her family had left the investigator's house the night before to see a movie, but that they did not return, leaving clothes and personal effects behind. The attorney informed me that the investigator had been to the apartment where M and the rest of her family had been living, and that the entire family was missing. According to neighbors, the entire family had left the night before and never returned. . . . My fear is that M's mother has once again "sold out" her daughter's interests and those of the unborn child, which is well-founded based on her actions to date. . . . I intend to utilize every effort to find out what happened to M and her family. I pray that I am not too late. . . .

Five days after the press release and two days after Fennell's affidavit rocked Saipan, Dotts stormed out of his office in the Nauru Building and into Judge Castro's humid courtroom to respond to both. He was joined in front of the bar by David Lujan; Kevin Moore, one of David Nevitt's partners; and, of course, Fennell, a tall, attractive, and supremely confident man with the toned thickness of an overgrown frat boy.

The purpose of the hearing was to determine whether or not the parties in the Hillblom probate had a right to learn the identity of Jane Doe and Baby Doe Hillblom. But it was obviously going to address much more than that; it might even determine whether or not Larry Hillblom would be remembered as a criminal and whether Joe Waechter was capable of kidnapping and murder. As soon as Castro took his seat, Dotts rose abruptly from his chair. The gerbil's anger was palpable. Although Fennell dwarfed him in size, Dotts seemed bigger as he demanded that Fennell's affidavit be struck from the record, calling it "scandalous" to refer to his former boss as a pedophile and someone who would have been arrested on the mainland.

Moore immediately picked up the thread: "Can I just add something to that, Your Honor?" he said breathlessly. "It's evident—from the most cursory reading in Mr. Fennell's affidavit, it is an amazing compilation of hearsay, double hearsay, triple hearsay. Mr. Fennell's conjecture, Mr. Fennell's gestures, and no facts! Mr. Dotts is absolutely right. It should be struck. It is—it is one of the most incredible things that I've ever seen."

Castro asked Fennell to respond. The lanky attorney uncurled his frame and explained that he'd had to rely on hearsay because the sources of his information did not want to implicate themselves in acts of pedophilia, which was, he noted, indeed a crime. As for keeping Jane Doe's and Baby Doe's identities secret, Fennell added, he was just trying to get everybody through this difficult process alive. The Philippines, after all, were filled with lawless elements who would kidnap his clients the moment their names became public.

Lujan rose. As usual, the only nonwhite lawyer present, he addressed the judge directly, reminding Castro that the Philippines was not the only place with criminals, that even in the United States, in Guam for example, there was "ice," aka crystal meth. "Not a simple sweat of evidence has been presented to this court," Lujan said, "that the lawlessness element in the Philippines is directing its attention to Baby Jane Doe.

"Incidentally," he added, "if Jane Doe were kidnapped and held for ransom, it would serve no one, really. Whoever the kidnapper is who decides to kidnap this child without this child being pronounced to be Hillblom's child would be the most stupid kidnapper."

"There are stupid kidnappers, contrary to what Mr. Lujan thinks," Fennell shot back.

Castro allowed the attorneys to vent a little longer, then, grim-faced as usual, he adjourned the hearing without ruling on whether or not Fennell's client could remain anonymous.

"M" would come forward on her own a short time later—at the behest of a pair of Manila family law attorneys named Luz Manlapaz and Gerry Paras. M's name was Mercedes Feliciano. She was a fifteen-year-old native of Parañaque, one of the dirtiest and most dangerous slums in Manila. The year before, she had met Hillblom at a strip club where her sister worked as a dancer. And she felt lucky to be there. Her mother needed money to take care of her blind sister, Rumila, and Mercedes had been turned down by several clubs for looking too young. Her affidavit contained a few heartbreaking details of her relationship with Larry: fending off much older men at the club until Hillblom immediately agreed to pay her "cherry fee"; her mother negotiating the end of her virginity with Hillblom and a DHL employee at a Manila KFC; being led into his bedroom at a resort in the southern Philippines, with her mother and Joe Lifoifoi (and his girlfriend) in adjoining rooms; waiting in vain for Larry to return after she became pregnant, because he had promised he would marry her.

Thankfully, Mercedes, aka "the Benz," had not been murdered or even kidnapped by Hillblom's former employees. Nor had her mother sold her out a second time. Rather, at the behest of her mother, Mercedes had been rescued by a family friend from the home of Randy Fennell's investigator, where she had become a prisoner, and ultimately, a pawn in the Hillblom probate. "The investigator," Mike Dotts explains, "was saying, 'You need to have a cesarean.' There was a deadline coming up in the probate for claims. And they wanted the baby born before the deadline, so they were telling Grandma, 'We need to get a cesarean for your grandchild.' And that freaked her out and that's why they fled."

Fennell moved forward with his remaining client. And he soon revealed her identity, though only after bringing her family to Saipan and secur-

ing a work visa for her mother, who would soon become the attorney Jim Sirok's maid. Jane Doe was Julie Cuartero; Baby Jane Doe was Jellian. Not that their names really mattered. Everyone knew there were thousands of Jane Does back in Manila and hundreds of those had probably slept with Larry. Hillblom's taste in girls had proven remarkably unremarkable.

Fennell then asked for a delay so he could be present for the testing of the Hillblom mole. And he issued a number of subpoenas, including one for Dotts's client, Josephine. It deserves mention here that had she been forced to testify that winter, her chances of receiving a settlement would have been quashed. Without immunity, she might have been deported— or worse. But Randy Fennell's subpoena would not fall into Josephine's delicate hands for some time. "Fennell's process server couldn't get his car up the hill to Hillblom's house." Dotts grins. "Larry always thought that Fennell was kind of lazy."

Judgment

fiduciary

1) n. from the Latin fiducia, meaning "trust," a person who has the power and obligation to act for another (often called the beneficiary) under circumstances which require total trust, good faith and honesty.

beneficiary

1) n. any person or entity who is to receive assets or profits from an estate, a trust, an insurance policy or any instrument in which there is distribution.

—www.dictionary.law.com

"We were furious when we found out that the FILC attorneys had given Donnici a sample of Junior's blood for nothing," Barry Israel tells me. "At the same time," he adds, "when they made a big settlement offer, then we knew that they knew Junior was his." The estate's offer was relayed to Israel and Lujan by David Nevitt in early December. Nevitt offered $5 million up front plus $50,000 per month for life, guaranteed for up to thirty years, plus $500,000 every five years, net of taxes. "Our first counteroffer for Junior that we made to Donnici included DHL shares and a board seat for Junior," Israel adds. Nevitt angrily rejected it, as expected; after all, Junior's owning those shares was the "nightmare scenario." But Israel and Lujan's partners at the Family Immigration and Law Clinic were equally furious that they'd turned down money on the table. In a tense conference call, the FILCers bemoaned the money they could have made, until Israel finally cut them

off. "You should be ashamed of yourself!" he growled and hung up the phone.

One hundred twenty miles to the north, the special master, Rex Kosack, plodded through more than three thousand pages of interview transcripts, and half again as many exhibits. By working endless days, he managed to produce a preliminary report in less than six weeks. When I request a copy from Dex, the assistant clerk of the CNMI Superior Court, I am mistakenly handed two versions—one heavily redacted and the other not at all. Without revealing what I am not allowed to reveal, I can divulge that virtually all of the sealed information concerns DHL's operations in Saudi Arabia; none has to do with the estate or its management.

Kosack's 124-page final report, which he turned in to Judge Castro in early February, begins with a brief history of DHL and an inventory of the estate's other assets. The special master then describes the creation of the Hillblom estate and the takeover of its executor, the Bank of Saipan, by CHC, before turning its full attention to its chief administrator: Joe Waechter. That's when Kosack throws down the legal gauntlet: the executor, he writes, is by definition a fiduciary of the estate and its beneficiaries. Therefore, according to the Law of Trust and Trustees, Waechter and his associates at the bank are bound by a two-part duty of loyalty: one, a prohibition against self-dealing; and, two, a requirement that any conflict of interest, either real or potential, be completely avoided. The language in Hillblom's will directing his executors to do what he would have done, as well as the argument that conflicts of interest existed to begin with and were simply carried over into the estate when Hillblom died are dismissed with a single word: *irrelevant.*

Kosack does acknowledge that the probate has been made unusually complex by virtue of the unconventional way in which Hillblom structured his empire. And he warns that he will not make either side happy before itemizing the ten major transactions that Joe Waechter has executed thus far, including the CHC deal, the DHL loans, and the inventory. Within these transactions, Kosack cites eleven instances in which Waechter and Peter Donnici have engaged in self-dealing or conflicts of interest. Kosack states unequivocally that the scheme to take control of the estate was illegal—just as Lujan had alleged. Moreover, Waechter's role as executor of the estate and Donnici's role as chairman of the trust while they remained directors and executives of estate-owned companies, Kosack asserts, create a pattern of being on both sides of every transaction. Even if they have not benefited personally from these transactions, they are just as guilty, because the duty of loyalty is absolute.

There is plenty in these first paragraphs that must have concerned Hill-blom's old friends, but Kosack's report is far from finished. Because, he continues, Donnici has claims against the estate—for stock that Hillblom had been holding on his behalf, in lieu of payment for legal services—participating in estate business virtually guarantees him a favorable resolution of his claims over others. And although, during the time of the hearings, Donnici, Waechter, and Lifoifoi dissolved CHC and transferred its Bank of Saipan shares to the estate—something they claimed to have planned to do all along—the bank's board remains stacked with their nominees. This, Kosack observes, could prove very much to their future benefit.

To say that Peter Donnici did not agree with Kosack's conclusions would be an understatement. During one of our two interviews, Hill-blom's former consigliere and friend intimated that Kosack was motivated by a personal grudge. At the time, however, Donnici made no such allegation. Instead, he toed the familiar line that Hillblom's friends were just doing what they knew Larry would have done—and they should be allowed to do it without being second-guessed. "I know more than any other living human being about the business activities of, assets owned by, and potential business-related claims against Mr. Hillblom prior to his unfortunate and tragic death," an indignant Donnici would write to Castro. "I know the nature of Mr. Hillblom's business relations with third parties and the extent to which Mr. Hillblom attempted to keep some of these business matters and relationships *confidential.*"

But the "trust us" argument failed to convince Castro, just as it had failed to convince Kosack. A short while later, the judge would adopt the Special Master Report in its entirety and ask for suggested punishments. So Donnici turned to a more academic argument: Throughout his report, Kosack had considered Junior and the two young Filipina girls as *beneficiaries* of Hillblom's estate rather than outsiders. If these children were suddenly the equals of the chief beneficiary named under Hillblom's will, the medical trust that Donnici was to establish, then the estate would be prevented from contesting their paternity claims because it could not favor one beneficiary over another. This scenario would leave the estate defenseless against a trio of children who had never been a part of Hillblom's life. Leaving them his fortune was clearly not what Hillblom had intended, nor did Donnici believe such a scenario was good law. Indeed, there was plenty of precedent to suggest that the unacknowledged children, "putative heirs" as the law called them, were outsiders challenging Hillblom's will. Therefore, Donnici believed, Hillblom's executor not only had the right but the obligation to defend the estate, and arguably by any means it deemed necessary.

Forty-Four

Lobbying

"**T**hey're saying that we stole from Larry!" Joe Lifoifoi groused into his cell phone. Waechter had just told him about Rex Kosack's report and the islander was stunned. How could anyone have accused him of being anything less than loyal to Larry? he demanded. He owed nearly everything in his life, including his wife, Amalia's, cancer treatments, to Larry. Larry had even named an apartment building on Saipan for him and paid—anonymously!—for the renovation of his church in Tanapag. If Kosack had found some legal problems with the way that CHC was structured, fine. Lifoifoi was no lawyer. But how could Kosack prove theft? Lifoifoi had never benefited from CHC—or from any part of Larry's estate.

On the other end of the line, Waechter offered no answers. He himself had become so vilified that, when his visage had flashed across the television at a popular Saipan bar a few days earlier, one of its customers had given it the finger and shouted "liar" until the bartender turned it off. The CHC deal had poisoned the well and Lujan's sucker punches were connecting. Judge Castro would certainly fire Waechter as executor, though he might have to keep the bank involved so as not to put the estate in default of the DHL loans. Lifoifoi, Waechter said, would need to meet a final time with the estate's lead attorney, David Nevitt, about plan B.

Unbeknownst to the court, Lifoifoi had been trekking to Carlsmith's office once a week since October to discuss "clarifying" the CNMI's probate code, to no effect, but Lifoifoi immediately promised Waechter that he would meet with Nevitt one more time. As Larry had promised the day he'd been hired at UMDA, Lifoifoi's time had finally come.

"We've had a couple of our guys in Los Angeles working on the probate code," Nevitt tossed out after Lifoifoi sank into his usual chair, "so Joe asked me to sit down with you today and work out something that you could present to the Legislature quickly."

"How fast?" was Lifoifoi's only question.

"This week, if possible." Nevitt added, "We were hoping that there were things we could do on a more limited basis than change the entire code."

Lifoifoi nodded. "Maybe just a few things. It's easier to amend an existing law than push through something brand-new."

"That's what we were thinking, too." Nevitt smiled and handed him a fax from an attorney at Carlsmith's Los Angeles office—a memo attached to what Lifoifoi would later call a wish list but what was really the outline of a bill to gut CNMI's probate code. Most glaring was a paragraph that would amend paternity laws retroactively; under the new bill, a father would have had to "openly and notoriously" acknowledge a child before his death, which included taking his son or daughter into his home in order for them to be considered heirs. The bill would also outlaw contingency fees and would specifically authorize an estate to use its assets in order to defend against heirship claims. Most audacious, however, was a clause that made DNA evidence inadmissible as proof of paternity.

Lifoifoi nodded his approval. You didn't need a law degree to understand that the bill checkmated Junior, Baby Jane Doe, Baby "M," and whomever else the attorneys dredged from the Manila slums. Then he lifted himself out of his chair. The drive to his next destination would take less than five minutes.

The CNMI government operates out of two dozen white bunkers erected atop Capital Hill by the U.S. Navy Seabees shortly after the end of World War II, a complex originally built for the training of Chinese spies by Office of Naval Intelligence (ONI) agents, the precursor to the CIA. The largest of these buildings, a two-story monolith that resembles a high school gym, houses the Legislature. The gallery is little more than an oversize conference room with a U-shaped table. When the Legislature is in session, the Speaker and a clerk sit or stand behind the curve. Seventeen representatives from Saipan, Rota, and Tinian cluster the sides in swiveling black office chairs. Their districts range in size from slightly more than 14,000 residents to well under 150. Lifoifoi could have found his way around the building blindfolded. He had been elected to serve here three times, once as Speaker of the House.

The gallery was empty this morning, so Lifoifoi strode down a white-washed hallway and into the office of his friend, Representative Oscar Babauta. After dispensing with the normal pleasantries, Lifoifoi handed him Nevitt's fax.

Babauta looked it over twice, chuckling. Then he shook his head. He read the newspapers. There was no question what this bill was designed to do.

"I can amend some of the language," Lifoifoi offered, almost as an apology. "I'm not entirely comfortable with it yet myself. But I think you should go ahead and draft the bill and have it introduced. We can polish it up later."

"What's the hurry?" Babauta grinned.

"We need to do it now," Lifoifoi said, "because it looks like there's gonna be a lot of these girls filing a claim. They're coming out of the woodwork."

"How many now, two?"

"Three."

"And you think there's gonna be more?"

Lifoifoi shrugged his shoulders.

"Why the hell didn't Larry take care of the boy?" Babauta said.

"I asked him," Lifoifoi replied. "I said, If that's your son, then you better start taking care of this boy, you know? You better give him some money for his school. His bags, his clothes. He just says no."

"Joe," Babauta finally said, "I'll help you improve the probate code. But this 'openly and notoriously acknowledge' language, and this stuff about 'bringing the child into his own home,' those just are not acceptable standards. You know, what if the father dies before the kid is born? Or moves away?"

"We can fix that later."

"I'll give it to Maya," Babauta finally said, referring to Maya Kara, the House of Representatives' chief legal counsel. "I'll see what we need to do."

"Thanks," Lifoifoi said. But if the court said it was unconstitutional, he would just revise it again and again until it stuck.

Babauta pushed the fax aside and changed the subject. They talked for a while longer about their late friend Jess Mafnas, in whose honor the building in which they now sat was to be named. Mafnas's widow was suing the estate for negligence and the rumor was that she had recently turned down a settlement offer of $2 million. But the Mafnas family had problems of their own: an illegitimate son of Jess's had popped up out of nowhere and was suing for his piece of the inheritance.

Then they talked about Larry—how he'd made his friends laugh by using the word *papalatto* to describe liars and otherwise deceptive people. For years, they had assumed *papalatto* was Tagalog—until a Filipino told them that there was no such word. Larry had just made it up to play a joke on them. Who knew what else he'd made up? Maybe he'd invented the word *papalatto* to describe himself. Or maybe he had meant the term to apply to his former friends, the ones who were a dime a dozen, the ones who were swarming Asia, the CNMI courthouse, and Capital Hill as they sought to dismantle his empire.

Forty-Five

The Hillblom Bill

"A re you James Scurlock?"

I will admit that, after living in Saipan for five months, the possibility that I might become *known* has crossed my mind more than once. The island is small, Larry Hillblom was by far its most famous resident, and dozens of attorneys who became involved in the case still live here. In my most delusional moments, I imagine being sought after by those who want to be certain that Hillblom's biographer gets their side of the story right. However, having spent most weekdays—from 7:30 a.m. until 4:00 p.m. at least—in a cubbyhole adjoining the CNMI Superior Court clerk's office for what already seems like an eternity, being spoon-fed files (one at a time) from *In the Matter of the Estate of Larry Lee Hillblom,* I have learned otherwise. The employees of the clerk's office are suspicious or aloof. The few attorneys who encounter me on their way to their wooden mailboxes ignore the figure hunched over an unsteady Formica counter, increasingly soft ass molded around the edge of a broken chair that sits far too low, transcribing entire pleadings by hand in tiny block letters. Until today, at least, when a quick twist of the head reveals a middle-aged man of medium height and military build in a pressed white shirt and tie, face framed by wire-rimmed lenses.

When I confirm that, yes, I am James Scurlock, he extends his right arm and introduces himself as Peter Woodruff.

Now I realize that every attorney on-island is aware of me, especially those who have pointedly ignored my presence. Woodruff hands me his card, offers that if I ever want to talk about Larry, he'd be glad to meet with me. After being ignored for so long, it's a welcome bit of luck; Woodruff was the CNMI Senate's counsel at the time that House Bill 10–147, soon to be known as the Hillblom Bill, was introduced to the CNMI Legislature by Oscar Babauta.

Days later, I climb the steps of Woodruff's law office—a modest two-story converted home across from the Saipan Cathedral that he shares with Joe Hill, Junior Larry Hillbroom's local counsel. From behind a desk piled with briefs and law books, Woodruff recounts his arrival on Saipan as a Peace Corps volunteer before the Commonwealth came into existence, how he worked as a political adviser and hotel food-and-beverage manager before going to law school at a late age. Upon graduation, Woodruff says, he was immediately hired by the CNMI Senate. He was not one of Hillblom's friends, but they knew one another as well as Hillblom seemed to know anyone and they'd even debated the Covenant from time to time. Hillblom had once invited Woodruff to join a flying school he started at the Saipan airport, but Woodruff (wisely) had declined. His admiration for Hillblom's political skills becomes clear as he recounts how Larry used his money* and his intellect to shape the law here, particularly his success at protecting the CNMI's tax rebate. Just as obvious is Woodruff's disdain for Joe Waechter, David Nevitt, and Nevitt's cronies at the Carlsmith firm. That they would contest Junior's paternity, Woodruff says, is patently dishonest because it was common knowledge on Palau, where Woodruff's wife was from, that Junior was Larry's. Any denial of Junior's paternity, Woodruff says with absolute conviction, must have been motivated by greed. But Woodruff saves his harshest criticism for the bill that Joe Lifoifoi drove up to Capital Hill in February 1996.

"It was just the worst piece of legislation!" Woodruff shakes his head. "The purpose of the Hillblom Bill was to cut off all of these claims. That was the intent. And the problem there, as all of the attorneys up there [at the Legislature] agreed, was that when Larry died, the rights of the heirs vested. And for the Legislature to come in later on and to change the rules and redefine who qualifies as a pretermitted heir so as to cut off all of these

---

* By this, Woodruff does not mean bribes but rather Hillblom's willingness to hire outside lawyers and lobbyists to push his agenda. Of course, it probably did not hurt that Hillblom took groups of legislators on junkets to his ranch in Half Moon Bay and a ski chalet that he purchased in Méribel, France—where, according to some of them, he played video games by himself into the early hours.

people is a violation of due process. And even equal protection. You can analyze it in a couple of different ways."

Of course, Peter Donnici and the estate's attorneys both took exception to this theory. The Hillblom Bill, they argued, was simply a *procedural* change, meaning that nothing substantive had been altered, so it could not have been altered retroactively. And Donnici had found at least one legal legend to agree with him: Charles Alan Wright, the nation's foremost expert on civil procedure and constitutional law. Wright was the author of *Federal Practice and Procedure,* a text that most of the Commonwealth's young attorneys, including Woodruff, had studied in law school. "I was appalled by that!" Woodruff says. "I was going, 'Professor Wright was willing to stoop that low?' And for what? For money would be the only reason for doing it. So, you know, that's one of those things that really makes you wonder, too, about the integrity of the system, because this is one of the most respected commentators on the law in the country and he's writing an affidavit like that in connection with this case. You know, you wonder, when large amounts of money are involved, what happens to people's judgment?"

That sentiment was echoed by several legislators, including Representative David Apatang, during its rushed debate on Capital Hill. "I do not see the urgency to pass this bill now," Apatang said in open session. "Why are we changing the law all of a sudden?" He implored his colleagues to protect the many, the CNMI's illegitimate children, rather than "the livelihood of those children whose fathers deny them their true identity."

But Apatang and Woodruff were in the minority back then. Over the objections of its own counsel, the CNMI House passed the Hillblom Bill on its first reading in late February 1996, after suspending the rules so that a legal opinion was not necessary. It sailed through the Senate on a 6–3 vote several weeks later. The Senate required a second reading when the bill encountered a stubborn headwind: Woodruff's refusal to rubber-stamp the law for "legal sufficiency," as required by law. After the final vote, Joe Lifoifoi and a Bank of Saipan board member high-fived in the Legislature's gallery, where they'd watched the vote through a glass picture window. Lifoifoi joked that the bill should really be called the "Lifoifoi Law."

But the difficult part still lay ahead. In order for the Hillblom Bill to become the Hillblom Law, Lifoifoi would need to obtain the signature of the governor: Froilan Cruz Tenorio.

Froilan, as everyone calls him, was known to be unpredictable and something of a maverick. He had not graduated from the University of Guam like Lifoifoi and most of the other Micronesian elite. Nor had he been involved in the Congress of Micronesia or the drafting of the Covenant. Froilan had attended Marquette University in Milwaukee, graduated with a civil engineering degree, and then worked for the City of Los Angeles for five years before starting his own construction company in Saipan.

And unlike most members of the Legislature, Froilan had not been a friend of Larry Hillblom's. In fact, he had originally lost the governorship to Hillblom's good friend Larry Guerrero, winning only after he created his own political party based on libertarian principles. Like most politicians, however, Froilan had sparred with Hillblom over the interpretation of the Covenant. If the United States wanted to claim sovereignty over the CNMI, Froilan had admonished Hillblom, that was fine with him and most islanders. Ditto for foreign policy. In Froilan's view, all the islanders wanted was a chance to run their economy in a way that made sense for them and not for New York City. During his single term as governor, Froilan tripled the number of sweatshops on-island and rejected tens of millions of dollars in federal aid, in the hope that the U.S. Congress would leave him alone.

In the spring and summer of 1996, as Joe Lifoifoi lobbied him relentlessly on Capital Hill and at barbecues, Froilan made it clear that he was in no hurry to do Larry Hillblom's estate a favor. The governor was focused on other matters, like protecting the island's profitable garment industry from stateside inspectors. When I meet Froilan twelve years later in a small café on Saipan, he feigns ignorance of the Hillblom Bill, though he allows that it sounds familiar. I will have to assume that neither Froilan nor his attorney general studied the Hillblom Bill's single precedent, a copy of which thankfully resides in the Hillblom Law Library, bound in a collection of Supreme Court opinions now at my fingertips, curiously untouched.

The case had begun in 1991, when the illegitimate son of a wealthy Chamorro landowner named DeLeon Guerrero had sued for a piece of his father's estate in CNMI Superior Court. DeLeon Guerrero had never acknowledged his son, David Camacho, now a middle-aged man; nor, during his father's life, had Camacho ever filed suit to prove his paternity. In fact, Camacho's birth certificate had made no mention of a father at all.

Camacho's alleged half sister, who had been appointed executor of her father's estate, had refused to allow him to participate in the probate and claimed that the CNMI law precluded him from doing so. Although she raised a number of objections to defend their father's estate from his challenge, the overriding issue was whether or not Camacho could be considered an heir or simply an outsider with an unproven claim.

Many islanders (including Joe Lifoifoi and Jess Mafnas) had illegitimate children whom they openly acknowledged and provided for. Being a bastard on Saipan was not as scandalous as it might be in parts of the United States, with its quasi-puritanical values, or in the Philippines, where President Corey Aquino had famously instructed hospitals to brand the birth certificates of illegitimate babies with a bright pink stamp. In researching the islands' young probate laws, the justices discovered not only that Camacho had a right to participate in his father's probate as a pretermitted* heir but that the court could establish a parental determination. And since Camacho's rights had vested at the time of his father's death, disallowing him from the proceedings would be unconstitutional, not only violating due process but denying the son a vested property right—exactly as Woodruff had explained to me earlier.

In its final opinion, the Supreme Court determined that Camacho's claim was "more accurately described as an heirship claim under probate proceedings rather than a paternity claim." In the CNMI, an illegitimate child was thus officially an heir, not a claimant. Camacho's incomplete birth certificate was disregarded as irrelevant. CNMI law, the court stated,

---

* The child of a person who has written a will in which the child is not left anything and is not mentioned at all.

"recognizes that the natural father of a child, under certain circumstances, may be different from the husband of the child's mother or what is stated in the child's birth certificate."

The decision was signed by Special Judge Larry Lee Hillblom, with the two other judges concurring.

Forty-Six

Reinforcements

"There's always been a history of racism," Mike Dotts throws out during one of our long beachside lunches. "That, you know, the people on the island sleep under coconut trees and really don't know anything about the law or the legal system. So, quite often, attorneys arrive from overseas to kind of teach us the way things work, and, quite often, they're handed their hat and they end up leaving with their tail between their legs. Historically, off-island hotshots have not done well on Saipan." Out of the dozens of stateside attorneys who became involved in the Hillblom probate, Dotts is referring to one in particular: Yeoryios Apallas.

Apallas, a bearded and dapper Greek immigrant fond of seersucker suits and fedoras, is now general counsel of a beer distributor; he works out of a nondescript two-story suburban office building just north of San Francisco—thirty miles south of the Larry Lee Hillblom Foundation's headquarters in Petaluma. In the spring of 1996, however, Apallas was employed by the California Attorney General's office in Sacramento. His business card read: "Deputy Attorney General/Charitable & Trusts Division." Part of Apallas's job was to ensure that philanthropic organizations received the funds bequeathed them by rich Californians.

Until February 1996, Apallas had never stepped outside of the state in an official capacity, nor had his boss or any of his fellow deputy attorneys general. But that month he received a phone call from the counsel to the University of California Board of Regents, who himself had been contacted by someone involved in the probate of Larry Lee Hillblom, the founder of DHL and member of the Forbes 400. Hillblom, the Regents'

attorney told Apallas, had died in a plane crash the previous summer and had left his fortune to a trust that he had instructed to fund medical research within the University of California system. However, events on a tiny island in the Western Pacific were conspiring to deny the UC system its windfall.

Apallas was overnighted a copy of CNMI Superior Court Case 95-626: *In the Matter of the Estate of Larry Lee Hillblom*. Poring over the thousands of pages of motions, pleadings, and affidavits, as well as Rex Kosack's Special Master Report, the deputy AG discovered a probate in crisis. An attorney named David Lujan was filing pleadings loaded with ad hominem attacks against both Joe Waechter, the executor, and Peter Donnici, the chairman of the Hillblom Charitable Trust; his latest referred to Hillblom's former associates as "rascals." Emergency motions were being filed on a nearly daily basis and for the most pedestrian of reasons. DNA samples had been collected but no testing protocol had been established, nor was it clear that any of the samples, mainly snippets of bloodstained sheets from Hillblom's ranch in Half Moon Bay, were usable. The judge, an islander named Alex Castro, seemed unsure as to whether the estate could legally defend itself against paternity claims and he had allowed an inordinate number of attorneys, claimants, and experts into the case as "interested parties," generating hundreds of pages of pleadings a day and allowing hearings to last for twelve hours or longer. On top of all this, the estate was insolvent. Peter Donnici's attorney had summed it up neatly in one of the more recent briefs splayed across Apallas's desk: "The proceedings with respect to the probate of Larry Lee Hillblom's Estate are in a state of disarray."

Apallas's first conclusion was that the judge had utterly lost control; such a large and complex case, he figured, required a larger and more sophisticated venue—preferably a California court. It also needed a viceroy to police the warring factions, a role that, the more Apallas read, the more eager he was to play himself. But when Apallas brought the case to his boss, a staunchly conservative and deeply religious man named Dan Lungren, the AG did not share his enthusiasm. Sending attorneys to Saipan would be expensive, Lungren knew, and few voters would understand the benefit of getting involved in a probate halfway around the world. And even if they *did* understand, taking sides on behalf of an alleged pedophile

against poor young women and their babies was certainly not the kind of street fight that a politician—or a religious man—like Lungren would be eager to join. But Apallas persisted. Estimates of Hillblom's net worth were rising by the day. At minimum, the trust established in his will would provide hundreds of millions of dollars for medical research—perhaps enough to fund a major breakthrough or even cure a disease. To sit back and allow that money to be snatched off the table by a bunch of greedy lawyers on a tiny island in the middle of nowhere would be immoral.

By the time Lungren finally caved, Apallas had prepared his first, supremely confident, pleading—a document so pretentious and grandiose that it purported to reframe the entire probate in the estate's favor. According to Apallas, Hillblom was "a great and generous man—a global visionary—who wanted to improve the quality of life for all mankind." Peter Donnici and Joe Waechter were "well-meaning friends" who had been a little clumsy. Rex Kosack, meanwhile, had produced an "extraordinary document," but it was also "fundamentally flawed" because the three children suing the estate could not legally be considered beneficiaries until they proved their biological relationship to Hillblom. In fact, before Apallas had set foot into Castro's courtroom, he had already coined a new term for Junior, Mercedita, and Jellian: *presumed* beneficiaries. As such, Apallas wrote the court, they were owed nothing whatsoever.

But the deputy attorney general's pleading went much further. The estate not only *possessed* the right to defend itself from paternity claims, Apallas admonished Castro, it was *obligated* to do so. In fact, if the estate did not fight back hard enough, Apallas wrote, the AG's office might sue the Bank of Saipan and its attorneys for negligence. But Apallas concluded his missive on a conciliatory note: "The protagonists in the Estate should sheath their swords and get down to doing what is best for the interests of Larry Hillblom's Estate and the vision he left behind. . . . March we all must do. . . . Let's get the business of who did what to whom behind us. . . . Let's get down to the business of getting this money to work for mankind as Mr. Hillblom had intended. Larry would have expected nothing less from us."

Apallas's missive landed on Saipan to a reception that might have awaited a giant turd. Randy Fennell demanded that "Mr. Apallas should promptly identify any authority on which he relies in support of his con-

tention that the California Attorney General can go wandering around the United States and its possessions looking for large probates to intervene in." David Lujan implored Castro to throw the deputy attorney general's letter into the trash can—"where," he scoffed, "it belongs." Both attorneys called out the hypocrisy of an attorney general demanding to enter a case without local counsel, as required by law. But on this last point, Apallas's excuse was incontrovertible: there were, he observed, no attorneys left on Saipan who were not already involved in Hillblom's probate.

Forty-Seven

Feeding Frenzy

One can only conclude that Donnici and Hillblom had been
in a criminal conspiracy regarding trading with the enemy
[in Vietnam] and the conspiracy continues to today with the
assistance and connivance of Waechter. . . . Their secretiveness
speaks volumes.

—Barry Israel, January 1996

Castro invited Apallas into his already overcrowded courtroom a week
later. Once inside, however, the deputy attorney general realized that
the documents he'd studied had not told the whole story. The most contentious question swirling around Hillblom's probate was not the validity
of Rex Kosack's Special Master Report or the constitutionality of the Hillblom Bill or whether the "mole" should be tested or whether Larry Hillblom was a criminal, for that matter. What all the parties really wanted to
know was: *How much was Larry worth?*

Officially, the number was $422 million—the sum of Joe Waechter's
latest inventory. Slightly more than half of that amount derived from
Hillblom's shares in DHL Corporation and DHL, International; the rest
was a hodgepodge of Hillblom's other investments: UMDA, Vietnam,
Continental Airlines, cellular licenses, and real estate, including the huge
ranch in Half Moon Bay, an island in Greece, and a ski chalet in Méribel,
France.

But Waechter's total was highly subjective; even he admitted that most
of the numbers were little more than informed guesses. David Lujan saw
something more sinister—a deliberate lowballing that would deliver Hillblom's former business associates the windfall they had never received

during his lifetime. How else to explain Waechter's valuing Hillblom's one-quarter interest in DHL, International—a fast-growing, $4 billion company—at just $126 million? Or a piece of property he owned near the Nikko Hotel for almost nothing, when Hillblom had collateralized it at $11 million a year earlier? Or the UMDA stock at $50 million, when Hillblom's stake in Air Mike alone was probably worth that?

Of paramount concern was the shell game that Hillblom's friends were now playing with the estate's largest asset. Po Chung, Hillblom's original nominee and now the head of DHL in Asia, was president of a Bermuda-based company called Monterrey, which held Hillblom's shares in DHL, International. (Monterrey, it had been revealed, had received $142 million in dividends from DHL, International as part of the Polar Bear Deal, plus 32,000 shares of the new DHLI, of which it was agreed that 24,000 shares belonged to Hillblom.) Theoretically, Po should have owed the Hillblom Estate in excess of $200 million, because Hillblom had immediately "sold" his stake in Monterrey to Po for that amount. But through a Hong Kong law firm, Po claimed that his debt with Hillblom had been settled as follows: $106 million in DHL, International shares; $50 million for 90 percent of Danao International Holdings, the Vietnam holding company; $42 million in a wire transfer to Hillblom before his death; $4.4 million in shares of a DHL affiliate called Dumbleton; $8.8 million in deposits to the JAL/Lufthansa/Nissho Iwai indemnity fund, an escrow account that had been set up to protect DHL's investors from unwelcome surprises; and $25.7 million in DHLC Class "B" shares. According to Po's math, he had paid back a total of $246.9 million on an original debt of roughly $226 million. He readily admitted to having no written proof of any of this. "One of the significant ingredients of the formula which built DHL from scratch into a multibillion dollar international corporation and which Larry and I shared with the other DHL principals," Po explained in an affidavit, "is the ability to delegate."

But untangling the Monterrey deal was only a starting point in understanding what Hillblom's stake in the company he'd founded was worth. Because both DHL corporations possessed the right to buy the estate's shares at "fair market value," it was in their best interest that fair value be as little as possible. So too with UMDA, where Joe Waechter, the estate's executor, was also chairman. Even Hillblom's stake in Continental Airlines, a public corporation whose shares are traded every day on the New York Stock Exchange, were held in a limited partnership and required the approval of his partners, including DHL, to sell. Hillblom's real estate holdings were even more problematic. The ranch in Half Moon Bay was owned by three separate corporations; the land holdings on Saipan were tied up in title disputes; the Vietnam properties, meanwhile, were bleeding cash, and banks were unwilling to finance potential buyers because of the communist government. Meanwhile, rumors of nominees stealing the assets Hillblom had placed in their name abounded, as did a long list of rumored assets that had not shown up on Waechter's official inventory.

"We don't necessarily know what they got away with," Dotts tells me, echoing the sentiments of not only David Lujan and Randy Fennell back then, but also Yeoryios Apallas, whose job, after all, was to protect the State of California's bequest and not Hillblom's friends. "There was another golf course in Vietnam that Larry had been involved with. I'm not sure what happened with that. There was a building in Hong Kong that he pointed out to me: 'That's my building.' But on the inventory, no buildings had shown up in Hong Kong, so there was kind of issues as to what happened with that stuff."

But Hillblom had also left more than a few liabilities. Dozens of claims ranging from the expected to the absurd had formed a pile on Waechter's desk. One of the largest was the income tax bill from the CNMI Department of Finance. There was also an unpaid medical bill of $2,501.20 due to the Commonwealth Health Center for treatment of Hillblom's injuries in the Cessna crash a year and a half before. There were demands that millions of dollars in personal guarantees for business loans be suddenly honored in full. There were sizable claims from Donnici and his legal associates for deferred compensation in the form of shares of Continental Airlines and DHL—shares they claimed that Hillblom had promised them in lieu of cash but which he had never delivered. There was an extraordinary claim from a Saudi prince for $15 million for something called share appreciation rights, as well as an emotional plea from John Spice, the loyal Englishman who was tending to the ranch in Half Moon Bay; he now claimed that Hillblom had promised to secure his green card and set up a pension. Carla had hired a lawyer to recoup more than $200,000—an unpaid loan and mortgage payments she'd made on the Kaneohe house in the early seventies, when they had lived there together. And Bruce Jorgensen, Hillblom's former lobbyist who had pulled him from the Cessna wreckage in 1993, had filed two personal injury claims as a result of that accident—one for himself and one for Adonis Gotas, the mechanic. Jorgensen was demanding $150 million in each case. Finally, the estate's legal fees were piling up at a rate of over $1 million per month. The costs of tax experts, investment bankers (to value the DHL shares independently), and accountants would add millions more.

Meanwhile, the only two things that might still settle who should inherit Larry Hillblom's estate relatively quickly had both stalled. The Hillblom Bill was still loitering on the governor's desk, unsigned, and the mole was resting at a lab in Northern California, untouchable as Lujan, Fennell, and the estate's attorneys squabbled over testing protocol.

On the early side of spring, an exasperated Randy Fennell telephoned Lujan with an ingenious (and inexpensive) way to break the legal stalemate: the three children and their mothers would submit to DNA testing, then the results would be cross-tested in order to establish siblingship. Once it was proven that Mercedita, Jellian, and Junior shared a common biological father, the identity of that father would be obvious: Larry Hillblom. Lujan and Israel were intrigued, but Lujan ultimately said no because he did not believe that the two Filipina girls could be Hillblom's. How, he asked Fennell, could one explain the thirteen-year gap between Junior's birth and the births of the two Filipinas? And if the children did *not* match, as Lujan expected, the sibship testing would only serve to weaken Junior's case, not strengthen it.

When the FILC attorneys found out that Lujan and Israel had rejected a second settlement opportunity, their already fragile partnership finally came undone. Lujan informed his partners that he had fulfilled his obligation of investing $250,000 into the case; if they wanted to continue their profit-sharing arrangement, he told them, everyone would have to contribute another $13,000 per percentage of the settlement that they were entitled to. A little later, Barry Israel faxed a sternly worded letter to Roland Fairfield, the FILC partner in charge of DNA, relieving him of those responsibilities; henceforth, he wrote, David Lujan would be in charge of DNA and the FILC was prohibited from taking any action without Israel and Lujan's consent. Fairfield responded by relieving Lujan of most of his duties; Ross Putnam, the FILC partner who had become Kaelani Kinney's boyfriend and drinking buddy, would now be Junior's "main lawyer."

In several pages dripping with sarcasm and contempt, Lujan abruptly resigned. He passed the torch—as well as his schedule, including three separate briefs and oral arguments due in a single day that month, besides lobbying Froilan to veto the Hillblom Bill—to the FILC via fax. "I'm sure that you will get an audience with ease and he will be receptive to your legal arguments," Lujan wrote of the governor, who still had one month to decide whether or not to sign the bill into law. As for Castro, Lujan cajoled, "I'm sure the Court will be looking forward to the brilliant oratory and masterful briefs you guys are capable of," before reminding them that they would also have to respond to Peter Donnici's Supreme Court appeal of the special master hearing. And, he added, "You should be prepared for a protracted all out war on who the next Executor should be. I predict this to be bitter and acrimonious and to last at least a week. Who the Executor will be has tremendous impact on whether Junior gets a good settlement offer. But, I'm sure you don't need me to tell you this."

Then Lujan moved on to the valuation of Hillblom's estate, particularly the DHL Corporation and DHL, International shares, whose "fair market value" would be determined by a judge in California and an arbitration proceeding in Paris, respectively. "Next to the issues of paternity," Lujan wrote, "this is probably the most important issue in this case. You must hire an expert, preferably a big Banking institution or someone like Goldman Sachs to review and dispute the depressed valuation which is tentatively being proffered. Once these cases are removed to Saipan and the Court schedules a valuation hearing, be prepared to be inundated by thousands of pages of reports and to be in a hearing which will last 2–4 weeks. I'm sure you'll be up to it, finances being one of your fortes, and have tremendous fun with it. Further, you should be prepared to spend $100,000 for your experts alone."

Of course, Lujan continued, these were only two of many other important actions that the FILC would now be litigating, including arbitrations concerning Hillblom's stock in the Bank of Saipan, Saipan Cattle, and

UMDA, all of which would have to be liquidated. "Remember," Lujan admonished, "Junior's claim is to the *entire* Estate and you have an ethical obligation to monitor and attend these proceedings."

As if his to-do list was not yet overwhelming, Lujan attached a proposed schedule of depositions that Yeoryios Apallas had just submitted to the court. If Castro approved these, and Lujan expected that the judge would, then at least one member of the FILC would have to travel to Saipan, California, and Brussels in order to attend. "It will be fun to go to all these places and live in hotels but I suspect each party will have to bear his/her costs," Lujan opined, before warning that these were "just a few" of the issues that the FILC would now have to be on top of in order to avoid liability for "unwarranted diminution" of Junior's interest in his father's estate. Oh, and of course they would need to file for *pro hac vice** immediately as Junior's new lead attorneys; otherwise, Castro would not allow them to present oral arguments in his courtroom.

With that, Lujan wished his former partners good luck and announced that he was going on a "well-deserved" vacation. Then the irascible boonie dog added a parting shot:

> *P.S.: When I return, expect to be served with a lawsuit from my attorney for breach of contract unless this matter is resolved to my satisfaction. And, don't try for an easy settlement simply because you don't want to spend the time and money—I will not allow this to happen to Junior!*

---

* A status granted by a court to lawyers who have not been admitted to practice in its jurisdiction, allowing them to participate in a particular case.

Forty-Eight

Celebrities

*I*n theory, there were plenty of reasons for Lujan to visit Koror, Palau, as he did a short time after "resigning" Junior's case. The island paradise was only a two-hour flight from Guam—on Air Mike, an asset that might soon be owned by Junior. The estate also owned Palau's cable system, as well as several large parcels of undeveloped land—the largest of which was tied up in litigation—and a good-size yacht docked in front of the Pirate's Cove, a waterside dive bar that had been favored by Hillblom and his politician friends.

But Lujan had not come to check up on the estate's investments, nor to dive in the archipelago's famed Jellyfish Lake, nor to enjoy a jaunt to the impossibly lush rock islands, as most wealthy tourists did. His destination was a small concrete block home framed by a tin roof and a small yard that sat just a few feet off of the main two-lane artery connecting Palau's airport with the handful of luxury hotels on-island. As in most such homes, a few chickens grazed the yard in back, while a single fighting cock paced impatiently, its neck tied to a post, awaiting its next fight. The cock was Junior Larry Hillbroom's prized possession. The home belonged to his grandparents, the Imeongs.

Naoko, Junior's grandmother, had raised the boy, but her daughter Kaelani, as his coguardian, had made most of his legal decisions—including who represented him. (Junior seemed more concerned with his fighting cock and spear-fishing than with the probate.) The gentle half-Japanese Naoko seemed uncomfortable in a legal war, particularly one involving copious amounts of money and sex. Years before, she had admonished Kaelani not to sue Hillblom for paternity when her daughter had learned his true identity. Palauans did not air their dirty laundry in public, like Americans, the old woman had lectured, though Naoko had hung a portrait of Larry above the mantel in their tiny home so that Junior would always know who his father was. Now, with her daughter living on Guam with her latest boyfriend, Naoko was shuttling Junior back and forth to Saipan for court hearings and praying for a quick resolution of his case. The estate's lawyers were ripping Kinney's reputation to shreds, calling her a prostitute and a drug addict. No wonder her daughter, always something of a wild child, was becoming indignant, paranoid, and increasingly violent. Naoko did not want to become rich; she just wanted it to end, with Junior acknowledged by his father's estate and her family's dignity intact. But none of the attorneys would listen to her.

When David Lujan showed up at Naoko's doorstep, she greeted him warmly. The attorney had already become something of a father figure to Junior—a positive influence, a role model. Three days later, Ross Putnam received a fax that she had terminated the FILC's services. She had hired Lujan as Junior's lead attorney.

The FILC lawyers collectively howled that Naoko could not fire them. As coguardian, they said, she lacked the authority to do so unilaterally. But that did not mean that they didn't want Lujan as Junior's lead attorney. In fact, whenever they could get hold of Lujan, they were pressing him to agree to a new addition to their legal team: Mr. "If-the-glove-does-not-fit-you-must-acquit" himself, Johnnie L. Cochran Jr.

Lujan knew what that meant: his estranged partners had finally hit the panic button and run to a celebrity attorney, believing that Cochran's fame was a magic bullet that would knock the Hillblom Bill off the governor's desk, cut through the brick wall erected by Hillblom's former business associates, and bring the parties to the settlement table.

But it also meant that they had called Lujan's bluff. They knew that he had no intention of quitting.

The trouble was that Lujan was not bluffing. Nor would he cave in to being replaced by Johnnie Cochran Jr.—or anyone else. When one of the FILC partners called, pleading for him to talk with "Johnnie," Lujan was cool. He wasn't necessarily opposed to Cochran's coming on board, he told them, especially if he could bring some money to the table. But, he added, Castro would never approve Cochran's hefty fee—an additional 8 percent of Junior's settlement. Nor would Lujan relinquish his title; if Cochran was brought on as lead attorney, Lujan warned them, he would sue them all for breach of contract.

The next day, Lujan received a letter from the FILC claiming that Governor Tenorio would not sign the Hillblom Bill if Cochran was involved, fearing the "worldwide media attention" that a member of O. J. Simpson's "dream team" would attract. Lujan knew the reality was just the opposite: a stateside celebrity like Cochran meddling in the CNMI's internal affairs would *guarantee* that the fiercely independent Froilan signed the bill. Tenorio hated the feds and the stateside attorneys even more than Larry Hillblom had. Anyone who knows anything about Tenorio, Lujan shot back, knew that he would not be intimidated by Johnnie Cochran.

As usual, Lujan was right.

On the morning of June 9, 1996, Governor Froilan Tenorio finally picked up one of the thick ballpoint pens on his desk and signed the Hillblom Bill into law. He might have allowed the moment to pass quietly, considering that the bill had been unanimously condemned by the government's legal experts, including his own attorney general—whom he'd subsequently fired—and considering that he was a well-known womanizer himself. Instead, the irrepressible Froilan issued a statement that celebrated the dubiousness of his decision. "Although this Bill had a number of serious defects," he wrote in an open letter, "I signed it with the understanding that the Legislature is willing to take the necessary action to correct those defects in new legislation." As it turned out, the governor's reluctance had not been due to the bill's questionable constitutionality—in the letter he congratulated both himself and the Legislature for ignoring the advice of legal counsel—but instead due to its failure to extract a windfall for the government, which, despite hundreds of millions in federal aid, always seemed to be broke. "Since one of the policy goals behind the Bill was to capture some income from the Hillblom Estate," Froilan wrote, "I trust the Legislature will take the necessary action to amend this provision at the earliest possible date." Only then did the governor speak to the public interest: by disinheriting Larry Hillblom's potential heirs, he asserted, the Hillblom Law would encourage other fathers to recognize their illegitimate children during their lifetime and provide for them in their wills.

Curiously, no one faulted the governor's bizarre logic. They faulted one another, and they faulted Johnnie Cochran. (Although they could not agree whether Froilan had signed the bill because of the celebrity lawyer's presence or because of his absence.) FILC partner Jack Avery immediately announced that their savior was now definitely coming to Saipan—with or without Junior's lead attorney. "Johnnie Cochran is willing to work with Naoko and attorney Lujan," Avery wrote in a fax addressed to a personal attorney that Naoko had been forced to retain, "but is prepared to proceed without them if necessary." Cochran's arrival was confirmed a few days later in the *Guam Daily News,* which announced—on the front page—that Lujan had been replaced.

Israel immediately flew to Los Angeles and met with Eric Ferrer, Cochran's right-hand man. He explained that he and Randy Fennell were both already preparing appeals of the Hillblom Law to the CNMI Supreme Court, and how Cochran's entrance into the case would only complicate a delicate situation. The last thing anyone needed was a famous statesider creating a media circus and offending the local judiciary at such a time. Israel admonished that the mere threat of Johnnie Cochran had provoked Tenorio into signing the Hillblom Law to begin with. But Ferrer told him that he and Cochran were definitely coming. They'd already booked their tickets.

On July 15, the FILC's messiah landed on Guam to as large a media storm as is possible on a small island. Jack Avery threw him a cocktail party that night at his home. Lujan's cell phone filled up with voice mails imploring him to attend, promising that no business would be discussed— just a social get-together with a celebrity attorney! or so a succession of the FILC partners' voices chimed in his mailbox—but Lujan was unmoved. He decided to go to Hawaii rather than stick around for an audience with Johnnie Cochran. At least he'd get a lot of work done on the long flight.

The next morning, Cochran, Avery, and Ferrer descended upon Saipan. Cochran gave an impromptu press conference at the airport. His quotes in the following day's newspaper were beyond inflammatory: "It's totally unconstitutional and against public policy," Cochran said of the

Hillblom Law in his now famous staccato delivery. "We're gonna turn it around because it's outrageous," he continued. "We're gonna take it all the way to the Ninth Circuit of the Supreme Court and it's gonna be overturned, you can count on that!"

Froilan's reply was terse, almost amused. "We'll see if he has as much luck here as he did in California," the governor was quoted beneath the same headline. Lujan's and Israel's worst fears were thus confirmed: the evangelistic Cochran had just made Froilan more stubborn.

Sensing a crisis, Joe Hill, Junior's local counsel, reached Lujan in Hawaii. Johnnie was starting to sniff about Lujan's "childish behavior," Hill told him. He wanted to work things out. But Lujan was enraged by Cochran's grandstanding. He'd even heard that, at Avery's cocktail party, Ferrer had bragged that Cochran's name alone would double any settlement offer from the estate. Utter bullshit, he said.

"What does he bring to the table that I don't already have, anyway?" Lujan asked, a rhetorical question he'd been posing to the FILCers for weeks. Like them, Hill did not have a good answer. Nor could he tell Lujan what Cochran's record was, or how many cases he had actually litigated. But Hill did have some good news: Cochran and Ferrer were leaving Micronesia that day. And when Hill added that Ferrer had requested to meet with him in Honolulu, during his layover from Guam to L.A., Lujan seemed agreeable.

But when Cochran's law partner arrived in Hawaii the following day, Lujan did not answer his phone. He'd come down with the flu and was suddenly unavailable. Ferrer waited three days for Lujan to feel better before returning to the airport. On the long ride home, Cochran's partner wrote Judge Castro an affidavit memorializing Lujan's failure to show. Castro would ignore it. So would Lujan. The judge didn't need a celebrity attorney in his courtroom, and Lujan had recently met someone far more useful than Johnnie Cochran.

To many New Yorkers, Myron Farber is one of those instantly familiar names whose relevance is not easily recalled. His byline has appeared many times on the front of the *New York Times*. A series of Farber's articles investigated President Ford for corruption; before then, he'd spent a year on the drug beat in 1970s Manhattan—the crime-addled Gotham of *Midnight Cowboy.*

The diminutive Farber had become a national sensation in 1977, when he was convicted of criminal contempt of court and confined to the Bergen County, New Jersey, Main Jail for forty days. The conviction arose from a two-part series that Farber had written on a surgeon named Mario Jascalevich. Farber's reporting had revived a twelve-year-old investigation into whether Jascalevich, the chief of surgery at a small New Jersey hospital, had secretly murdered a dozen of the hospital's patients using an exotic South American drug called curare. When Jascalevich's criminal attorney, a relentless African-American named Ray Brown, had subpoenaed all of Farber's notes and documents, Farber had refused to turn them over, citing the First Amendment and a New Jersey law that shielded journalists from such requests. Egged on by Brown, however, the judge had thrown Farber in prison and fined the *New York Times* $5,000 for every day that he refused to reveal his sources. In the end, Jascalevich was acquitted, but Farber was also exonerated. He was pardoned by New Jersey's governor, who concluded that the journalist's intent had not been "to insult or frustrate the judicial process, but to stand on a noble, if sometimes imperfect principle." The *New York Times* was refunded $101,000 in contempt fines. Later, when the New Jersey Legislature passed a bill expanding on the earlier protections of its so-called shield law for journalists, it would become known as the Farber Law.

Farber had written a book about the Jascalevich case in 1978 titled *Somebody Is Lying.* It was nominated for the Pulitzer Prize. When, nearly twenty years later, an editor at *Vanity Fair* magazine learned about the billionaire whose plane had disappeared in the Western North Pacific and the children suing for his estate, he contacted Farber to cover the story. But then *Dateline NBC* had hired him on as a producer of their own piece. One of Farber's first calls had been to David Lujan, who had agreed to interviews of himself, Junior, and Kaelani. But the more Farber talked to Lujan, the more Lujan began to interview Farber. The journalist knew how to track down witnesses in small towns, gather evidence, and work with forensic pathologists. Moreover, the key to the Jascalevich case had been the testing of preserved human tissue for curare, identical in principle at least to the testing of the mole for DNA. Finally, Farber had demonstrated extraordinary loyalty and discretion, rounding out all of the talents that someone would need to research—and win—a complex paternity case like the Hillblom probate.

After *Dateline* wrapped, Lujan asked Farber to lunch on Saipan and suggested that he join Junior's legal team. Lujan and Israel needed someone who could move between all of the warring factions and produce at least the outlines of a settlement. But the journalist was on his way to a small village in France in less than a week, to spend the summer with his wife's family. Lujan pressed him, but Farber demanded the summer to think it over. Lujan seemed to give in, but almost as soon as Farber arrived in Europe the little village's only fax machine began to purr with daily missives addressed to Myron Farber. Lujan was more convinced than ever that he needed a mole himself.

Forty-Nine

Press

It's time for [David Nevitt] to prostrate himself before this Court and beg forgiveness for all the sins he has committed and helped to commit against this Court and this Estate. . . . Waechter and Nevitt would be well-advised to acknowledge and atone for their transgressions. In this, they may find their salvation and be saved from the fires of Hell. Repent, sinners, lest your souls be lost!!!
—*David Lujan, in a pleading to Castro, March 20, 1996*

Anyway [*sic*] you slice it, they're farther from the money now than they've ever been. Worst of all, Larry's name and reputation are being trashed.
—*Joe Waechter,* The Wall Street Journal, *May 15, 1996*

"Anything's possible!" scoffs Peter Donnici on Farber's *Dateline NBC* episode, which finally aired in November of 1996. It was his retort to the interviewer's question: Was it possible that Larry had slept with Kaelani Kinney? When the reporter follows up with whether or not Donnici *thinks* that his old friend slept with Junior's mother, Donnici shrugs his shoulders. "She doesn't seem like his type," he finally offers. And by then, of course, Kaelani Kinney was definitely *not* Larry Hillblom's type. Kaelani, though not quite thirty at that moment, looks many years older—decades beyond Hillblom's age limit. Fat hangs from her arms in thin brown hammocks; her cheekbones are invisible behind swollen skin and her once-radiant smile has sunk to form a permanent scowl. But the eyes are by far the saddest feature—dull as a drug addict's, yet paranoid.

Cut to painfully shy fifteen-year-old Mercedes Feliciano, whose braces and pageboy haircut make her seem even younger. In a barely audible, pubescent voice, she tells the same reporter that she thought Larry loved her. Smash cut to a montage of dancing islander girls in matching bikinis, then off to commercial. Painful stuff for a stateside audience but also hard to turn off. *Is that what American men do out there?* a lot of women must have wondered. But plenty of men, particularly those who'd served in Asia, would have recognized themselves in Larry; those watching the program with wives or girlfriends were probably compelled to do some denying of their own.

What effect, if any, the prime-time airing of Hillblom's dirty laundry had on the case is difficult to say. Over the summer of 1996, Castro had suspended the Bank of Saipan as executor and fired the Carlsmith firm, exiling Donnici and Waechter. The judge had appointed a CPA from Texas named William Webster to perform the duties of the executor—at $70,000 a month—and hired a giant law firm out of San Francisco called Morrison Foerster, aka MoFo, to represent the estate. They did not come cheap. "These are not boney [*sic*] dogs that wander in free," Lujan squealed when MoFo's first seven-figure invoice arrived. "They are extraordinarily expensive hybrid, pureblooded dogs with an insatiable appetite for money."

("How do you bill a million dollars a month?" Mike Dotts laughs. "You research everything. You read everything. You send off expeditions to Vietnam to measure the bricks on the wall, and catalog everything and interview everybody and depose everybody.")

While Donnici huddled in his San Francisco office, Waechter remained in Micronesia, where he sat for depositions and told his remaining friends that he never should have taken the job of executor. Going out, he was constantly at risk of being served with subpoenas. Lujan was already crowing that Waechter's and Donnici's legacies to their children and grandchildren would be a blizzard of lawsuits. (He was wrong.) But few felt sympathy for the ousted gatekeeper of Larry Hillblom's empire. Mike Dotts smirks. "Donnici and Waechter got what they deserved. They all got caught up in their hatred of Lujan and in winning; they lost sight of Hillblom's life."

In December 1996, David Lujan awoke in his hotel room on Saipan to a double rainbow. He interpreted it as a sign from God. After all, his two favorite targets had been neutered, and he had discovered a giant loophole in the Hillblom Law. By disallowing DNA evidence, the CNMI Legislature had simply thrown paternity testing back to the old days, when Lujan's father, the judge, would summon parent and child for a good look. The law's standard that a father must have "openly and notoriously" "held out" a child "as his own," actually gave Junior an insurmountable advantage over the other children, whom Hillblom had never met. Mercedita had not even been born at the time of his death. So all that was required for Junior to win the entire Hillblom estate was (1) find photographs or video of Larry at Junior's age or call witnesses who would attest to the fact that the boy resembled his father; and (2) produce witnesses who would attest to either seeing Larry with Junior, or swear that Hillblom had acknowledged that he had a son. There were, Lujan knew, dozens of such people on Palau alone.

Not that he and Israel had given up on proving Junior's paternity biologically. Upon his return from France, Myron Farber referred Lujan to two of the most respected DNA experts in the world: Barry Scheck and Peter Neufeld. Both men had become famous due (ironically) to their success denigrating the DNA evidence collected by the Los Angeles Police Department in the O. J. Simpson double-murder trial—the same evidence that Brad Popovich had vouched for. Scheck and Neufeld were expensive, but Lujan would not allow Larry Hillblom to disappear again. He and Israel agreed to pay their expenses, plus a percentage of Junior's inheritance, even though a $10,000 DNA test of the mole would still be sufficient to settle the matter once and for all.

In Morrison Foerster, they faced a more nuanced foe than Carlsmith. At first, MoFo's attorneys argued that the Hillblom Law rendered DNA testing obsolete. When that failed—Israel successfully argued that, even if the law held, they should still be allowed to use DNA testing to impeach witnesses who'd claimed that Hillblom had had a vasectomy—the estate's new attorneys submitted an impossibly long set of standards for testing, then they chose a testing method that destroyed the sample after a single test: RFLP, aka Restrictive Fragment Length Polymorphism. Neufeld and Scheck accused MoFo of being scientifically irresponsible; the small size of Hillblom's tissue sample would mean they had only one shot. Scheck and Neufeld wanted to amplify the tissue in a thermocycler so that the results could be analyzed and verified.

But testing the mole had become a foregone conclusion. All that remained to be decided was when the mole would be transferred from the doctors to the court-appointed lab and, after that, how soon Hillblom's genetic code would finally be known.

The answer to the first question is very cold and foggy day in mid-February 1997; the place a conference room at the Davies Medical Center facility in San Francisco—only a couple of miles from Donnici's Market Street offices. Assembled were several attorneys and experts from both sides. Underscoring the momentousness of the occasion, Peter Neufeld had been flown in from New York City. Lujan and Israel were well aware that everything about the mole, from its chain of custody to its anticipated match with Junior, would be vigorously opposed by the estate's new 550-attorney law firm. However, they also knew that a positive match would provide a huge psychological advantage—maybe a knockout punch would force Donnici and the Charitable Trust to the bargaining table on their knees.

The Davies pathologist arrived a little late, as doctors are apt to do, wearing a white lab coat on which his name was stitched in blue cursive. For purposes of identification, the "mole" would be referred to not as Larry Hillblom but as tissue specimen number DMC-69755. (In forensic pathology, every human being, even one as complex as Hillblom, can be magically distilled into a series of numbers.) Neufeld glanced at the number attached to the specimen and then back at the number on the original pathology report, a copy of which he'd brought with him for verification. The sample number on the report was DMC-697**55**. But the number of the tissue sample on the table was DMC-697**75**.

"Excuse me," Neufeld said, stunned. "The pathology report reads DMC-697*55*, right?"

"That's correct," the pathologist replied nonchalantly.

"This is sample number DMC-697*75*."

The pathologist looked at the readout attached to his sample. "That's odd," he finally said. "I'll be right back." Then the doctor disappeared, leaving the room in a pregnant silence. Everyone was upright in their seats now, silently wondering the same thing: the Davies lab was famous for *not* making mistakes, so how the hell could something like this be happening?

The pathologist returned a few minutes later—an eternity. His hands were buried deep in his pockets and his gait was unflinchingly apathetic. Still standing, he casually removed a tiny paraffin cube from his right pocket, tossed it onto the conference table with a grin, and announced, "Heeeeeeeere's Larry!"

Incredulous, Neufeld excused himself from the room and started dialing his cell phone. It was early morning in Honolulu, but David would want to know about this right away.

Fifty

The Journalist

"**D**on't touch it!" Lujan snapped.

He was pacing a hotel suite in Honolulu, only a mile or so from the rat-infested loft where DHL had started twenty-seven years earlier, and several floors above the conference room where Castro had ordered the estate, the trust, and the children to reach a compromise. For the past several days, a federal judge hired by the estate had mediated discussions that Lujan found so pointless that he'd stormed out of the first morning—after telling Mercedita's local counsel to fuck off. But if the two sides did not settle soon, he knew, the Internal Revenue Service and the estate's law firms might end up with the entirety of Hillblom's empire. MoFo was charging in excess of $1 million a month, and a tax expert had told them that the IRS would calculate the estate tax retroactively from the day of Hillblom's death. Penalties and interest were already accruing. If the case dragged on for several years, whatever the estate's lawyers didn't take, the IRS would.

The report should have motivated the parties to compromise; instead, they flocked to the media to air their grievances. Hillblom's brothers, who had refused to offer the DNA samples that could have quickly and cheaply settled the issue of paternity more than a year earlier, whined about the estate's multimillion-dollar legal bills. "The situation is totally out of hand as far as costs go," Terry Hillblom was quoted in a *Marianas Variety* cover story. Echoed his half brother, Grant Anderson: "We are witnessing the destruction of the Estate, which Larry created over 25 years."

In May, the Hillblom probate made the front page of the *Wall Street Journal*; the warring factions used the newspaper as an arena to threaten, cajole, and intimidate one other. A few even offered up new theories. Joe Hill was quoted surmising that Larry had purposefully left his will out-dated and his estate in disarray in order to give his children a chance at inheriting it.

Oddly enough, the *Journal* had started one more feeding frenzy by dis-covering three more Filipino children who claimed Hillblom might be their father. The two girls and one boy shared the same mother, a dancer named Angelica Nonan, whom Hillblom had been obsessed with for a time. Lujan didn't believe for a moment that Larry would have fathered three kids by the same woman, but under the Hillblom Law's standards, she could "prove" paternity with a few photographs. Lujan dismissed the Nonans as the "phantom children" because they had not yet filed or appeared in court. Yet he worried that they might be part of a Hillblom Trust conspiracy— that Peter Donnici might have paid them a few million dollars to buy out their claims in advance. That way, even if Junior, Mercedita, and Jellian all proved paternity, the trust would still take half of the estate.

Now, as he listened to one of his high-priced DNA experts telling him how the august Davies Medical Center in San Francisco had fumbled the mole, Lujan was reminded that anything was indeed possible. But the boonie dog would not be tricked. Nor would he run home with his tail between his legs.

Lujan said good-bye to Neufeld and dialed another room in his hotel. When a man's voice answered, Lujan said they needed to talk. Immedi-ately.

A few minutes later, Lujan walked past his unmade bed, turned the knob, and ushered in a small, rather excitable middle-aged man: Myron Farber, the *New York Times* reporter he'd wooed for months. Lujan motioned for him to sit at the suite's dining table, then told him about the mole. He was ready to make Farber an offer he couldn't refuse.

"Let's face it," Lujan began, "I need you."

Myron Farber's first few missions had been diplomatic in nature. He'd introduced Lujan to Barry Scheck and Peter Neufeld, and he had flown to

San Francisco to convince Peter Donnici to accept a neutral mediator—the former dean of Berkeley's business school. (Donnici had declined.) Then Farber had traveled to the settlement talks in Hawaii after months of venomous pleadings had further frayed the communications lines between the estate, the California Attorney General's office, the trust, and the children's lawyers; no one person involved in the Hillblom probate was on speaking terms with all of the parties.

Lujan sat down at the table. He still believed that Junior was the only heir, he said, but the emergence of the "phantom children" and now, the possibility that Davies had switched Hillblom's tissue sample with someone else's, necessitated a major strategy shift. They would need to gather overwhelming evidence for a *prima facie* case—photos, affidavits from people who had heard Hillblom acknowledge Junior, and so on. But also, the journalist would have to go to Kingsburg, California, to find photographs of Hillblom at Junior's age, films too if possible, and hire forensic experts to do it the old-fashioned way—to hold up Junior and Hillblom side by side. He hoped that the resemblance would be evidence enough.

That was part of Farber's new mission, Lujan explained, though not all. Due to both its importance and the depth of Farber's experience, the journalist's fee would be $1 million, minimum. But there was another, more discreet task . . .

Lujan had not yet given up on DNA. When he returned to Guam, he announced that he had had a change of heart: He was ready to accept Randy Fennell's offer of one year ago, though he would reframe it as his own. "An obvious solution to dealing with these other three children," Lujan wrote the Nonans, "is to test them in order to determine if they have the same father among themselves or with Junior, Cuartero, or Feliciano. Kinney will be putting on evidence that it is simply not credible that Hillblom fathered three children by the same woman. A man who seeks out young virgin girls and demands abortions when they get pregnant is not likely to be fathering children repeatedly with the same woman. . . . Here is the real problem: If the phantom children are forced to test, no bluff will exist for whomever plans to assert these rights, or for the Trust to insert an interest in the Estate through them. . . . One way to demonstrate paternity in the absence of a reliable DNA sample from Hillblom will be for these children to cross-test DNA against each other."

Fifty-One

Kingsburg

Beneath the Mayberry sheen of Kingsburg, Helen Anderson had not, as the farmers say, had an easy row to hoe. But how much of her own struggle she had managed to hide from her eldest son is impossible to know because Helen passed away several years ago. What is common knowledge in "the Burg" is that Larry was an extremely bright, curious child who saved much of his adolescent resentment for his mother. Larry had easily fulfilled every expectation of hers, becoming the best piano player, the smartest student, and the most devout churchgoer—playing the organ, teaching Sunday School, and even delivering sermons when the preacher was out. What he could not do, of course, was replace the man she'd loved, whose name he and his brother, Terry, would keep for the rest of their lives. Helen had a good man now, but he had married her out of obligation. Larry was her flesh and blood. After he'd gone to law school, she'd kept his bedroom like a shrine, often sleeping there rather than with her husband.

Yet the more Larry achieved, the more distance he seemed to place between them. Before long, she was reduced to seeking out his friends around town, asking if they had talked to him, fishing for news. From 1976 until 1991, Larry did not come home a single time, and more and more she blamed herself for his exile. She confided to her best friend that she had once sent a letter to Larry asking him if he couldn't pay his brothers more. (Grant was then developing DHL's offices in the Middle East, and Terry was a pilot for Island Airways, one of Larry's side projects.) Helen thought the request was modest. Moreover, she wasn't asking for herself. She had never asked her eldest son for anything. But her friend immediately realized that Helen had done the worst thing possible. Not only had she intruded into Larry's adult life—she'd sought to impose some authority over it.

The first week of May 1995, Helen had picked out a card for Larry's fifty-second birthday and sent it to her son care of a PO box on Saipan. Then she'd prayed for a response. Larry had come home a year earlier, and, although he hadn't stayed with her and Andy, they had driven out to the airstrip in Selma with Grant and his family to meet his small plane. Larry had looked terrible, of course, having lost an eye and shattered nearly every bone in his face. He wore torn jeans, a T-shirt, and large dark glasses. Clinging to his lean frame, unchanged since high school, was a very shy, young Filipina named Josephine who had stayed with him while he'd recovered at the hotel near the San Francisco Airport. Helen had visited him once there—to tell him that she loved him.

Reunited, maybe reconciled. Hillblom with his estranged mother, Helen, in Kingsburg. (Courtesy of Michael W. Dotts)

Back at the farm, they'd arranged themselves in front of a small bunch of haystacks and taken a family photograph, the first one in years, Andy in worn overalls and Helen in a cotton summer dress, squinting in the sun's glare, everyone smiling for the camera except Larry.

Sensing a thaw in their little cold war, Helen had attached a note to

Larry's birthday card asking his forgiveness for anything she might have done wrong in raising him. All she'd wanted to know since then was whether or not he'd received the note before he'd taken off in that funny-looking airplane and been lost at sea.

In town she heard talk about the television show with the dancing girls, and she knew that people were collecting newspaper clippings of the scandal. Knowing her neighbors were whispering about her son's "life-style" was painful. That wasn't her Larry. Her Larry was *her*: smart, ambitious, stubborn, sometimes a little too direct for other people's tastes, but that had gotten them through the tough times together. She still cried when she thought about him. When Helen's friends traveled overseas, they would take photographs of the red-and-white DHL trucks and vans and send them to the farm, but that was cold comfort.

Her friends said that of course he had received her card, but Larry traveled so much, it was difficult to know. According to Joe Waechter, they'd been in Vietnam just before the crash, opening a new hotel there. Maybe she'd visit someday, or fly to Saipan to see everything that Larry had accomplished there. But as long as the estate case was open, the lawyers had warned her that it wasn't safe. She might be subpoenaed. The children's attorneys wanted her DNA.

Throughout 1996 and the following year, Helen had written Josephine a number of letters; at the end of the year, she'd sent a pretty Christmas card. From time to time, she even picked up the phone and called Larry's house. Most of her letters and all of her phone calls went unanswered but Helen had continued to write to Josephine, anyhow, communicating the doings of her rather uneventful life in Kingsburg—the monotony of small town life was punctuated only by her two young granddaughters' music lessons, a sustained outpouring of affection from Hillblom's former associates, and visits to the doctors who treated her arthritis—and expressing her hope that they could become friends.

Helen's letters, nearly lost amid a sagging box of pleadings in Mike Dotts's office, do not mention the arrival of a former *New York Times* reporter in Kingsburg during the spring of 1997, a small but persistent man who was going around town interviewing Larry's friends and numerous cousins, asking for old photos, football films, and even his high school yearbook. It is possible that Helen remained unaware of Farber, though his presence certainly would have been discussed in a small, religious community like Kingsburg. When she and Andy drove up to the Fresno medical complex to finally take care of her arthritis, neither of them would have been looking in the rearview mirror; nor, as she awaited the doctor in the examination room a short time later, would she have been suspicious of a man dressed in a proper lab coat, even as he swabbed the inside of her cheek for no apparent reason.

Fifty-Two

The Number

> While involved in the "fact" investigation [of Junior Larry
> Hillbroom's paternity] I performed what ultimately proved to be
> a . . . critical service for Lujan, one that had a profound impact
> on both Lujan and the case. Through contacts in California who
> were unavailable to Lujan, I kept Lujan, Barry Israel and others
> on our team abreast of the movements and habits of Hillblom's
> family, including his mother, Helen Anderson, who had ignored
> a CNMI court order to provide blood for DNA analysis. As
> Lujan readily acknowledged to me, this timely, highly detailed
> information was pivotal in achieving his key immediate
> objective   a genetic profile that could be matched with Junior
> to see if he was, irrefutably, a son of Larry Hillblom.
> —*From Myron Farber's affidavit in* Farber v. Lujan, *2001*

Patrick Lupo empties his glass of its last sip of sauvignon blanc, sets
it confidently on the table beside an empty plate, and casts a wist-
ful glance around the dining room of the quaint pub where we have just
finished our lunch. These hourlong respites are technically off the record,
but I doubt that he will mind my sharing what he expresses next: a lingering anger that whoever snuck into Helen Anderson's hospital room and
swabbed her cheek had been allowed to vanish as utterly as Hillblom himself. "You'd think . . ." Lupo starts, but his jaw clenches shut. There is much
about the Hillblom probate that gnaws at him, but nothing so much as
what happened to Larry's mother in Fresno.

When, in the summer of 1997, David Lujan was informed that he
possessed Helen's DNA, his response was very different. "Total victory!"

he crowed into his cell phone. Finally, Lujan had the two things that he wanted: DNA that linked Junior to Larry Hillblom, and a clear advantage for his client over the other potential heirs. He dispatched Peter Neufeld to tell the estate's attorneys that Junior's team now had biological proof of his paternity. Of course, they were stunned. Despite all of the mud-slinging and name-calling, no one had ever expected Larry's mother to be violated. Yet, as the news reverberated across the Pacific Ocean, only one person threatened retribution: Yeoryios Apallas. Apallas e-mailed Barry Israel that his agents were in Fresno investigating what he called "some hospital staff's intrusion on one of the people connected to this case." The threat might have worked had there been any truth behind it, or if Apallas had not embellished the e-mail with a threat to destroy Kaelani Kinney by forcing her to testify, as Apallas wrote, "about how many times she fucked Larry and the other folks around the same time." Or if he had not ended with this promise: "He who laughs last laughs best my friend. It will be a cold day in hell before you and your ilk get any of the Hillblom money if I have anything to say about it." Israel promptly forwarded Apallas's e-mails to Castro. Shortly afterward, the deputy AG with the exotic accent was reassigned by the California Attorney General's office, and even the estate's attorneys refused to be in the same room with him.

The Global Settlement Conference began in July 1997 in San Francisco, under the mediation of a retired federal judge named Coleman Fannin. It was reconvened at Saipan's brand-new oceanfront showcase, the 300-room Diamond Hotel, on August 6, just three days before the Hillblom probate would go to trial. There was still no agreement on any issue besides the obvious: that Hillblom's fortune would be divided somehow between Junior, Mercedita, and Jellian, who had tested positive for sibship a month earlier, and the medical trust called for under his will. Adding to the tension, lab results would soon reveal that a young Vietnamese boy named Be Lory matched the three confirmed siblings, so whatever the children received would now be split four ways instead of three. At least Ted Mitchell had finally been expunged. Castro had delegated the Clash of the Titans to another court, which had promptly ended it.

"Mostly," Mike Dotts recalls, "what drove the settlement from then on were the tax issues. Everybody hired their own tax attorneys to try and advise them on what to do about the tax problems. And it just kind of reached a point where everybody understood how taxes were going to affect the estate and that the only solution was a settlement, and also I think MoFo really did help out in the settlement because their billings were so high, and nobody liked seeing them get paid so much money, and that was a motivation to settle—just to wean them off the tit, basically."

But a magic number proved elusive. Peter Donnici thought that the trust deserved at least 60 percent of the estate—in large part because his tax experts believed that if the heirs got a majority of Hillblom's estate, then the entire thing would be subject to the 55 percent estate tax. If, on the other hand, the trust inherited at least 60 percent, it was theoretically possible that the entire estate could avoid the estate tax. But Lujan and Israel were just as adamant that the children get at least 60 percent, and their experts thought the transaction could be structured in such a way to use the trust's tax-exempt status regardless—by having the trust inherit Hillblom's entire fortune and then afterward settle with the children. A compromise might have been struck, but both sides still refused to speak directly with one another. Attorneys for the trust, for the children, for the estate, and for Josephine were kept in separate rooms while an ambassador was recruited to deliver the latest offer to each room. Occasionally, Judge Fannin would show up personally in one room or another to see if he could push a concession, but Peter Donnici was so pessimistic about bridging the twenty-point difference that he'd remained in San Francisco. During the second day of the talks, one of the phantom children's attorneys served a breach of contract lawsuit on his partner, further poisoning the atmosphere. Meanwhile, rumors permeated the hotel like viruses, including one that Mike Dotts had cut a secret deal with David Lujan—"that," as Dotts explains, "in exchange for supporting Josephine's claim, she would testify that Larry had admitted being Junior's father during pillow talk." Dotts won't say who started the rumor, but neither he nor Lujan did anything to squash it. That the children's attorneys had offered to pay Josephine millions of dollars from their share of the estate was by then an open secret.

Literally towering over the settlement discussions was Raoul Kennedy, MoFo's head of litigation, and, as such, the estate's attorney in charge of negotiations. One of the estate's new lawyers had called Kennedy a "dog of war," but in the flesh, the lanky marine reservist came across as a cerebral, soft-spoken preppy with a slight lisp and a fondness for plaid golf pants. By his own admission, he normally represented what he called "ultra-unsympathetic clients": insurance companies refusing to pay claims, oil companies polluting the environment, et cetera. The Hillblom case, he would later admit, exposed an unexpectedly weak stomach. Deposing the two teenage Filipina mothers, Mercedes Feliciano and Julie Cuartero, had been deeply embarrassing for the conservative Republican. Asking fifteen-year-old girls when they'd gotten their period and if Larry Hillblom—a fellow Boalt Hall grad whom, in private, Kennedy characterizes as "utterly repulsive"—was circumcised and exactly how much betadine he had poured onto his penis after sex to protect himself from *them* was not palatable to a man who believed deeply in women's rights. How could men of wealth and education take advantage of poverty so sordidly and so blatantly?

Kennedy might have been a warrior but he was not, like his main opponent, scrappy. Nor, more to the point, was he a gambler. He was not inclined to roll the dice on the Hillblom Law, not with close to a billion dollars on the table, and certainly not after a well-connected local attorney had assured him that the Hillblom Law would *not* be upheld by the CNMI Supreme Court—perhaps because of Larry Hillblom's own precedent. If the Hillblom Law fell, Helen's swabbing would still not be admissible evidence, but the children's cross-testing would, and Kennedy would have a very hard time explaining how four children from three Asian countries whose mothers were known to have slept with Larry Hillblom could have a different father—or why, despite interviewing most of the urologists on the West Coast, the estate's investigators had never found any evidence that Hillblom had had a vasectomy.

Unlike Johnnie Cochran and Yeoryios Apallas, Kennedy maintained a sense of humor; he joked to his friends back in San Francisco that practicing law in Saipan was like eating Chinese food with one chopstick.

The Hillblom estate *had* to settle, Kennedy knew, which is why he had suggested his friend Coley Fannin to mediate this last-ditch effort. And Coley had certainly tried his best. He had even cajoled Hillblom's brothers, who were furious over the swabbing incident, back to the bargaining table the week before. When they'd dug in their heels, both Kennedy and the former judge had tried to reason with them: *What if they might be able to benefit from their genetic kinship to these kids one day? What if a kid in Palau turned out to be the key to healing a genetic disease, such as Terry Hillblom's diabetes?* But raising the possibility that these children might be their kin seemed to infuriate Larry's brothers all the more. They'd burst into tears and rant that the kids would never see a dime. "The Hillblom Minuet," Kennedy called it.

On the opposing side, David Lujan remained a roadblock. The other attorneys had all agreed to accept $10–$15 million apiece long ago, but Lujan had refused to go along, demanding $150 million for Junior and claiming he had 140 witnesses lined up to testify that Larry was Junior's father. Why $10 million wasn't enough for *any* child *anywhere* blew Kennedy's mind. (He was familiar enough with David Lujan's response: *Because the law allows it.*) If Lujan walked away from these talks, as he had all of the others, Kennedy had let it be known that the law also allowed filing a malpractice suit to punish Guam's boonie dog for refusing a patently generous offer.

On August 8, 1997, the last day of the final settlement conference, Kennedy stepped onto the sidewalk in front of the Diamond Hotel, out of its air-conditioned chill and into a stale heat. The trial had been scheduled to begin in Courtroom A of the CNMI Superior Court, across the street. God knows how long *that* would take, he thought to himself. Then the appeal would be heard next door, in the Supreme Court building, sometime next year or beyond. The appeal of that appeal would be tossed across the Pacific Ocean to the Ninth Circuit in San Francisco. . . .

Kennedy watched the sun beginning to lower across the Philippine Sea. Coley Fannin was standing a few feet away at that very moment, locked in conversation with one of the children's attorneys about The Number. Three of the children were now onboard for a 50/50 split: half for medical research and half for the kids—and their attorneys, of course. But David Lujan and Barry Israel were demanding 63 percent and the trust refused to give more than 58. There was only one possible solution left.

Kennedy straightened his tall frame in the hot sun.

"Hiya, Judge," he said, interrupting. "What's the latest?"

"Next stop, mutually assured destruction," Fannin deadpanned. "We've been discussing whether or not it's time to present a mediator number* before I leave tomorrow."

"To be frank," Kennedy replied, "we're at the point where I think you've got to earn your money and put that number on the table. Somebody's got to cut through this Gordian knot or we'll be here forever."

"Some of the attorneys are worried that it may be premature."

"I'm worried that it's long overdue," Kennedy retorted. "And if you do give us a number, remember that you've only got one shot. It's like firing a Derringer. You can't come back tomorrow and it's a new Nixon."

Fannin nodded. He'd known Kennedy for a quarter century and appreciated his candor. But the judge also got the hint about earning his fee; you didn't want to disappoint a client, at a rack rate of $20,000 a day, which is what the estate was paying. "Let's go back inside," Fannin said after a long pause. "I'll give you both a number to take to your constituents. I'll be on-island for another day or so. After that, you can reach me in San Francisco by telephone."

Kennedy and the other attorney followed Fannin slowly down the Diamond's driveway, past several gargantuan orange-and-white tour buses, through the hotel's open lobby, teeming with Japanese newlyweds wrapped in monogrammed towels, and finally into the conference area they'd left five minutes ago. By the time Fannin reached his makeshift desk, the number was engraved in his mind. He pulled a hotel pen from his pocket and scribbled two numbers onto one of his term sheets: 60/40– 60 percent for the children and 40 percent for the Hillblom Charitable Trust. After a tense conference call with Patrick Lupo, Peter Donnici, and the Hillblom brothers, Fannin announced that it was a done deal.

---

* The number that a mediator determines has the best chance of acceptance, rather than the number that he or she considers fair. It is typically given to both sides at the same time, with the condition that neither party can submit a counteroffer. It can only be accepted or rejected. And only if both sides accept the number are they made aware that the other side accepted.

Phan Thiet

The only life worth living is the adventurous life . . . of such
a life the dominant characteristic is that it is unafraid. It is
unafraid of what other people think . . . it does not adapt
either its pace or its objectives to the pace and objectives of its
neighbors. It thinks its own thoughts, it reads its own books,
it develops its own hobbies, and it is governed by its own
conscience. The herd may graze where it pleases or stampede
when it pleases, but he who lives the adventurous life will remain
unafraid when he finds himself alone.

    —From the Kingsburg memorial service program, May 1995

At the heart of Larry was a deep patriotism, and it's proved by
the very things that people use to suggest he's not patriotic.

    —Steve Kroll

The woman in the photograph is short, though no longer slight; her
designer jeans hug curves that most Vietnamese women will never know.
She is not ugly, as a waitress at the Dalat Palace once told me, probably out
of jealousy, though *pretty* might be an overstatement. Considering the beauty
of many women here, I can easily imagine her being the one *not* picked, the
one standing awkwardly in the second-floor hallway of Villa No. 1 until an
oversexed Larry calls from his bedroom that he will take her. There is an
independence to her that I wonder if he could have felt from that distance, a
look in her eyes that borders on stubborn that he probably would have found
sexy. Or maybe the woman from the photograph is just angry right now.

    "How did you know I was here?" she demands on the doorstep of her family's hut outside Phan Thiet, the pungent odor of fish sauce from the nearby factories punctuating her breath. I tell her that I didn't know; my translator found her address and we decided to pay a visit, then her father told us that she was coming very soon and invited us to stay for tea.

She doesn't believe me, of course, nor should she, even though this unlikely story happens to be true. "Why should I tell you anything?" is her next question, and my response is that I don't know. That I am so unprepared for her interrogation seems to soften her gaze just a little. Rather than order me to leave, she says that she's writing a book herself, with the help of a friend in suburban Virginia, which is where she and her son, Be Lory, moved after the case, because it is close to the guardian hired by her attorneys. When she says that her book will be a romance, based on the Hillblom probate, I offer to help her find a publisher or a literary agent; after all, there's no chance of our books competing with one another. I have come to believe what one of Hillblom's friends told me long ago: Larry was incapable of love. The idea of romance was too nuanced for a man with such outsize ambitions and such insatiable appetites. Of course, I don't tell her this.

Thi Be asks me why she shouldn't kick me off her parents' property. Then, almost as quickly, she invites me to stay for lunch. At the back of the hut is a long dining table, on which her mother has laid out a spread of dragon fruit and unfamiliar vegetables, mostly raw. A few moments later, she is telling me that she not only fell in love with Larry in that one night but later also with her young American attorney, John Veague, who could pass for a J.Crew model. So maybe her weakness for Caucasian men has inspired her to tolerate me. The talk veers from Larry Hillblom to other things as she scolds me for not eating enough.

After the meal, we walk through the small rice paddies next door, where a couple of old women in pointed hats squat in waist-deep brown water, swatting strands of rice with machetes. There are thousands of strands, which must be stripped of the rice kernels and dried out on blankets—typically laid out on the side of the road—but the old women stop their work for several minutes to acknowledge Thi Be and smile wide, toothless grins as she says something in Vietnamese that makes them both laugh.

Our destination is a large shade tree that rises out of the marsh maybe a hundred feet from the rice. "This," Thi Be says, "is where I gave birth to Lory. Under the tree."

There is no hint of bitterness in the remark, no suggestion of anything inappropriate in the fact that the heir of Larry Lee Hillblom, near-billionaire globalizer and onetime king of Saipan, arrived on this earth in the midst of such poverty, amid air that stinks of fish sauce, to a plain farmer's daughter. Thi Be seems to think that this is where Lory should have been born, among the poor and on the soil where Larry expected to build his last empire.

Lory does not remember a doctor taking a sample of his blood when he was less than three years old. Nor was he anywhere near Berkeley, California, in September 1997, when a quirky forensic mathematician named Charles Brenner determined that he and three other children, all of whose mothers had been lovers of Larry Hillblom but none of whom had ever met one another, were related. Like his three half siblings, Be Lory's share of his father's empire totaled just under $100 million. Even after attorneys' fees and taxes, this made him one of the wealthiest people in the country. But it should have been more than that. Pat Lupo groans that several of the estate's larger assets were sold at fire-sale prices, including the ranch in Half Moon Bay, though none more so than the one Lupo helmed at the time: DHL, International. DHL ultimately paid $140 million for Hillblom's 24 percent of the company; less than a year later, DHL would flip it to Deutsche Post, the German postal monopoly, for more than three times that amount.

Lupo has never met Thi Be, and Thi Be's son has never met his grandmother Helen, although he, along with the other children, agreed to pay her a million dollars for a drop of her blood, money that Lupo helped to make. Hillblom's children—through their guardians and attorneys—also agreed to donate a sum in the low six figures from their inheritance to establish the Larry Lee Hillblom Law Library on Saipan and to pay $3 million to Josephine and $4 million to each of the "phantom children." They also bought a $30 million insurance policy in case any more potential siblings came forward.* After the first agreements were signed, their guardians and lawyers received extra-large T-shirts printed with cartoon effigies of

---

* In 2001, three more children would come forward, when a stripper from Buffalo, New York, named Susan Bauer filed a triple paternity claim. Bauer demanded that her children's DNA be tested against that of Hillblom's family members, but her lawsuit was ultimately dismissed by Judge Alex Castro, citing the Hillblom Law, which remains in effect.

themselves, hand in hand, circling the globe. Underneath were the words *Everlasting Peace.*

Hillblom on his powerboat, in a rare moment of contemplation. He is probably in Palau, a favorite getaway and a paradise where he had hoped to build a tourism empire. (Courtesy of Michael W. Dotts)

Standing under the shade tree, Thi Be appears to be living that peace. I assume the same of her son, who attends a prep school on the East Coast. For the others, however, everlasting has proved temporary. At the behest of their attorneys, Jellian Cuartero and her parents moved from Saipan to the Cayman Islands and back—supposedly to avoid paying taxes. Last year, Julie Cuartero complained that her attorneys have plundered Jellian's trust fund for luxury travel, among other things, while they are not only broke but unable to work because of the constant moving. Allegations have surfaced that most of Mercedes's inheritance has been spent funding a lavish lifestyle for her extended family, who have all moved into her home in a posh gated community in Manila. And Junior Larry Hillbroom, who has bounced in and out of rehab for crystal meth addiction, is back in federal court at the moment, suing his attorneys David Lujan and Barry Israel for changing the terms of his contingency agreement retroactively in order to grab nearly 60 percent of his inheritance—plus millions more in fees. Bad investments have also taken their toll, though it's impossible to know how much. Junior's trust is based in the Cook Islands, a notoriously opaque tax haven.

But there is more to peace than financial security, of course; there is also identity and there is trust. As they grow older, Hillblom's children are confronting the endless, unanswerable questions of their father's life: Why didn't he change his will? Why didn't he buy a decent plane? Why didn't he acknowledge them? Why didn't he tell the truth? Was he in the pilot's seat? Was he a criminal? A murderer? A monster? Is he still alive? Was he ever a billionaire? They will be largely alone as they seek to answer these questions; Hillblom's family does not acknowledge them. Only two—Junior and Jellian Cuartero—have even met each other in the fifteen years since their father's death. Yet Hillblom has left his mark on them, as he has everyone.

Nine thousand miles west, in the conference room that overlooks the charming suburban marina, Peter Donnici tells me that his secretary regularly receives calls and e-mails denouncing Larry as a pedophile and the Hillblom Foundation as a disgrace, even as it doles out millions of dollars to fund important medical research on aging and diabetes. Well, no one remembers Howard Hughes for making the largest gift to medical research in history, do they? They remember the women and the long toenails and speculate that the wasted, disease-ridden body his Mormon handlers flew in from Mexico wasn't really him. The old law professor doesn't want to talk about the salacious stuff, though, so it's time for me to leave after a few more stories from the good old days. On my way out, Donnici shrugs his shoulders, as though he, too, has become one of Larry's abandoned children, trapped in the shade of his infamy. Trapped no matter how many millions of dollars are spent trying to escape it, no matter how much good his fortune may do.

1969	Larry Hillblom, Robert Lynn, and Adrian Dalsey incorporate DHL.
1971	DHL Philippines is incorporated.
1973	Joe Waechter is hired by DHL while a student at San Francisco State.
	DHL is ordered to "cease and desist" by the U.S. District Court in Honolulu.
	Hillblom meets Peter Donnici at USF Law School.
	Hillblom and Po Chung found Mattawan, later DHL, International.
1975	Donnici wins appeal of "cease and desist."
	Hillblom's DHLI shares are given to Po Chung as nominee.
1976	Citizens of the Northern Mariana Islands ratify the Covenant.
1977	Hillblom testifies before the Subcommittee on Aviation of the House Committee on Public Works and Transportation in favor of airline deregulation.
1978	CNMI becomes a self-governing commonwealth.
1979	U.S. Postal Service relinquishes its monopoly on letters.
	DHL is operating in 120 countries.
1980	Hillblom quits DHL.
1981	Hillblom moves to Saipan.
1982	Hillblom files will; DHL shareholders sign pledge agreement.
	Hillblom buys 90 percent of Bank of Saipan.
1983	Joe Waechter becomes president and CEO of DHLC.

Hillblom and Donnici travel to Palau for the 34th APPU Council meeting as part of the CNMI delegation—Hillblom as special senate counsel and Donnici as special counsel to the CNMI Legislature.

Hillblom meets Kaelani Kinney at the Nanyo Ocean Club, Palau.

Larry incorporates San Roque Beach Development and Saipan Cattle Company, owner of the Cowtown rodeo-brothel.

1984 Junior Larry Barusch is born on Palau.

Continental Airlines sues Larry in FSM Supreme Court.

1985 Larry (POM) sues Continental in U.S. District Court on Saipan.

Larry runs for CNMI Legislature.

1986 Joe Waechter is fired by Pat Lupo.

Ronald Reagan terminates the Trust Territory of the Western Pacific.

1988 DHL starts negotiations with JAL and Nissho Iwai.

Joe Lifoifoi becomes a consultant for UMDA.

Hillblom is issued a student pilot certificate.

1989 Hillblom agrees to sell Po Chung his stake in Mattawan (DHLI) for a $200 million note.

Larry becomes a special justice of the CNMI Supreme Court.

1990–2 DHL's original shareholders receive $250 million in cash plus 42.5 percent of a restructured DHL, International, under the terms of a two-phase deal with Japan Airlines, Lufthansa, and Nissho Iwai.

1990 UN Security Council formally terminates the Trust Territory.

Joe Waechter moves to Saipan to run UMDA.

Hillblom's student pilot certificate expires.

1991 Danao and Lamdong Provincial Government sign 40-year joint venture to develop properties in Dalat, including the Palace Hotel.

Danao announces a 30-year joint venture with Vietnamese government for an apartment development near Ho Chi Minh City (Saigon).

1992	Ted Mitchell files his first Article XII lawsuit vs. Hillblom.
	Larry testifies before congressional "sweatshop" hearings.
	DHL shareholders sign share pledge agreement, guaranteeing that no outsiders are able to buy stock without their consent.
12/1992	CNMI taxpayers file Article XII lawsuit.
	Ted Mitchell files second Article XII lawsuit against Hillblom.
1993	Larry invests $8.7 million in Air Partners, the general partner of Continental Airlines.
	Peter Donnici files *Hillblom v. Mitchell.*
	Danao signs 50-year joint venture with Binh Thuan Tourist to open the Hotel Mercure Phan Thiet in Binh Thuan, Vietnam.
	Larry crashes his Cessna single-engine aircraft on Tinian.
	Governor Larry Guerrero signs SB 8-124 into law. The law places caps on contingency fees lawyers charge in Article XII cases and shortens the time in which Article XII cases can be brought by original landowners; it also limits fees to 20 percent or $700.
1994	Nguyen Be Lory is born.
	Vietnam embargo is lifted.
	Po Chung agrees to give Larry 90 percent of Danao in settlement of the $200 million note.
	Joe Waechter moves to Vietnam to become chairman of Danao.
1995	The Palace Hotel Dalat opens.
5/4/95	Julie Cuartero gives birth to Jellian Cuartero in Manila.
5/21/95	Larry dies in plane crash.
5/26/95	Carlsmith looks into ways to take control of Bank of Saipan.
5/28/95	Hillblom memorial service in Kingsburg.
5/31/95	Hillblom memorial service in Saipan.
6/5/95	CHC files articles of incorporation.
6/24/95	Waechter is hired as VP of Trusts and Fiduciary Affairs of Bank of Saipan.
6/27/95	Hillblom's death certificate issued by Judge Alex Castro.
6/30/95	IRS issues DHL tax deficiency of $194,534,167; plus penalties totaling $74,777,222.

7/28/95	Joe Hill makes first request for Hillblom's DNA on behalf of Kaelani Kinney.
9/15/95	Waechter files first inventory of estate at $422 million.
9/28/95	Rex Kosack is appointed special master.
	Fennel is retained to represent Julie and Jellian Cuartero.
10/10/95	Attorneys and consultants inspect the Cessna wreckage on Tinian.
12/1995	Mercedita Feliciano is born in Manila.
2/9/96	Kosack releases first draft of the Special Master's Report.
2/16/96	Hillblom Law introduced into CNMI Legislature.
7/15/96	Johnnie Cochran arrives on Saipan to challenge Hillblom Law.
11/6/96	*Dateline NBC* airs program on Hillblom estate case.
5/1997	Waechter replaced as estate administrator.
8/1997	Coleman Fannin holds settlement discussions in San Francisco and Saipan.
6/1998	Excavation at Hillblom estate.
6/21/07	Federalization Bill introduced in the U.S. Senate.
6/21/07	Vietnam and United States sign historic trade agreement.

Characters

David Allen—Founder, Middleston, NV (DHL, International)
Andy Anderson—Larry's stepfather
Grant Anderson—Larry's half brother and trustee
Helen Anderson—Larry's mother
Yeoryios Apallas—Deputy attorney general, State of California
David Bonderman—Investor, owner, Continental Airlines
Carla Bostom (Summer)—Larry's girlfriend/DHL executive
Charles Brenner—Forensic mathematician
Ed "Champ" Calvo—Larry's friend and Bank of Saipan board member
Alex Castro—CNMI Superior Court judge
James "Jim" Campbell—Political consultant, postal matters
Marilyn "Mares" Corral—DHL's first employee
Jellian Cuartero—Purported heir of Hillblom
Adrian Dalsey—Cofounder of DHL
Peter Donnici—Larry's personal attorney and DHL board member
Michael Dotts—Larry's personal attorney on Saipan
Family Law and Immigration Law Clinic (FILC)—Attorneys for Junior
Mercedita Feliciano—Purported heir of Hillblom
Randy Fennell—Attorney for "Baby Doe Hillblom," aka Jellian Cuartero
Be Lory—Purported heir of Hillblom
Adonis Gotas—Cessna mechanic
Roger Gridley—Real estate investor and friend
Joe Hill—Local counsel (Saipan) for Junior
Junior Larry Hillbroom—Purported heir of Hillblom
Naoko Imeong—Grandmother of Junior Larry Hillbroom
Barry Israel—Attorney for Junior Larry Hillbroom

Bruce Jorgensen—Hillblom's former attorney; lobbyist on Saipan
Raoul Kennedy—Attorney for the estate
Kaelani Kinney—Mother of Junior Larry Hillbroom
Steven Kroll—Larry's friend and former general counsel, DHL
Joe Lifoifoi—Larry's best friend and Bank of Saipan board member
Henry Litton—Queen's Counsel (Hong Kong)
Bob Long—SeaBee pilot/mechanic
Charles Loomis—Chairman of Loomis Corporation
Robert Lynn—Cofounder of DHL
David Lujan—Attorney for Junior Larry Hillbroom
Patrick Lupo—Chairman of DHL, International; DHL's second general
    counsel
Jess Mafnas—Larry's friend and former CNMI Speaker of the House
Bill Millard—Founder of Computerland; tax fugitive
Ted Mitchell—General counsel, UMDA
Alex Munson—District judge, CNMI, 1988–
David Nevitt—Managing partner, Carlsmith law firm
Peter Neufeld—DNA expert
Josephine Nocasa—Larry's live-in girlfriend
Bob O'Connor—Larry's personal attorney on Saipan and friend
John Osborn—Partner, Carlsmith law firm
Douglas Ousterhout—Craniofacial surgeon
Brad Popovich—Molecular biologist/geneticist
William Robinson—Founder, Middleston, NV (DHL, International)
Barry Scheck—DNA expert
Barry Simon—General counsel, Continental Airlines
Robert Timm—Chairman of the Civil Aeronautics Board (CAB)
Mr. Toan—Assistant to Larry Hillblom in Vietnam
Froilan Tenorio—Governor of the CNMI, 1993–98
Ted Thomas—Publicist, Hong Kong
Joe Waechter—Executor and chairman, UMDA and Danao International
    Holdings; president of DHL Corporation, 1983–86

Companies Owned or Partly Owned
by Larry Hillblom and/or His Estate

A.R.W. (DHL ranch, cellular licenses)
AIR MICRONESIA ("Air Mike")
AIR PARTNERS, LP (Continental Airlines)
AIR SAIPAN, INC. (Continental Airlines G.P.)
ALEXANDER DRILLING
ALEXANDER REAL ESTATE
BANK OF SAIPAN, INC.
BEL AIR APARTMENTS (Manila studio)
BVI CORPORATION (DHL)
COMMONWEALTH HOLDINGS CORPORATION (CHC)
DAEDALUS dba MCV—GUAM (cable TV)
DALAT RESORT INCORPORATED (DRI)
DANAO INTERNATIONAL HOLDINGS (DIH)
DHL AIRWAYS
DHL AUSTRALIA
DHL COMMUNICATIONS (fax)
DHL CORPORATION
DHL, INTERNATIONAL
DUMBLETON PROPERTIES (real estate)
FAST CASH, INC. (pawnshop)
FIRST SKYLINE CORP. (DHL ranch)
GREEN HEIGHTS, INC. (Kannat Gardens apartments)
ISLAND AIRWAYS (inter-island airline, Hawaii)
KSPN (Saipan television network)
LAO LAO BAY, LLC (golf course)

MANAGEMENT RESOURCES, INT'L. (consulting)

MARIANAS CABLEVISION (cable television)

MARIAS FALLS INSURANCE

MATTAWAN, aka MONTERREY (DHL, International stock)

MIDDLESTON, NV (DHL affiliate)

MERIZO SHORES, LLC (Cocos Island)

MICRONESIAN TELECOMMUNICATIONS CORP.

NAOG PROPERTY (Saipan real estate)

NEWCO (DHL)

NHA TRANG, INC. (Lifoifoi building)

NIRADA, INC. (Greece real estate)

PEOPLE OF MICRONESIA (POM)

POTAWATOMIE, INC. (Coral Island condos)

PURISSIMA PROPERTIES, INC. (DHL ranch)

RED INDIANAPOLIS F. (wireless cable)

SAIPAN CATTLE CORPORATION ("Cowtown" ranch/brothel/drive-in theater)

SAIPAN CHARTER dba LEISURE TIME INVESTMENT (SeaBee airplane)

SAIPAN COMPUTER SERVICES

SAIPAN LONG DISTANCE, INC.

SAN ROQUE BEACH DEVELOPMENT, INC. (SRBD)

SAN VICENTE APARTMENTS

TAGAYTAY HIGHLANDS (PI real estate)

TAPACHAO PARTNERSHIP (condos)

ULUNIU SHORES (Hawaii real estate)

UNITED MICRONESIAN DEVELOPMENT ASSOCIATION (UMDA)

Acknowledgments

*T*wo people in particular deserve mention here: Brant Rumble, a supremely patient and wise editor; and my mother, Marianne Scurlock, who read several manuscripts over the past few years and provided advice and encouragement. I should also thank Nan Graham and Susan Moldow at Scribner for their patience, as well as my agent, Melissa Flashman at Trident Media Group, without whom there would be no book. I am fortunate that Larry Hillblom surrounded himself with interesting and intelligent people, some of whom were very generous with their time. At the top of this list are Steven Kroll and Carla Summer, as well as Mike Dotts, Bob O'Connor, Patrick Lupo, Marilyn Corral, Jesse Choper, and Jim Campbell. There were many others who gave of their time, including Parker Folse, Sandy Phillips, Peter Donnici, Douglas Ousterhout, Joe Lifoifoi, Champ Calvo, David Bonderman, Herman Guerrero, Howard Hills, John Jones, Peter Woodruff, Jose De La Cruz, Ferdie De La Torre, Barry Simon, Charles Brenner, Roy Alexander, Travis Coffman, Tim Goodwin, Alice Braziler, Mr. Toan, Joe Hill, Dave Crass, Jack Atwood, Paul Kimoto, John Veague, Raoul Kennedy, Yeoryios Apallas, Thi Be, Julie Cuartero, Russ Sands, Manny Villagomez, Manny S. Tenorio, Pete Guerrero, Jim Sirok, Pete A. Tenorio, Froilan Tenorio, Bob Christian, Roger Gridley, John Anderson, David Grizzle, Henry Litton, George Proctor, Mary Fischer, Geoffrey Farrow, Ed Pangelinan, Roger Clark, Moses Uludong, James Ripple, Allen Hazlip, Bob Kline, Gerry Paras, Fred Radewagen,

Sam MacPhetres, Manny Villagomez, Ron Shinkai, Lennis Scheline, Bud White, Mike White, Barry Israel, and David Lujan, among others. Judge Francis Tydingco-Gatewood, Marconi Calindas, Kevin Wilson, and Grant Anderson either opened doors or kept them from slamming shut. The overworked staff at the CNMI Courts Building on Saipan, particularly Bernie Sablan and Dex, fetched the Hillblom Estate case, volume after volume, day after day, so I am grateful to them indeed. Staffs at other courthouses, including the federal courthouse on Saipan, were also generous but their names I can no longer recall. Thanks is also due to the federal archives center in San Mateo, as well as the courthouse there. Then there are those whose names I am not at liberty to disclose here but whose help proved invaluable. Finally, of course, I must thank Larry Hillblom himself. If I have not done justice to his life in these pages, it has not been for lack of help or lack of effort.

Index

Page numbers in *italics* refer to illustrations.